WITHDRAWN

KT-443-149

UNIVERSITY OF
WOLVERHAMPTON

CAME IN FROM
THE COLD

WP 0836087 1

The Royal Institute of International Affairs is an independent body which promotes the rigorous study of international questions and does not express opinions of its own. The opinions expressed in this publication are the responsibility of the author.

This project has been supported by generous funding from Capital Research and Management Co., one of the Capital Group Companies.

THE WORLD THAT CAME IN FROM THE COLD

PERSPECTIVES FROM EAST AND WEST ON THE COLD WAR

GABRIEL PARTOS

UNIVERSITY OF WOLVERHAMPTON
LIBRARY

Acc No.
836087

CLASS 123

CONTROL

327.
0904
PAR

DATE
15. NOV. 1993

SITE
RS

 Royal Institute of International Affairs

BBC *WORLD SERVICE*

This book is based on the BBC World Service Series
The World that Came in from the Cold
presented by Gabriel Partos, produced by Keshini Navaratnam and
David Edmonds, and edited by Liz Mardall
Original transcript material © The British Broadcasting Corporation, 1993
Text © The British Broadcasting Corporation and Royal Institute of
International Affairs, 1993

First published in Great Britain in 1993 by
Royal Institute of International Affairs
Chatham House, 10 St James's Square, London SW1Y 4LE

Apart from any fair dealing for the purposes of research or private study, or
criticism or review, as permitted under the Copyright, Designs and Patents Act,
1988, this publication may not be reproduced, stored or transmitted in any
form, or by any means or process, without the prior permission in writing of
the copyright holder. Except for reproduction in accordance with the terms of
licences issued by the Copyright Licensing Agency, photocopying of whole or
part of this publication without prior written permission of the copyright
holder in single or multiple copies whether for gain or not is illegal and expressly forbidden. Please direct all inquiries concerning copyright to
the Publishers at the address above.

British Library Cataloguing in Publication Data

A CIP catalogue record for this book is available from the British Library.

ISBN 0 905031 58 X (paperback)
ISBN 0 905031 62 8 (hardback)

Text designed and set by Hannah Doe
Cover design by Youngs Design in Production
Printed and bound in Great Britain by the Bath Press, Avon

CONTENTS

PREFACE

There was no declaration of war when it began and no victory parades when it ended. Yet the Cold War lasted four and a half decades and during that time no corner of the world escaped its impact. From the break-up of their wartime alliance to the collapse of the Soviet empire, the Western powers and the Soviet Union waged a relentless struggle against each other. East and West employed a huge arsenal in this global confrontation: the arms race and trade embargoes, direct military involvement in local conflicts and fighting wars by proxy, espionage and propaganda were the weapons used in the Cold War. No wonder that the term itself, first used in public by the American statesman Bernard Baruch in 1947, quickly gained universal currency.

Three key characteristics defined this age. First, the scale of the confrontation between the United States and the Soviet Union – each supported by its allies – was unprecedented in its global proportions. Second, the ideological divide between the two sides made their mutual enmity more bitter; both of them sought to demonstrate the superiority of their own system and envisaged – most of the time explicitly, sometimes more vaguely – the collapse of the adversary. Third, the menacing presence of nuclear weapons made Washington and Moscow determined to avoid any direct military conflict for fear of precipitating a nuclear war that could conceivably end human civilization on earth.

Until recently, accounts of the Cold War tended to be based on predominantly Western perspectives. The nature of the Soviet-style regimes made it virtually impossible to show the East's side of the story, other than in terms of official communist propaganda. However, the emergence of *glasnost*, or openness, in Mikhail Gorbachev's Soviet Union, and the subsequent collapse of communism, have removed many of the shackles of secrecy that once weighed heavily on the sources of information in the Soviet bloc. Based on nearly 200 interviews conducted for a 10-part BBC World Service radio series of the same title, *The World that Came in from the Cold* takes advantage of the fresh opportunities of the post-Cold War era by presenting perspectives from both sides of the former 'Iron Curtain'. All the quotations in this book are taken from interviews recorded between July 1992 and March 1993.

Given the immense scope of the subject, I have not attempted to give a systematic or comprehensive account of the postwar decades in this book. There are several excellent histories of the Cold War, and its individual battles, that do that. My aim was to explore a few of the major themes and events of this era, relying as much as possible on the personal accounts of those who made some of the crucial decisions, those who advised them, those who carried out the decisions and those who suffered their effects. However, to let the voices of the participants and the eyewitnesses speak clearly and in the context of their times, I felt it necessary to provide a simple historical framework.

The themes chosen for this book are somewhat lopsided. There is a chapter on the failure of the command economy, but the strengths and weaknesses of the various brands of the market economy are not discussed. Another chapter deals with relations between Moscow and its East European allies; there is no corresponding discussion of America's relations with its NATO allies or, perhaps more appropriately, with its Central American 'backyard'. Moreover, some important topics, such as the parts played by China and the Middle East in the East–West confrontation, are not discussed in detail. The concentration on the Soviet and East European side of the story is, I believe, justified for two reasons. A great deal of new information has recently come out into the open from the ex-communist countries, some of which has not until now found its way into print. Moreover, the peoples of the former Soviet bloc have been affected in more ways by the demise of the Cold War than anyone else. For them the new world order that has emerged in recent years has meant more than just an end to the two-generations-long era of East–West hostility; it has also seen the adoption of Western-style capitalist democracy, the end of foreign domination (in the shape of the Soviet Union or Russia) and the break-up of several states.

In discussing some of the major themes that characterized the Cold War within the confines of a relatively short book, I had no alternative to using a broad-brush approach. However, I tried to paint in some of the detail by focusing on a number of important events or developments that can throw light on the broader themes. In some of the chapters this is explicitly stated; elsewhere I did not want to interrupt the flow of the narrative that comes from the contributors by explaining my aim. What follows here is a brief guide to what I set out to achieve in the book.

Chapter 1 looks at the origins and early battles of the Cold War;

Chapter 2 focuses on Berlin as a microcosm of a divided world;

Chapter 3 describes the nuclear arms race until the first arms control agreements, with a closer look at the Cuban missile crisis;

Chapter 4 highlights some aspects of the propaganda war, mainly in the medium of foreign-language broadcasting;

Chapter 5 tells the story of Soviet–East European relations with particular reference to the Hungarian uprising;

Chapter 6 describes the shortcomings of the command economy;

Chapter 7 compares the failure of America in Vietnam with that of the Soviet Union in Afghanistan;

Chapter 8 looks at superpower involvement by proxy in the Angolan conflict;

Chapter 9 takes as its theme the espionage war;

Chapter 10 deals with detente, particularly in arms control, and the return to greater tension in East–West relations;

Chapter 11 looks at Mikhail Gorbachev's role in bringing the Cold War to an end, concentrating on Moscow's relations with the United States and Eastern Europe; and

Chapter 12 tries to address very briefly some of the major themes of the Cold War, such as the war psychosis, the role of ideology in foreign policy and the importance of the nuclear deterrent, before asking a few questions about the nature of the world that has emerged since the end of the Cold War.

In choosing the title, *The World that Came in from the Cold*, for the radio series and for the book, the production team did not wish to imply that somehow international tension and domestic strife have come to an end. It is simply a way of saying that a relatively well-defined era in history has passed, and that the various problems that states, nations and ethnic groups now have to tackle are of a different kind.

Any book is a collective achievement; when it accompanies a radio series the team is even bigger, and I am grateful to many people who have helped me research and write this volume. The book and the programmes, together with a number of seminars, are part of a project jointly undertaken by the BBC World Service and the Royal Institute of International Affairs (RIIA), and helped by generous funding from Capital Research and Management Co., one of the Capital Group Companies. John Tusa, former Managing Director of the World Service, and Professor Laurence Martin, Director of the RIIA, were instrumental in launching and sustaining the project. Liz Mardall, the editor of the radio series and coordinator of the project, was a constant source of advice, encouragement and practical help. Pauline Wickham, Head of Publications at the RIIA, guided the book through its tight publishing schedule with great tact. She was assisted in that with considerable skill by Hannah Doe. The producers of the series, David Edmonds and Keshini Navaratnam, persevered against the odds to obtain the interviews without which the book would never have been written. Stephen Court, who compiled the appendices, checked the text with meticulous care. Arthur Collinsworth, representative of the RIIA in the United States, gave very practical support to the project from its early stages.

Members of the RIIA study group, chaired by Professor Jack Spence, the Institute's Director of Studies, provided valuable comments on and corrections to the draft chapters; I wish to thank Michael Cox, Gina Despres, Anne Deighton, Carol Geldart, Adrian Hyde-Price, Neil Malcolm and Trevor Taylor for the interest they have shown in the book. For the same reason – and for other forms of practical help – I am also grateful to my present and former colleagues at the BBC, Donald Armour, Judit Beach, Mark Brayne, Nick Childs, Stephen Dalziel, Ron Gerver, Milada Haigh, Malcolm Haslett, Andrew Joynes, Hugh Lunghi, Rachel Osario, Rob Parsons, Mary Raine, Elizabeth Smith, Keith Somerville, Peter Szente, Alex Vincenti and Tim Whewell. The inquiry assistants at the World Service Information Centre, especially those at CARIS (Current Affairs Research and Information Section), Sue Eastwood, Nancy Reynolds and Jonathan Rowe, dealt with my queries in their usual enthusiastic and experienced way. Karen Webb provided diligent secretarial help.

The many contributors whose names are mentioned in the book – as well as those whose interviews are used in the radio series – deserve special thanks for giving up their time in recalling their personal memories of the Cold War.

Above all, I am grateful to my family for putting up with conditions which were difficult for us all; I spent three months largely away from home and another three (metaphorically) chained to a desk-top computer. During that time I received every possible form of support as well as understanding from my wife, Vesna; and many welcome inquiries from my daughters, Rebecca and Hannah, about the book they thought I was writing for them – in which they were right.

London, March 1993   Gabriel Partos

Churchill, Roosevelt and Stalin at the Yalta Conference, February 1945. It was the last meeting of the three towering giants of the wartime alliance.

1

FROM WORLD WAR TO COLD WAR

'I was writing dispatches from Moscow, as George Kennan [at the US embassy] was doing early in 1946,' says SIR FRANK ROBERTS, who was then the minister at the British embassy, 'warning people that we were not going to be able to continue in peacetime anything like the working relationship which we'd had in wartime, and that what had been Roosevelt's ambition and hope of a peacetime organization of the world based on understanding – and, in his view, I think, even friendship between the Soviet Union and the United States – was just not on because their objectives and ours were quite different. You had in the war a period when Churchill and Roosevelt were talking about Stalin – if only we treat him like a member of our club, he will behave like a member of our club – completely forgetting that he had a club of his own which he ran and which he was much more interested in than becoming another member of our club. But towards the end of the war Churchill was realizing that that had been a pipe-dream; and I think probably had Roosevelt not died [in April 1945], he'd have come to realize it, too.'

Sir Frank Roberts, the author of these cautionary dispatches, had attended a year earlier the Yalta conference – the event that later generations came to see as the symbolic foundation of the two 'clubs', even though the 'Big Three' wartime allies had already discussed the postwar spheres of influence at the Teheran confer-

1

ence in 1943. Yet even at the time of Yalta, it was not altogether clear how sharply the world would be divided into two camps, East and West, in a matter of less than three years.

'The Roosevelt–Churchill relationship was pretty close,' says Sir Frank, 'but Roosevelt was always anxious to persuade Stalin that it wasn't just a cosy pair against him, as it were, and that it was a threesome. At Yalta – I remember seeing it – well, at times he was frankly rather rude to Churchill and playing up to Stalin. And the interesting thing was that Stalin didn't want to join in in that kind of thing, and he used to go out of his way to sort of mollify Churchill and say, "No, no, no, we know, Mr Churchill, that you are not what Mr President has just been saying you might be."

'It was very odd. And, of course, there was this very strong American feeling that Churchill, who was a great believer in the British Empire, didn't want to see the independence of India and, from that point of view, was not Roosevelt's ideal partner for the postwar period. But he had a strange idea that Stalin might be.'

Yet within a year of Yalta it had become obvious where the real postwar divisions lay. In March 1946 Churchill delivered his famous speech in Fulton, Missouri, in which he used the term 'the Iron Curtain' to describe the boundary between Soviet-controlled Eastern Europe – which was soon to come under communist rule – and the Western world. Churchill's speech was followed a year later by the declaration of the Truman doctrine, pledging American support for countries facing communist pressure from inside or outside. Hard on the heels of the Truman doctrine came the Marshall Plan, announced in June 1947, which was to set the seal on the economic division of Europe, splitting the continent into a prosperous West and an East that was forever lagging behind.

Rifts in the wartime alliance

The postwar division of the world did not start at Yalta. There was constant friction between Moscow and the Western allies during the war. One of Stalin's concerns was over the length of time it was taking Britain and the United States to open a second front in Western Europe and take more of the German pressure off the Red Army. VALENTIN BEREZHKOV worked during the war as an interpreter for Vyacheslav Molotov, the Soviet Foreign Minister. Although an engineer by training, Berezhkov was invited to join the staff of the foreign ministry in 1940 in the wake of Stalin's prewar purges, which had left the diplomatic service with very few officials who could speak foreign languages. Berezhkov recalls the reasons for Stalin's suspicions: 'Our war started in the summer of 1941, but the second front opened only in the summer of 1944. Stalin understood this as an attempt not only to destroy Germany but to weaken the Soviet Union – that the Soviet Union should fight, fight and fight alone. Stalin also knew about the [atomic] bomb since 1942. We had our agents who told him about the Los Alamos project [US nuclear research laboratory], and he was thinking, "Why do they never say anything about that?"'

Stalin's accusations against his allies were somewhat contrived; he had not informed them about the Soviet atomic bomb project, which had been running parallel to the American effort. Besides, Britain and the United States had reasons for not rushing ahead opening a second front in Western Europe: they had wars to fight in North Africa, Italy and the Far East. This did not dissipate Stalin's suspicions about their intentions. HUGH LUNGHI arrived in Moscow in 1943 as aide-de-camp to the head of the British military mission and later attended all the three wartime summits as an interpreter. 'Well, there were articles published constantly, denouncing mainly the British for not opening the second front earlier,' says Lunghi. 'There were articles by military people saying this was perfectly possible – it was quite impossible, of course, because we didn't have the landing craft or the trained troops. There were also constant accusations that the British, and the Americans, were trying to make a separate peace with the Germans. Now it became quite clear to us that this was Stalin's guilty conscience. He had double-crossed the

3

allies, first of all, by signing the [1939] pact with Hitler; Hitler had double-crossed him by invading Russia, which was then his ally; and Stalin kept thinking that we, Churchill in particular for historical reasons, would double-cross him.'

The Soviet leadership's all-pervasive paranoia extended to much of the Western allies' war effort, including their liaison personnel who worked in the Soviet Union. Lunghi says: 'I arrived in Moscow from Britain, where the press, the radio and people in general were brimming over with admiration and enthusiasm for the Soviet Union, our brave Soviet allies who had stopped the Nazi war machine in its tracks. After about six months this was knocked out of us. Quite apart from the restrictions, the petty persecutions of living under a police state, the microphones in our living and working quarters, the surveillance by the secret police and the arrests of Russian friends, there were things which were much more serious and which we regarded as deliberate obstruction of our mutual war effort.'

Lunghi recalls one example of the obstructionism the British encountered from their Soviet allies: 'We wanted to protect our convoys particularly during the lighter period of the year because during the arctic nights of the winter the convoys were a bit safer. We wanted to continue sending these war materials to Russia during the lighter period and we asked if we could have *Hampden* torpedo bombers stationed in Russia to protect the convoys. At first the Russian naval command agreed to all this. And then suddenly, for no apparent reason to us at the time, word came from on high, obviously from Stalin, that we would not be allowed to station any more personnel in Russia. There was always a quarrel. Stalin kept saying that we had far too many people there; in fact, we were terribly tightly stretched. Stalin didn't want any more foreigners in Russia because we were all regarded as spies; this was made quite plain to us. So we couldn't protect the convoys during the summer months, but then Stalin complained we were not sending supplies.

And in retrospect it was really at that time that I realized the Cold War had started.'

On the whole, Roosevelt, if not Churchill, did not reciprocate Stalin's mistrust. SIR FRANK ROBERTS describes the relationship between the wartime allies: 'Roosevelt had a vision of avoiding the mistakes made in 1918. He wanted to have a different world, based on the United Nations and, above all, on the two big bosses and the two big countries.' Roosevelt's idea was not altogether naive; his plan was to try to involve the Soviet Union in the world community. The alternative of either excluding Moscow or encouraging it to isolate itself would have seemed potentially more dangerous. The prewar precedent of the League of Nations had demonstrated how a world organization could be reduced to virtual impotence by the absence from its ranks of many of the major powers.

However, Roosevelt's ideas were not fully shared by Churchill, who remained far more suspicious of Stalin. 'Churchill was different,' says Sir Frank. 'He had been very anti-communist for most of his life, but for him there was one major thing after 1939–40: we had to defeat Hitler. Therefore, when Hitler attacked Russia, he said he would sign a treaty with the devil to get rid of Hitler. And then he began to sort of admire Stalin. You see, Stalin was not a typical dictator. He was small, a little chap who had a soft voice and a bad arm and didn't rant and roar like Hitler and Mussolini and really handled the two extremely intelligently. And they began to say, he's not as bad as all that, it must be his colleagues who are always stopping him doing what he wants to do; and this was very naive. But because of Stalin's treatment of the Poles – the last thing being when the Russians wouldn't go to the help of Warsaw in 1944 – Churchill began to realize that no, it wasn't possible to have this kind of Rooseveltian relationship with Stalin.'

The Warsaw rising was an attempt in August 1944 by the Polish Home Army, the non-communist resistance loyal to the government-in-exile in London, to liberate the Polish capital from German

5

occupation before the Red Army could do the job. It was undertaken in the hope that this act of heroism would impress the Western allies enough to stand up for Poland against Moscow after the war. JAN NOWAK was a young courier between the resistance at home and the government-in-exile in London, who came to understand after his talks in Britain that the Poles' game was already lost. 'I realized what Poles at home did not – that we'd lost the war, that we would not be free, that we would be under Soviet domination. And when I reached Warsaw, just before the uprising, I was trying to say this to the leadership: "Look, the uprising will not have the slightest influence on the policy of the West. We've lost. Nothing will save us from Soviet control." I am not sure if people could act on the testimony of one man, who was so young, even though I'd talked to Churchill and [Foreign Secretary Anthony] Eden. I had a clear picture that we were being offered on a silver plate, in the sense that the West had told the Soviet Union very early in the game that there would be no resistance to its advance in Eastern Europe. And it was a great mistake, which led to the Cold War, because Stalin had the wrong perception that it was so easy to conquer half of Europe that he would have no resistance when he tried to extend it to Western Europe and countries such as Korea, for instance.'

While the Warsaw uprising was being crushed by the Germans, the Red Army was standing by on the outskirts of the city on the other side of the River Vistula. It did not go to the aid of the Polish Home Army, even though Radio Moscow had earlier exhorted the people of Warsaw to rise in arms against the Nazi occupiers. VALENTIN BEREZHKOV explains Stalin's motives: 'Stalin understood that if he helped at that moment, he would have to deal himself with the men he considered unacceptable. So a man like Stalin certainly calculated that it was better that the Germans get rid of them first, and when he arrived there was already nothing to fear and nobody to fight. That may be very cynical, but he was thinking, why should he now be involved in that?'

Within days of the crushing of the Warsaw rising, Churchill was in Moscow to discuss with Stalin the parcelling out of the British and Soviet spheres of influence in Eastern and Southeastern Europe. In a famous incident, the British Prime Minister presented his host with a piece of paper, showing in percentage terms the influence each country was to have. Churchill's explanation of this episode was that the arrangements he proposed were for the duration of the war and immediate postwar occupation and did not explicitly refer to a long-term demarcation of different spheres of interest. Stalin had other ideas. Apart from wanting to keep Germany weak, his main goal was to bring Eastern Europe under Soviet control.

The Yalta agenda

Moscow and Washington had different priorities to advance at Yalta. Sir Frank Roberts remembers the main items on the agenda: 'One was agreeing on how to end the war and get the arrangements for the occupation of Germany signed and sealed, which there wasn't much difficulty about – except for reparations, which were postponed until Potsdam. Then the second issue – one very close to Roosevelt's heart – was the United Nations, which he was very keen on getting the Russians in. He always had at the back of his mind that Churchill was splendid, but he was an old imperialist, whereas he and Stalin could somehow get on. The third major question was the war against Japan. At that time nobody was sure that the atom bomb was going to work and there was a fear that the eventual attack on Japan might cost a million lives. So it was very important in his view to get the Russians to attack Japan from Manchuria. And for that he needed Stalin's agreement. The fourth chapter was, of course, the East European one – the one Stalin was interested in – which was, in effect, restoring what he regarded as the old boundaries of the Tsarist empire and what he had got out of Hitler in the secret agreement of 1939. That conflicted entirely with our commitments to the Poles and our hopes for the rest of Eastern Europe.'

Stalin's objective was to bring Eastern Europe under Soviet

7

the West it was not immediately clear whether Stalin was
determined to impose communist regimes in the region or would
accept relatively independent states, albeit with governments friendly
towards the Soviet Union. MILOVAN DJILAS, who was one of Tito's
lieutenants in the Yugoslav communist leadership during and after
the war, got a glimpse of Stalin's thinking when they met shortly
after Yalta. 'Towards Eastern Europe Stalin was aggressive and
imperialistic,' says Djilas. 'As regards the rest of Europe, he believed
that a period of preparations should pass before the day of reckon-
ing. Stalin believed that it would be possible to win Germany over
to the Soviet side because he expected social unrest. And it was
characteristic of Stalin to say that the Second World War was not like
other wars because after this war each country on the winning side
would be able to impose its own system on the lands it occupied.'

Whether for reasons of expansion or security, Stalin was determined to create a *cordon sanitaire* along the Soviet Union's western
borders. Later on, after the Americans exploded their first nuclear
device in July 1945, this became even more important for him.
VALENTIN BEREZHKOV explains: 'Until 1949 we didn't have the
[atom] bomb. And the Americans had the bomb. Stalin's idea was to
have reliable rulers in Eastern Europe; that was his response to the
threat of the bomb.' Yet, well before the Americans detonated their
first nuclear bomb in July 1945, there were strong indications that
Stalin was bent on extending his control in Eastern Europe. This was
particularly so in Poland, where the rounding-up of Home Army
officers and politicians loyal to the government-in-exile in London
got under way. This led to 'a complete breakdown of the Yalta
regime for Eastern Europe,' says SIR FRANK ROBERTS. 'At Yalta we
had got written agreements, diplomatic arrangements for free elections in Poland, democratic governments and so on. Now I was at
Yalta and we were very sceptical about that because the Russian
interpretation of these concepts was going to be very different from
ours. In fact, they were completely flouted.'

There was always an element of ambiguity in Western attitudes

8

towards the Soviet sphere of influence in Eastern Europe. Extracting the promise from Stalin of allowing free elections in the countries occupied by the Red Army may have been an attempt to cover up the fact that Eastern Europe had been effectively surrendered to Moscow. After all, the nature of the Soviet regime could hardly have inspired any trust that Stalin's pledge would be kept.

The first indications of Soviet misconduct came from Poland, where the offensive against the non-communist side was gathering momentum. Roosevelt's more pugnacious successor, President Harry Truman, took Molotov to task for the Soviet Union's failure to abide by the Yalta agreement and ensure conditions for holding free elections in Poland. OLEG TROYANOVSKY was a young diplomat, brought up in the United States in the 1930s, one of whose first jobs was to act as Molotov's interpreter. 'On 23 April 1945, when the war was still going on,' Troyanovsky says, 'Molotov had an interview in Washington with Truman who was very stern with him. As Truman later said, "I gave him the one-two, right to the jaw." This was a real shock, not only to Molotov but to [Andrei] Gromyko, who was our ambassador in Washington at the time and who accompanied Molotov to his talks with Truman. When they came back to the embassy, Molotov started by himself writing a cable to Moscow, and then he just couldn't get it straight because he was very nervous as to how this would be received in Moscow. It was such a surprise, this "one-two to the jaw", that he invited Gromyko to help him out and the two of them formulated the cable.'

Although the United States and Britain were disappointed by Stalin's moves, which tightened his stranglehold on Eastern Europe, initially there was little reason to fear that these would have wider implications around the world. Eastern Europe had traditionally been part of the German and Russian spheres of influence. For the United States, in particular, Eastern Europe lay beyond the areas it considered vital to its strategic interests – Western Europe, the Middle East and the Far East. With the Third Reich now defeated, it was almost natural that the Soviet Union should step into the power vacuum. Nor did the West equate at that stage Soviet influence in Eastern Europe with the full imposition of the Soviet system on the countries of the region.

The era of American preponderance

Besides, there was every indication that the postwar years would be an era of American domination – if Washington chose not to retreat into the policy of isolationism it had embraced after the First World War. The United States had come out of the war as by far the most powerful country in the world. Its economy had been much strengthened by wartime demand for weapons and munitions; now it was ready to flood five continents with manufactured goods while its competitors' plants lay in ruins.

France and Britain, the prewar colonial powers, had been devastated by the war; the former had suffered the further ignominy of defeat, while the latter was weighed down by debt caused by the huge cost of the war. America's only likely postwar rival, the Soviet Union, had suffered devastation on an even larger scale. Much of its economy in the European part of the country lay in ruins, although Stalin's industrialization drive in the 1930s and the wartime evacuation of plants had created a large production capacity beyond the Urals. Still, the Soviet economy was in no way comparable with the American. In 1945, for example, the United States produced 75 million tonnes of steel, six times as much as the Soviet Union. This kind of huge disparity, no doubt, prompted Stalin to observe that his country's military security could be assured only when its output of steel reached 60 million tonnes.

With America acquiring the nuclear bomb in the summer of 1945, there seemed no limits to its military and political power. In the words of NOAM CHOMSKY, one of the most prominent critics of American foreign policy over the years, '1945 was an historic moment in which there was one country with such extraordinary wealth and power that it could in fact organize the whole world.

That had never happened before and we have lost that moment now. At that point the US had 50 per cent of the world's wealth. It had overwhelming military domination. It had total security. American planners knew it and they were going to run the world in terms of their interests.'

American aid began to flood into Europe at the end of the war – well before the Marshall Plan was ever conceived. The Soviet Union had received massive supplies from the United States (and Britain) during the war, and it was believed that by providing further assistance Washington could maintain a leverage over Moscow. SIR FRANK ROBERTS was the minister at the British embassy in Moscow in the immediate postwar years. 'There was a very strong concept in many people's minds that, after the terrible destruction it had suffered in the war, the Soviet Union would be very dependent on American aid for its reconstruction; therefore there would be a weapon, if you like, that would make the Russians hesitate. It became fairly clear soon after the war that the Americans were prepared to offer the Russians a continuation of what was known as UNRRA [United Nations Relief and Rehabilitation Administration] aid. I remember [Averell] Harriman, who was the American ambassador at the time I was in charge of our embassy – we saw a lot of each other – coming back from a meeting with Stalin and being absolutely amazed that he'd offered this and it was turned down. Stalin wasn't interested. He didn't want to be part of the American scheme of things; he'd rather make the Russians suffer more and do it themselves without the Americans getting involved.'

Stalin tightens his grip

As Moscow was consolidating its hold on Eastern Europe – secured through the presence of the Red Army – the West looked on, largely powerless to do anything. Tens of thousands died in the war that Soviet forces and their local allies waged against anti-communist guerrillas in Poland in 1945–6; there was also much fighting in

11

western Ukraine and the Baltic states, incorporated in the Soviet Union under the Hitler–Stalin pact of 1939. In all the East European countries where multi-party regimes survived for two or three years after the war, the stakes had been loaded in favour of the communists from the very beginning with the banning of local parties accused of wartime collaboration with the Germans. The Soviet occupying authorities, whose task it was to identify these 'collaborators', used this power to exclude many anti-communist parties and politicians from the democratic process.

With right-wing parties being the main target of the Soviet onslaught, social democrats had a crucial role in several East European countries to resist the drift towards communist rule. DENIS HEALEY, a prewar communist himself, had the job, as international secretary of the British Labour Party, of trying to keep the flames of social democracy burning in the cold climate of Soviet-occupied Eastern Europe. 'Churchill reluctantly, Roosevelt without very much concern, had agreed', says Lord Healey, 'that the Red Army should occupy the bulk of Eastern Europe, and the Soviet Union should be the dominant influence afterwards. The fact that they chose to do so by installing communist governments which were under the direct control of the KGB [then known as the MGB] was in a sense a detail. The British government had very little bargaining power, although they did support me whenever I asked them for the sort of help they might be able to give. I was trying to help the socialist parties in Czechoslovakia, Hungary and Poland avoid being swallowed up by the communist parties.'

But as the East European communists, aided by Moscow, gradually got rid of their political opponents through a mixture of intimidation, terror, bribery and ballot-rigging, Western governments began to fear that the communist threat might move across the Iron Curtain. In France and Italy the communists were at the height of their popularity, which they had earned, in part, as a result of the prominent role they had played in the wartime resistance. The economic dislocation caused by the recent war also caused considerable social tension. Until 1947 the French and Italian governments included communists.

PAUL NITZE, a banker who became an American government official during the war, recalls the expectation of communist take-overs in Western Europe. 'I was in London right after the war', Nitze says, 'and there was a meeting of the World Federation of Trade Unions. I used to see one of the union leaders every day and he would tell me what had been going on. His descriptions of the debates in the WFTU were as to which European countries would become communist first and which would become communist second. Their view was that Italy would become communist first, and shortly thereafter France, and some of the other continental European countries next, and perhaps the last to become communist might be the United Kingdom – and that might take two years. They were arguing about these timetables and the way in which one country after another would cause a chain effect. And the communists really were very confident.'

Such expectations of communist victories were wildly unrealistic. But the threat to Western Europe was also emphasized by the maintenance of a huge Soviet army in Central and Eastern Europe – its size remained unknown – at a time when the United States had already rapidly demobilized and was pulling out its troops from Europe. It was not until September 1946 that Washington announced that its forces would stay in Europe as long as the occupation of Germany continued. The Western governments began to fear that Moscow might want to make further gains beyond its sphere of influence. (Elsewhere, in Iran in 1946, Moscow had pulled its troops out only under intense Western pressure.) However, OLEG TROYAN-OVSKY argues that postwar Soviet policy was primarily defensive: 'It was based on fear of a resurgence of German aggression and the fact that if a rearmed Germany became part of the Western alliance, it would create a great threat to the Soviet Union. The country was absolutely devastated by that time – we had lost over 20 million people – and under those conditions only a madman would have started a war.'

In fact, Stalin does appear to have had some lunatic ideas. 'I have heard from [former Chief of Staff] Marshal Akhromeyev that Stalin was so irritated by the policy of the United States to surround the Soviet Union with a chain of airforce bases that he was eager to have some force for retaliation,' says LIEUTENANT-GENERAL NIKOLAI LEONOV, former deputy head of the KGB's foreign intelligence directorate. 'And he had an absolutely mad idea to create an army of invasion against the United States. One of the ideas he gave was to deploy an army of 150,000 men in Chukotka at the Bering strait. This idea was worked on laboriously but proved to be so expensive that the general staff decided to tell the terrifying father of the people that it was impossible to maintain there a big army which could represent a danger of invasion, through Alaska, to the United States.'

In any case, Stalin's record before, during and after the war was a strong source of concern for the West. The Soviet Union had occupied eastern Poland and the Baltic states in the wake of the Nazi–Soviet Pact and had attacked Finland in the years 1939–40; it had crushed the Polish Home Army in 1944–5; and it was busy establishing Soviet-style regimes in Eastern Europe. Moscow could justify almost any move on the grounds of creating a defensive *cordon sanitaire* on its borders, but many in the West feared that this buffer zone would be constantly expanding.

There were further reasons for the deterioration in relations between Stalin and his wartime allies. The ideological struggle – one of the key features of the Cold War – was also starting up after something of a lull during the war. After his war service in Moscow, HUGH LUNGHI returned to the Soviet capital in 1946 to work at the British embassy. 'Quite soon after my arrival', Lunghi remembers, 'a campaign started in the media – terribly anti-American and anti-British – a campaign whose viciousness and intensity were barely surpassed even at the height of the Cold War. At the higher level, in the philosophical and political journals, there was a great deal about the inevitability of a clash between the Soviet system and the capitalist system.

'At the lower level', Lunghi continues, 'there were plays, such as that notorious one called *A Matter of Honour*. This was about two Soviet scientists who put forward the slogan that science has no boundaries so we ought to share any scientific discoveries. But they very quickly found out that when they made contact with Americans these were American spies working for the military, and the message obviously was that there are boundaries between scientists, between writers and others. We were trying to establish good relations and yet we had this vicious campaign waged against us. This was really the Cold War.'

Washington adopts the doctrine of containment

Among the American diplomats who were working in Moscow at that time was George Kennan, who provided the inspiration for a coherent American policy to deal with communist expansion. His famous 'Long Telegram', sent to Washington from the Moscow embassy in February 1946, and a subsequent article published in the following year provided the framework for the policy of containment which became the cornerstone of American diplomacy in the Cold War. Kennan later became director of policy planning at the State Department, a post in which he was succeeded by PAUL NITZE.

'The whole theory of containment', says Nitze, 'was that if you could ever contain Soviet outward expansion to a point where they began to look inward and see what this effort was doing to them internally, they'd begin to try to tinker with that watch which Marxism-Leninism-Stalinism had built and try to fix this and try to fix that. And they would disorganize the watch and it couldn't possibly stand tinkering and then it would implode and then explode and the Soviet Union or Russia would never be the same

15

after. And that did, in fact, happen. The main question in George Kennan's and my mind was how long would it take? Well, George thought it would take one generation and I thought it might take two or three – and it took 50 years before it really blew up.'

The ideas contained in Kennan's 'Long Telegram' gained speedy acceptance by the American administration; the State Department sent copies of it to all American missions abroad. It was formally adopted as part of American foreign policy in March 1947 with the declaration of the Truman doctrine, by which Washington pledged to provide assistance to all countries facing subjugation by armed minorities or outside pressures. In practical terms that meant support for regimes threatened by attempts at staging communist takeovers. The explicit formulation of the Truman doctrine had been prompted by the civil war in Greece between the communists and the royalists. Britain's financial difficulties compelled it to give up its support for the royalists, and that left the door open for the Americans to step in.

Greece was one of the first demonstrations in Europe of Washington's determination to apply the principles of containment – though there had been an earlier example in the case of Iran. In fact, Stalin largely kept out of involvement in the Greek civil war, observing the tacit agreement reached with Churchill in 1944 that Greece would be predominantly under British and, in general, Western influence. As VALENTIN BEREZHKOV says, 'The Greek communist leaders appealed for help to Stalin in desperate telegrams – and I've read these telegrams – but Stalin ignored them because he'd probably decided that if it was 90 per cent British, as agreed with Churchill, then it was theirs.' The Greek communists were finally defeated in 1949, mainly because of first British and then American support for the royalists and because assistance from Yugoslavia to the communists was halted after Tito's break with Stalin in 1948.

The Marshall Plan

The Truman doctrine was followed three months later by the Marshall Plan initiative. It later came to symbolize another successful example of containment through the massive injection of aid into Western Europe's war-ravaged economies. Yet the offer of American assistance announced by Secretary of State George Marshall in June 1947 was extended not only to Western Europe but also to the Soviet Union and two countries in its sphere of influence, Poland and Czechoslovakia. Why? GEORGE BALL came to know a great deal about the damage the war caused when he worked as one of the directors of the United States Strategic Bombing Survey. After the war he worked closely with Jean Monnet, the French economist and leading exponent of European economic integration. 'We were very conscious of the mistake that had been made after the First World War,' says Ball, 'which was to load the Germans with an enormous burden of debt which they could not repay. And as a result we had the Hitler phenomenon. We were not going to see it repeated, so the Marshall Plan was a perfectly obvious reaction. The Marshall Plan, in my judgment, was a matter of historic importance; it was a policy which I think very few people could quarrel with.'

However, the Kremlin did quarrel with the project. After some hesitation Molotov announced that the Soviet Union would not accept it. OLEG TROYANOVSKY, who attended the Paris conference held in July 1947 to inaugurate the Marshall Plan, says that Molotov rejected the offer of assistance because 'the Soviet Union insisted that each country should set forth its financial and material requirements and present them to the United States, whereas the Western powers wanted to set up some kind of a committee that would apportion the aid to the different countries. But behind that there were two different approaches to the Marshall Plan, in that the Soviet Union was suspicious that this would increase Western influence in Eastern Europe.' SIR FRANK ROBERTS remembers the implications of Moscow's rejection for the East European countries:

'Stalin not only turned it down for himself but told the Poles and the Czechs they had better get out quick. And I recall [Czechoslovak Foreign Minister] Jan Masaryk explaining once to me how humiliating that had been. It was fairly clear Stalin was not thinking in terms of cooperation even on things which would normally have seemed to be to his advantage.'

OLEG TROYANOVSKY believes that while it would have been embarrassing for Washington not to offer aid to Moscow, its wartime ally, it was certainly not disappointed by Moscow's rejection of the Marshall Plan. 'I think it was pretty obvious', Troyanovsky says, 'that the United States from the very beginning preferred the Soviet Union not to get involved in the Marshall Plan.' CHARLES KINDLEBERGER, who worked as an economist at the State Department after the war and met Marshall while they were both in Moscow in April 1947, disagrees. 'There are some people who say', Kindleberger explains, 'that Marshall knew it would be turned down. That suggests that he was a devious character. I believe that's wrong. There were plenty of devious characters about, and they may have permitted this to get through because of their deviousness. But Marshall, I am sure, was offering it, saying in a way, "We want Europe as a whole to recover." I believe that's what he meant.'

In the years 1948–52, aid worth some $14,000 million (half the amount requested by the Europeans) was distributed to Western Europe within the framework of the Marshall Plan. On an annual basis the amount was not more than what had been channelled to Europe in the immediate postwar years, but it was now being done on a more coordinated basis. As a condition of aid under the Marshall Plan, the Organization for European Economic Cooperation (OEEC) was set up in 1948 to liberalize trade, promote European economic integration and administer the assistance.

The Marshall Plan had a considerable impact on Western Europe's economic recovery. For some of its recipients, funds received under the scheme accounted for 10–20 per cent of their annual industrial investment. The United States profited from it, too, because it exported to Europe a large proportion of the machinery needed to restart production. Everybody seemed to benefit. 'The Marshall Plan was like a children's party,' says CHARLES KINDLEBERGER. 'Everyone had to have a prize. Some countries needed a lot of help, some needed almost none. And Sweden, for example, didn't need it but got a small piece.'

The political impact of the Marshall Plan was almost as important as its economic effect. The Soviet Union's rejection made it into a highly divisive issue at a time when the Cold War's fault-line was cracking open. MAURICE COUVE DE MURVILLE, who was director-general of political affairs at the French foreign ministry, says: 'The Marshall Plan confirmed the formation of the two blocs, East and West, which was already going on at the time. The Americans were not angels and they were convinced that the help they offered would help to develop their influence and power. In fact, the Marshall Plan was the beginning of the Western bloc and of the predominance of the United States on all the Western countries.'

The emergence of the two blocs

Having prevented its allies from accepting the Marshall Plan, Moscow tightened its grip on Eastern Europe by establishing the Communist Information Bureau, the Cominform, in October 1947. Its task was to coordinate communist party activities and bolster ideological conformity among its members. By now it had become clear that in Eastern Europe Stalin would no longer settle for anything less than undisputed control by local communists who, in their turn, owed their positions to his power. Earlier hopes in the region that the Kremlin would accept regimes that were friendly to Moscow but not totally subservient to it had been quashed. This pattern was now being replaced everywhere by a process of Sovieti-zation, with each East European country transformed into a carbon copy of the Soviet Union.

The last country to fall was Czechoslovakia, where the coup of

19

February 1948 established total communist domination. Yugoslavia, though under communist control since 1945, was expelled from the Cominform in June 1948 because its President, Josip Broz Tito, had showed signs of reluctance to accept orders from the Kremlin. SIR FRANK ROBERTS, who was British ambassador to Yugoslavia in the 1950s, recalls Tito asking him: '"Do you think the Russians are ever prepared to accept anybody who is leaning to their side but is keeping a relationship with the other side?" He said, "No, that's not their view, that's why we broke with them, you have to be 100 per cent on their side." And that was made clear from the communist takeover in Prague almost more than anything else.'

Rather menacingly for the West, the Cominform included not only the communist parties of the emerging Soviet bloc but also those of France and Italy. This was seen as another indication that Moscow was trying to foment internal unrest and possible communist takeovers in the two West European countries with the largest communist parties. Soviet pressure also increased in Germany, particularly in Berlin with the blockade of its western sectors which was imposed in June 1948. The year-long blockade, apparently aimed at forcing the Western allies out of the city, did much to speed up American and British plans to establish a West German state and to obtain French cooperation with that.

Soviet intransigence over Berlin also acted as midwife to the North Atlantic Treaty, which was signed in April 1949, just a month before Stalin decided that the continued blockade of West Berlin was pointless. (A year later the treaty acquired an organization – NATO – to give a permanent military framework to the alliance.) Its 11 founding members pledged to provide assistance to any member of the alliance in the event that that country came under attack. The establishment of NATO followed considerable lobbying by the West Europeans, whose own fledgling alliance would have been woefully inadequate in military terms to counter any possible Soviet advance.

SIR FRANK ROBERTS was private secretary to Ernest Bevin, the

British Foreign Secretary, at the time George Marshall, the American Secretary of State, visited London in the autumn of 1947. 'Bevin had dinner with Marshall', Sir Frank says, 'and he said to Marshall that for our plans for the economic rehabilitation of Europe to go ahead, there had to be political and security confidence in Western Europe. And for that we need some security organization and, to be frank, we need American troops back in Europe. Marshall explained that he quite understood, but it would be extremely difficult to get that through Congress – it ran entirely counter to all American precon-ceived policies. And he said to Bevin: "You have to do all you can now in Europe." We then already had our Treaty of Dunkirk with France and that was built up into the Brussels Treaty [in April 1948], bringing in the Benelux states. And only then could Bevin go to Marshall and say, "Well, we've now done all we can in Europe, now it's up to you." And on that basis the negotiations took place in 1948 for setting up NATO, much assisted, of course, by the communist takeover in Prague and the Berlin blockade.'

By the time NATO began functioning, Stalin had turned his attention in Europe in a different direction. He was bent on punish-ing the renegade Yugoslav communists, who had defied him in 1948 and who now represented the first crack in the monolithic unity of the newly established Soviet bloc. Moscow's allies, especially Hun-gary, Romania and Bulgaria, each of which shared a border with Yugoslavia, were allotted their parts in the coming operation. MAJOR GENERAL BÉLA KIRÁLY was commander of Hungary's infantry forces until his arrest on trumped-up charges of treason in 1951 which landed him in prison to serve a sentence of life imprisonment. 'The war plan against Yugoslavia', says General Király, 'was com-pleted in the summer of 1950. From 1951, at the pleasure of Stalin, we would have marched against Yugoslavia. The Korean war saved Yugoslavia from a Soviet invasion because the Soviets gradually came to the conclusion that in Yugoslavia, as in Korea, the West would not have behaved like a paper tiger.'

21

'We received a threatening note from Moscow in 1949 and began carrying out preparations for defence, although on a modest scale because of lack of money,' says MILOVAN DJILAS. 'These preparations were oriented towards guerrilla warfare and defending particular points on the Adriatic coast. In 1950 the Soviet Union was preparing an invasion of Yugoslavia in which the countries that were later to form the Warsaw Pact would have taken part. The idea was not to dismember Yugoslavia but to replace the central and republican governments.'

The Cold War goes 'hot'

North Korea's invasion of South Korea in June 1950 strongly accentuated the shift in the main focus of the East–West conflict away from Europe to Asia and later to other parts of the world – a process that had already begun with the communist victory in China in the preceding year. Although Moscow would continue to make threatening noises and issue ultimatums over Berlin for another decade, it would make no further attempts to try to force the West out of the city. The possible consequences of a direct American–Soviet confrontation became much riskier with the Kremlin's acquisition of nuclear weapons in 1949. Deterrence, based on the two superpowers' mutual fears of each other's nuclear arsenals, became one of the crucial factors in their relationship.

The war in Korea posed a major challenge to Washington. Its policy of containment in the cases of the Greek civil war and the Berlin blockade had worked well without deploying American troops in combat. In Korea the choice was between sending American (and allied) forces to the peninsula or allowing Kim Il-sung's communist North Korea to reunite the country through the use of force. Failure to act would set an unfortunate precedent for another divided country, Germany, and more immediately for the *de facto* divided city of Berlin. Moreover, the Korean war came less than nine months after Mao Tse-tung's victory in the Chinese civil war. Communism appeared to be on the march in Asia and, from Washington's point of view, it had to be stopped.

GENERAL ALEXANDER HAIG, who later became NATO commander in Europe, fought as a junior officer in Korea. He saw the North Korean invasion as part of a pattern of Soviet-inspired policies. 'As a member of General MacArthur's occupation staff in Japan,' says Haig, 'I was aware that the Soviet Union had a very active insurgency and propaganda programme to penetrate Japan; MacArthur fought that day and night – and I witnessed that at first hand. And I had no doubt after the [Korean] war broke out, and I entered it landing at Inchon and seeing the evidence of Soviet presence in the north, that they were the executor, the logistician and the grand strategist behind all this.' As American and allied troops defeated the invading force and crossed into North Korea, Chinese troops joined in the battle to support the North Koreans. On a much smaller scale, Soviet anti-aircraft and fighter units were also deployed in North Korea. Their presence was shrouded in secrecy. The consequences of acknowledging that Soviet and American troops were fighting each other would have been too frightening to consider for fear of the escalation that it might lead to.

With the Korean war, the Cold War went 'hot', but the limits imposed by Washington and Moscow ensured that conflict would not escalate beyond the regional context. After three years of fighting, an armistice was signed in July 1953 which put an end to the biggest blood-letting (along with the Vietnam war) of the Cold War. Other regional conflicts involving the United States or the Soviet Union – one of the features of East–West confrontation – would punctuate the history of the next 40 years.

By the beginning of the Korean war in 1950, the main pattern of the Cold War had come into being. Two hostile blocs, one led by America and the other one under Soviet control, were facing one another. The West had NATO; the East European countries – apart from being bound together in the Cominform – were tied to Moscow by a series of bilateral treaties (which would be complemented by the Warsaw Pact in 1955). The West had the Marshall Plan; the East had the Comecon trading organization. The propaganda war was well under way; America was setting up Radio Free Europe – joined a few years later by Radio Liberation – specifically for the purpose of broadcasting to the communist countries.

Few areas of life could remain free from the effects of the Cold War confrontation. MIKHAIL BOTVINNIK from the Soviet Union, three times world chess champion in the postwar era, recalls his earliest attempt to win the title in 1948. 'The first part of the championship was in The Hague and the second in Moscow. And there I was leading after the first half. When we got to Moscow, I was unexpectedly invited to the secretariat of the Communist Party's central committee. Andrei Zhdanov, its Chairman, told me that they were really scared that Reshevsky, an American player, would become the champion. "Let's do it the following way," he said, "the two other Soviet players, Keres and Smyslov, will lose their games against you." Sounds nice, doesn't it? In fact, it was completely pointless because in the seven competitions I had played in between 1941 and 1948 I always got first place. So there was no need to fix these games.' (A quarter of a century later – at the height of detente – the Fischer–Spassky contest for the world chess title in Reykjavik, which ended a long succession of Soviet victories, would elicit an even greater degree of interest.)

Chess was only one example of the way in which the Cold War mentality permeated all aspects of life. During the first phase of the Cold War, in particular, when travel between East and West was at best very difficult and in many cases impossible, contacts between ordinary people on the two sides of the divide became a rarity. This gave rise to much misunderstanding. OLGA SANTOVÁ, a Czech journalist, was one of the few among her compatriots who managed to visit Britain during the 1950s. 'I came to Britain as an interpreter with a group of children who'd been invited for a visit as part of an exchange scheme organized by the Czechoslovak-British Friend-ship League. And at the end of our stay in South Wales, there was a party at which the Czechoslovak children danced and sang. Over tea, the grandmother of one of the British children asked me: "How did you manage to get here?" I said, "Well, we came on an airplane." "Oh, really, I didn't know that was possible," she said. "Why not?" I asked. "Because I didn't realize", she said, "that planes could fly so high as to go over the Iron Curtain."'

The Berlin Wall; the front line between East and West. At some points along Bernauer Street (in the foreground of the picture), where apartment blocks just inside East Berlin backed onto the street inside West Berlin, people managed to escape on 13 December 1961 by jumping from the upper storeys into sheets held by the West Berlin fire brigade.

2

BERLIN: A TALE OF TWO CITIES

Berlin, the capital of the defeated Third Reich, quickly emerged as the most vibrant and emotionally charged symbol of the Cold War – a role it retained for more than four decades. Even before the Wall went up, making it the divided first city of an already divided Germany, it was the place – by virtue of its position on the front line between the Eastern and Western blocs – where many of the battles of the Cold War were fought out.

Barely three years after his forces captured Berlin in May 1945, Stalin tried to force his erstwhile allies out of the city by imposing a blockade on its western sectors. He failed. Yet for more than another decade the city remained the only gap in the Iron Curtain – until the East German authorities began to build a wall across the city to prevent the flow of their people to the West. In the weeks that followed, American and Soviet tanks confronted one another – for the first and last time during the Cold War – their turrets turned towards each other at a distance of barely 50 metres. 'Berlin had become the symbol of the Cold War, starting with the blockade of 1948,' says YULI KVITSINSKY, a former senior Soviet diplomat who spent many years at the Soviet embassies in East Berlin and Bonn. 'It was also something that the former governing Mayor of Berlin, [Ernst] Reuter, called "a spearhead permanently put into the flesh of the GDR". So this city and its destiny were somehow symbolic of the whole postwar history of Germany.'

For nearly three decades Berlin remained an artificially divided community. But it also became the place where East–West detente made its presence felt most directly when access from West to East Berlin was made easier in 1972. Nevertheless, the East Germans remained the poor relations to their Western cousins; they wanted to enjoy the same level of prosperity and range of personal freedoms available on the other side of the Iron Curtain. Their protests and exodus in the autumn of 1989 led to the collapse of East Germany's communist regime. With the breaching of the Berlin Wall in November 1989, the most visible symbol of the Cold War turned into its crumbling monument. The noise of hammering and chiselling that accompanied the tearing down of the Wall sounded the death-knell for East–West confrontation.

Berlin under occupation

Back in the spring of 1945 the noise came from guns and small arms as the Red Army fought its way through the streets of Berlin to the Reichstag. At the end of the war the city was a place of utter devastation; much of it lay in ruins, its people were starving, expecting – often rightly – the worst from the Soviet occupying troops.

As the allies celebrated victory in Europe in May, they began to put into operation their plan for the occupation of Germany, which had been worked out during the previous year by American, British and Soviet diplomats. They had demarcated the three occupation zones in Germany and the same number of sectors in Berlin – both of which were increased to four at Yalta in February 1945 to accommodate their junior ally, France.

In theory the separate occupation zones were all under the joint control of the Four-Power Allied Control Council (ACC), with its headquarters in Berlin. Its decisions required unanimous agreement and were intended to apply to the whole of occupied Germany. SIR FRANK ROBERTS, one of the British diplomats who took part in the Yalta conference, recalls the reasoning behind these arrangements: 'This was in no way conceived of as a partition of Germany. It was a matter of military convenience and safety, to avoid unfortunate incidents or misunderstandings between the four victorious allies.'

These arrangements were largely confirmed at the Potsdam conference, the last meeting of the 'Big Three' wartime allies, which took place on the outskirts of Berlin in July and August 1945. There was broad agreement on the need to keep Germany weak and prevent the re-emergence of a powerful and aggressive German state. For that reason the wartime allies insisted on applying the five 'Ds' to their defeated enemy: denazification, demilitarization, decentralization, decartelization and democratization.

Controversy at Potsdam centred on two other issues: border changes and war reparations. As the Red Army advanced into Germany during the spring of 1945, Moscow assigned large areas of eastern Germany to itself and Poland, not as occupied territory, but as lands to be administered by the Soviet and Polish governments. The Western allies acquiesced in these huge territorial revisions – involving one-quarter of Germany's pre-1938 territory – but on condition that Germany's final boundaries were to be fixed at a peace conference.

Stalin also secured the Western allies' reluctant agreement that Germany be required to pay reparations to the Soviet Union for the devastation caused during the war. The provisions of the agreement were not very clear, but reparations were to take the form of transferring machinery and industrial plant from Germany to the Soviet Union. Some of these were to come from the highly industrialized Western occupation zones in exchange for foodstuffs from the more agricultural Soviet zone.

The rift over reparations

But the issue of reparations soon became one of the main bones of contention between the Western allies and the Kremlin. Reparations were seen as crucial by the Soviet Union, both to rebuild its own war-ravaged economy and to keep the expected German economic recovery in check. OLEG TROYANOVSKY, one of Molotov's aides, recalls the Soviet Foreign Minister's feelings at the time: 'Reparations from Germany were promised at Yalta in a rather vague manner, but still there was a promise, a mention of 20 billion dollars. And I recall that when I was interpreting for Molotov at the Moscow conference in 1947, when we came to the reparations issue he said, "We are not asking, we are insisting on reparations." And then he whispered to me: "Please say this as forcefully as you can."'

By the time of the Moscow conference the Western allies had halted the delivery of the promised machinery and plant from their zones. By dismantling western Germany's production capacity and transferring it to the Soviet Union, they were merely preventing the zones under their control from being able to feed their inhabitants. The bill for staving off starvation had to be picked up by Washington and London. Although the Potsdam conference confirmed that Germany was to be treated as a single unit, CHARLES KINDLEBERGER, one of the US economists working for the reparations commission at the time, remembers that the reality failed to live up to the plans. 'The United States was feeding its zone, and the British were feeding their zone, as best they could, while they were running out of money. The Russians were looting their zone. It was really like a cow with the mouth in one zone and the udder in the other.'

The decision of the Western allies, beginning with the Americans in May 1946, to stop the transfer of reparations material from their zones to the Soviet Union angered the Kremlin, which denounced this move as a violation of the Potsdam agreement. The resulting dispute paralysed the work of the ACC, and the chances for consensus on governing Germany faded away. To facilitate German economic recovery, the United States and Britain brought together their zones for administrative purposes at the beginning of 1947. The new unit, known as 'Bizonia', granted a limited but expanding degree of self-government to the local German authorities, and it gradually became the embryonic West German state.

The Berlin blockade

In the absence of any progress on reaching agreement with the Kremlin about a peace treaty with Germany, the three Western allies and the Benelux countries held a conference in London in the spring of 1948 at which they called for the setting-up of a West German government and decided to extend the Marshall Plan to Germany. Moscow denounced this as yet another violation of the Potsdam agreement, which had specified that all decisions affecting Germany had to be reached jointly by the four occupying powers. When the Western allies introduced a new currency in their occupation zones and in their sectors in Berlin, Stalin retaliated by imposing a blockade on West Berlin in June 1948.

Moscow was in a strong position. Berlin lay within the Soviet occupation zone, nearly 200 kilometres from what was to become the border with West Germany. Access to Berlin by road, rail and river had not been guaranteed to the Western allies in writing. The Red Army had reached Berlin first, and, as SIR JOHN KILLICK, a British diplomat in Berlin at the time, remembers: 'We were in a very weak negotiating position when it came to discussing the details of access to Berlin and the practical arrangements for its survival as a city. It was a great pity that we had not all reached Berlin together and thus [could not] negotiate on a level playing-field.'

However, there was a written agreement on granting access to Berlin through three air corridors. The Western allies were now faced with a dilemma: to abandon their plans for West Germany and perhaps be forced out of Berlin altogether, which would have been a tremendous blow to their morale, or to attempt to supply the entire population of West Berlin through an airlift. 'Berlin was very

31

important to the Germans and it was part of Allied occupation rights,' says SIR FRANK ROBERTS. 'If we'd just said, we don't mind about Berlin, a great many people would have assumed that we didn't mind about anything else very much. So it became a major symbol of Allied resolution and readiness to stand up for our rights and support our allies and friends.'

The task was daunting. Britain, for example, had contingency plans to airlift supplies to its 5,000-strong garrison in Berlin, but to provide food, fuel and other basic essentials to a city of two million inhabitants seemed more like 'mission impossible'. 'We thought it was very odd that people like myself, who had been bombing Berlin a few years earlier, should now be intent on supplying it and keeping it alive,' says AIR COMMODORE FRED RAINSFORD, who as Deputy Director of Air Transport at the British Air Ministry was one of the organizers of the airlift during the blockade. 'We did think it was rather odd. But we were professionals and we did what we were told. And we were not unsympathetic.' As the airlift built up, there were flights every 90 seconds into or out of the city along the three air corridors. To reduce the time needed for these flights, bulky

People in the western part of Berlin greet a plane coming in to land at Tempelhof airport on one of the last flights before the ending of the 10-month blockade in May 1949.

32

items, such as coal, were often dropped from the air onto fields designated for the purpose.

To save weight, dried potatoes and powdered milk were substituted for the fresh articles, flour replaced bread, and coal-fired power stations were converted to using oil, even though that had involved flying in heavy machinery to convert the plants. Air Commodore Rainsford remembers other examples of inventiveness. 'There was a panic about salt because of its corrosive properties. But flying boats are made of salt-resistant materials and we carried vast quantities of salt on these Sunderland flying boats, landing on Berlin's Havel lake until it froze up.'

Although the massive airlift kept West Berlin going, it could barely provide more than about one-third of the city's normal daily requirements. Life was tough for Berliners, who had only a few years earlier undergone relentless bombing raids and then an even more destructive siege. Much of the city still lay in ruins. But the recent experience of wartime hardship made it easier to adjust to another bout of privations. KLAUS SCHÜTZ, who 20 years later became West Berlin's Mayor but at the time of the blockade was a young student, puts it this way: 'If the blockade struck us today, it would be much more difficult to adjust to a situation where you didn't have electricity for hours, where you didn't have enough coal and, although you had enough to eat, you always had the feeling that this could break down. At that time, after the war, we were used to all that, so the blockade wasn't a deep shock for us.'

Stalin had imposed the blockade in the hope that he could force the Western allies to abandon their plans for a West German state and to expel the Western powers from Berlin. However, he was not prepared to risk an armed conflict over Berlin only three years after a war that had devastated the Soviet Union's European parts. America still had a nuclear monopoly and it had pledged to keep its troops in Germany as long as that country's Four-Power occupation lasted. But Stalin's caution was not taken for granted by contemporaries. SIR JOHN KILLICK recalls those tense times. 'Well, to us on the ground in Berlin, sitting as I was one night playing bridge by candlelight, when we got the news of the buzzing and destruction of a BEA [British European Airways] aircraft, it seemed almost as though World War Three was just around the corner. With hindsight, I would have to say that the chances of Stalin going to war over Berlin must have been very small. But Berlin's political importance was enormous. We regarded it in the stock-phrase of the time as the bastion of freedom.'

The foundation of the two German states

If one of Stalin's aims in imposing the blockade on western Berlin was to prevent the establishment of a West German state, the result of his action was the exact opposite of what he had intended. Fear of Moscow's aggressive behaviour concentrated minds wonderfully in the West. In April 1949 the French – who had previously obstructed moves towards German unity – joined their occupation zone to 'Bizonia'. The German authorities in this new 'Trizonia' abandoned their hopes for the speedy establishment of a united German state, and in May 1949 approved the Basic Law – or constitution – of the Federal Republic. This was the West German state that was to exist for 41 years – along with East Germany, which was formed in the Soviet occupation zone five months later.

The foundation of the two German states came as a shock to many Germans, who had hoped that the postwar division of their country would be short-lived. 'In those days we had a very strong feeling that German unity was just around the corner – that in maybe one or two years, if we were steadfast, it would happen,' says KLAUS SCHÜTZ. 'We had this type of illusion and it lasted in a strong way far into the 1950s.' That illusion was further fostered by the refusal of the West German authorities to recognize the existence of the other Germany on the grounds that the people of East Germany had not had their say in this matter through free and democratic elections.

That policy of non-recognition, laid down by Chancellor Konrad Adenauer's administration, was to continue for two decades.

West Germany's Basic Law declared Berlin to be part of the Federal Republic, but this was not fully acknowledged even by the Western allies, let alone the Soviet Union. The United States, Britain and France wanted to preserve Berlin's special status, which furnished them, along with the Soviet Union, with continuing occupation rights over the whole of Berlin. Different interpretations of those occupation rights gave rise to endless disputes between the Soviet and the Western sides.

The two economic systems

Though legally not part of West Germany, what West Berlin did share with the Federal Republic was the economic miracle that was soon to emerge, helped by the Marshall Plan and the currency reform of 1948, which replaced worthless banknotes, printed in large quantities by the Soviet occupation authorities, with a stable currency. Before that, conditions had been appalling. 'Because money was worthless, we had the cigarette economy, the soluble coffee economy and the silk stockings economy,' says CHARLES KINDLEBERGER, who was with the American State Department's division of German economic affairs at the time. 'Cigarettes were much better because you could make exchanges with them, whereas with stockings it wasn't clear that you would get the right size and you couldn't split a pair. The only real money were the ration tickets.'

As conditions in West Germany improved, huge subsidies began to be channelled to West Berlin. The American economist JOHN KENNETH GALBRAITH, who was then in charge of German and Japanese economic affairs at the State Department, was struck by Germany's rapid postwar recovery. 'The singular feature about attacks on industry was how quickly they were repaired,' says Galbraith. 'This was something that John Stuart Mill mentioned almost 150 years ago. He said that one always notices the destruction following war, not recognizing that much of that capital will be quickly replaced anyway. This point has been strongly emphasized by Joseph Schumpeter, who called capitalism a system of creative destruction. Yet I was still surprised at the speed, particularly of the German recovery.'

Yet the economic miracle eluded East Germany, the country its leaders called the 'first workers' and peasants' state on German soil'. The Soviet Union continued to fleece East Germany for reparations: after the foundation of East Germany, more than one-quarter of its income from industrial production was earmarked for reparations or the maintenance of Soviet troops in the country. To avoid economic privations and a repressive communist regime, many East Germans fled to the West. In 1952 the East German authorities converted the demarcation line between the two Germanies into a fortified border, but Berlin, with its special Four-Power status, remained a yawning gap in the newly constructed Iron Curtain.

The East Berlin workers' rising

Those who stayed behind faced chronic shortages of essential goods, aggravated by a policy of collectivization, which prompted many farmers to abandon the land. Expectations of milder policies were raised by Stalin's death in March 1953, but they were quashed with the adoption of higher production quotas for industrial workers – whom the regime called the main beneficiaries of socialist society – which amounted in practice to a wage cut.

The new quotas were scheduled to come into effect at the end of June to coincide with the 60th birthday of Walter Ulbricht, leader of the (communist) Socialist Unity Party (SED). But Ulbricht received an unexpected birthday present on 16 June, when construction workers staged a demonstration against the higher work quotas. Their demands – including a call for a general strike – were quickly disseminated by RIAS, the Radio in the American Sector, and much of the East Berlin workforce downed tools on 17 June. The protest movement spread like wildfire: there were strikes and demonstrations in a further 200 towns. The workers' demands became more political: they called for Ulbricht's resignation and free elections. KLAUS SCHÜTZ remembers those electrifying days: 'Nobody thought that anything like this could be possible. These people had lived through twelve years of the Nazi regime and then seven years of communist rule; they had never seen anything free and democratic; so there wouldn't be anything possible like this, a demonstration for freedom and democracy. That was the first astonishing experience – that it was possible. I never really felt – with one or two exceptions later – the city in such movement as during those days. That was due to the fact that some of the workers' columns were marching through West Berlin on their way to East Berlin to protest there.'

The protesters ransacked the headquarters of the secret police in East Berlin and attacked gaols to release prisoners. But the movement was almost entirely spontaneous and, lacking leaders and clear objectives, was already disintegrating when the Soviet tanks appeared on the streets in the afternoon of 17 June to disperse them. Dozens of demonstrators were killed at the time or executed in the retribution that followed. The East German authorities justified the repression of the uprising on the grounds that it had been a fascist and imperialist plot to overthrow the workers' state. PETER FLORIN, who at the time was in charge of foreign relations at the SED central committee, now points to a more authentic reason: 'The Soviet Union used its tanks in East Berlin and the GDR to prevent what they feared might be a complete change in the political situation; to prevent people coming to power who would not guarantee to the Soviet Union that they would stand for Soviet policies in East Germany.'

Whether the East Berlin workers' rising ever posed such a threat is questionable. It was certainly the first example of large-scale collective protest against communist rule since the establishment of Stalin's East European empire. It was also the first occasion on which Moscow used force to prevent the collapse of a communist regime in the region. The spectacle of an uprising against a communist government raised doubts even among its supporters, such as the writer STEFAN HEYM, a refugee from Nazi Germany, who moved from the United States to East Germany in 1952 to escape the McCarthyite witch-hunt: 'I began to think that something was seriously wrong. After all, how come, in a workers' state, that workers were on strike and rising up against the workers' government? Somebody was wrong, either the workers or the government. It was Bertolt Brecht who said at the time that in this situation it might be better for the government to look for another people. But they couldn't find another people: the people were already there. So perhaps the government should change: but it didn't.'

The Berlin rising showed up the weakness of the communist regime, but its result was to bolster the future of the East German state. Barely a year before the events of June 1953, Stalin had proposed the unification of the two Germanies – holding out, furthermore, the prospect of free elections, which would have meant political oblivion for East Germany's communist rulers – but only on condition that a peace treaty would bind Germany to neutrality. At the time the Western allies had rejected that proposal, arguing that it should be left to the democratically elected government of a reunited Germany to decide its own foreign policy, including whether it should be neutral or not. But after Moscow's denunciation of the imperialist West for plotting to overthrow the workers' state in East Germany, it became more difficult to bargain with the three Western allies about a unification of Germany that would have led to the liquidation of the East German state. True, Stalin's successors did revive the idea in 1955, but only in a somewhat half-hearted way in order to prevent West Germany joining NATO.

The West's rejection of the Soviet offers reflected its ambiguous attitudes to German unity. Though publicly in favour of the idea, privately Western politicians felt that without West Germany's membership, NATO would not be strong enough as an alliance. 'It was the Germans' right to be reunified, and we were saying so, but none of us expected it to come for a long time – and the majority of us felt, so much the better,' says CLAUDE CHEYSSON, the French diplomat who became President Mitterrand's first foreign minister in 1981. 'And there was this very poor joke at the time – we love Germany so much that we are pleased there are two Germanies to love.'

If East Germany could not be bargained away, Moscow's objective was to transform it into a more viable ally. The Kremlin agreed to stop all reparations from East Germany in 1954 and wrote its debts. East Germany became a founding member of the Warsaw Pact on 14 May 1955 – less than a week after West Germany joined NATO.

Yet no amount of Soviet economic aid or political recognition could help East Germany redress the balance in its contest with West Germany. People continued to leave in their droves, and Berlin was the place through which they changed countries. By 1961 some three million people – one-sixth of the population – were to leave, creating serious skill shortages in the East German economy. (The contrast in economic conditions prompted the rhetorical question as to what was Karl Marx's legacy to the two German states. The answer was that to East Germany he had left *The Communist Manifesto* and to West Germany *The Capital*.)

The flight from East Germany not only devastated the East German economy but seriously embarrassed Moscow, punching a big hole in the credibility of an ideology that claimed the superiority of the communist system. Khrushchev made no secret of his problem over Berlin. SIR FRANK ROBERTS, the British ambassador in Moscow in the early 1960s, recalls Khrushchev's attitude: 'Khrushchev used to say to me, "What would you do if you had a tooth in your mouth which was causing you great pain? You'd want that tooth out and that's how I feel about the East German side." So he was looking for some solution. I remember once he was telling me, "Well, why don't you have a United Nations presence in Berlin – much nicer for you and you'll be able to get out". And he rather thought we wanted to get out, but of course the Berliners would not have accepted the UN as an adequate substitute for the Americans and the rest of us.'

Khrushchev had tried to lance the boil in November 1958, when he addressed an ultimatum to the Western allies. Unless the problem of Berlin was solved within six months, the Soviet Union would sign a peace treaty with East Germany, handing over to it responsibility for the whole of Berlin, which Khrushchev claimed lay on East German territory. West Berlin was to be given the option of becoming a demilitarized 'free city', but access from it to West Germany was to be negotiated with East Germany – a state Bonn and the West in general continued not to recognize. Another blockade – this time to be imposed by East Germany – appeared to loom on the horizon. But the West called Khrushchev's bluff and the ultimatum faded away.

The Berlin Wall

Meanwhile, the problem of Berlin would not go away. East Germany was becoming the top half of a sand-glass with its population draining away. Something drastic had to be done. And finally in the early hours of the morning of 13 August 1961 it happened. DETLEF KÜHN, who 10 years later became Director of the Institute for All-German Questions, was a West Berlin student at the time. 'On the evening of 12 August one of my uncles, who lived in East Germany, came to see us,' says Kühn. 'And he told us that he had experienced some difficulties in reaching West Berlin, which was not normal at that time: practically everyone could enter West Berlin from the East. We were together until midnight. And early next morning my father came to my room and said, "Get up, hurry up; the East Germans have closed the border between East and West Berlin." We needed more than two years until we were allowed to see my uncle again in East Germany, at Christmas 1963.'

The East German authorities had mounted a massive operation, by putting up barbed wire and other obstacles around West Berlin virtually overnight. The Wall itself took many months to complete. The initial reaction of Berliners and the outside world was complete bewilderment. East Berliners who had a chance to escape tried to do so while it was still possible. Detlef Kühn remembers the dramatic escape attempts at the time in Bernauer Street, where the apartment blocks on the southern side were in East Berlin but where the outer side of the pavement attached to them was inside West Berlin. 'The doors of these buildings were, of course, locked immediately on 13 August, but people who lived in these flats had a chance to escape by jumping from the windows,' says Kühn. 'On that day I saw several people jump from the third or fourth floor into sheets held by the West Berlin fire brigade on the pavement outside. Later on the buildings were demolished.'

Although the building of the Berlin Wall came as a shock, its origins went back a long way, to the time when the border between East and West Germany was transformed into a fortified border. YULI KVITSINSKY, who was the interpreter of the Soviet ambassador to East Germany when the Wall was built, relates the background: 'This idea was first born in 1952, but it was rejected by Stalin, and for a number of years nothing happened. Then, in the summer of 1961, Ulbricht told us that the situation in the GDR had become rather dangerous and he was not able to guarantee the stability of his republic unless extraordinary steps were taken. A couple of days later we conveyed a positive answer from Khrushchev and that was the start of the preparatory work for the operation.'

Initially, the Western allies were at a loss as to how to react. The cordoning-off of West Berlin was carried out by the East German security forces, who had no right to interfere with the movement of people across Berlin, which remained in theory under Four-Power control. However, any attempt by Western forces to tear down the obstacles was likely to provoke armed Soviet intervention, with incalculable consequences. EGON BAHR, who was head of information in the office of West Berlin's mayor, Willy Brandt, still feels bitter when he recalls those tense days: 'When the barbed wire was put in place,' says Bahr, 'Brandt went to the three Western commandants, and he had quite a job on his hands to convince them that they should protest. And it took 48 hours before they delivered their protest to their Soviet counterpart in East Berlin. This must have given the impression that the West would not react. So on 16 August – three days later – they started to build the actual Wall. And there was a real breakdown in confidence between the Berliners and the three Western powers.'

Prompted by Willy Brandt, President Kennedy responded. His National Security Adviser, MCGEORGE BUNDY, believes the action was decisive: 'We were slow to understand the strength of emotions in West Berlin. But we did send General [Lucius] Clay [hero of the Berlin airlift] and Vice-President Johnson, as well as a detachment of troops, to Berlin. And I don't think the Berliners held it deeply against President Kennedy, because I was with him in Berlin in 1963 and he received the most overwhelming ovation that I have ever seen in my life.'

By the time Kennedy visited Berlin, the construction of the Wall had been completed. It was a monstrous creation: four metres high, made of concrete slabs and with a heavy concrete pipe running along the top, measuring altogether 111 kilometres in length. There were nearly 300 watchtowers and over 50 bunkers. It provided employment for hundreds of guard dogs and thousands of border guards.

The Wall became a fitting symbol for the entire communist bloc, a system that tried to keep its citizens in a gigantic prison. For their part, the East German authorities referred to it as 'the anti-fascist protection Wall', which kept potential Western aggressors at bay. In fact, in military terms it had no real function. However, with the Wall in place, Berlin 'was no longer the ideal place to operate from,' says

GEORGE BLAKE, the British intelligence officer, based in Berlin, who was giving away secrets to the KGB. Before the Wall, 'Berlin had been the main battleground for the intelligence services,' says Blake, 'because it was easy to move from one sector to another and it was easy to recruit agents.'

Among the older generation of former SED officials, some still support the original explanation for dividing Berlin. 'The very existence of the Wall was not, of course, good for the foreign policy of the GDR,' says PETER FLORIN, 'but it was built to make clear where our state's border stood and it was very important to guarantee the security of this international border. However, it would have been better if another way could have been found to guarantee that border.' East German Politburo member GÜNTER SCHABOWSKI (whose announcement on allowing East Germans freedom of travel was to herald the breaching of the Wall in November 1989) no longer tries to justify it on security grounds. 'I accepted the Wall at the time it was built,' says Schabowski. 'Our position was that our state, which embodied the socialist future of Germany, had to be protected from the threat of being undermined by the imperialist opponent. And the same was true for the people. They had to be protected from themselves because they were vulnerable to the influence of our opponents' media. The bleeding to death of the East German economy had to be prevented.'

For East Germans – even those sympathetic to the regime – the building of the Wall amounted to an admission of failure on the part of their rulers. STEFAN HEYM says: 'In 1961 I found that a socialism that needed a Wall to keep its people in the country wasn't the right kind of socialism. If it had been a real, functioning socialism, it would have been the other side – the West, the capitalists – who would have built a Wall so that their people wouldn't come running over to the East. I spoke to Walter Ulbricht's private secretary, [Otto] Gotsche, suggesting policies that would make it possible to tear down the Wall as soon as possible. And he told me after the Wall was built, "Well, now they can't run away, now we have them."'

For Moscow and East Berlin the construction of the Wall ended the Berlin crisis. It also spelt the end of Soviet threats to intimidate the West over Berlin – a weak and exposed link in the Western alliance. This was not an unwelcome development for the West. 'If you read some of the American memoirs', says OLEG TROYANOVSKY, the Soviet diplomat who spent much of his career in the United States, 'you will see that Kennedy heaved a sigh of relief when the Wall was put up because he realized correctly that that was the end of the Berlin crisis.' But the grim stability brought by this new development was not immediately obvious to contemporaries. As EGON BAHR recalls, there was a resurgence of concern at the time of the Cuban missile crisis in October 1962: 'We got a letter from President Kennedy in which he told the governing mayor that he could not exclude repercussions against Berlin if things became critical around Cuba. Brandt wrote back, saying that he was absolutely convinced that the President should act in Cuba as if Berlin were not a critical point. After this he told us in his office that we might be on the eve of a long march within a few days. "Please bring some warm socks," he said. And we thought that if the East Germans, backed by the Soviets, were to start an attack to occupy West Berlin, then we could think about calling an uprising in the GDR because we had had the experience of 1953.'

The impact of the Wall on Berlin's inhabitants was devastating. West Berlin became an island-city, completely surrounded by a hostile environment. For East Germans the easy option of flight to the West via an undivided Berlin came to an end, and many years were to pass before small numbers of them were allowed to travel to the West. Many tried to escape; and there were over 80 recorded deaths at the Berlin Wall alone. As a psychiatrist, DR HERBERT LOOS used to treat some of the psychological victims of the Wall in East Berlin. 'We often had people here who had applied to emigrate to West Berlin or West Germany. Because of this there were many who suffered, who had difficulties with their surroundings and who couldn't sleep properly. They needed treatment. For most people the Western part of the city was further away than South America. Very few of them had a chance to go to West Berlin, and for that reason they had no idea what it actually looked like, apart from what they could see on television.'

For the East German regime the building of the Wall represented a lifeline without which it could hardly have survived, let alone prospered. After 1961, with the escape route out of the country blocked, East Germans had no choice but to buckle down and work hard in the hope of achieving at least a degree of prosperity. The result was the East German economic miracle of the 1960s, which was nowhere near as spectacular as its West German counterpart but did at least make the ailing East German economy the most successful in the Soviet bloc.

A new approach to the East: Ostpolitik

Another, though delayed, effect of the Wall was the change in West German policy towards the East, a shift that became particularly pronounced after Willy Brandt became Chancellor in 1969 at the head of a coalition government of Social Democrats and Free Democrats. Before this new, far more accommodating policy, known as *Ostpolitik*, was adopted, West Germany had claimed to represent the whole of Germany, refusing to recognize the East German state because its citizens had never had an opportunity to express their political views in free elections. Bonn had also failed to accept Germany's postwar borders without a peace conference; and it was not prepared to have diplomatic relations with any country – with the important exception of the Soviet Union – that had recognized East Germany.

This policy was strong on principle, particularly as regards German unity and the German people's right to self-determination. But it was weak on the postwar realities, and it laid Bonn open to accusations of revanchism, of wishing to recover territories lost to Poland and the Soviet Union. By failing to recognize East Germany,

45

it made conditions for West Berliners much worse, and the lack of diplomatic relations with the Soviet bloc countries (which, of course, recognized East Germany) considerably reduced Bonn's influence in Eastern Europe.

Ostpolitik was to change all that. EGON BAHR, who was one of the architects of the new policy, points out its origins: 'When the Wall was built dividing Berlin, we came to the conclusion that nobody was helping us. So we had to help ourselves to bring holes in the Wall and to bring people together. We realized that since we were unable to change the situation completely, we had to look for a *modus vivendi* and we had to negotiate with the communist governments. This brought us to the Moscow negotiations because we were fully aware that the people in Moscow were the real masters, so we had to start there.' The result was the Moscow treaty of 1970 – a non-aggression pact in which Bonn finally recognized Germany's post-war frontiers as inviolable. These included the intra-German border as well as the Oder–Neisse line as the frontier between East Germany and Poland. Moscow was prepared to accept a separate letter, in which the West German government expressed its view that the treaty did not rule out Germany's peaceful unification at a future date.

Bonn made ratification of the Moscow treaty dependent on Soviet willingness to negotiate a new Four-Power accord on Berlin. The wartime allies reached agreement in 1971, though the Soviet side refused to discuss East Berlin altogether. However, Moscow gave up its earlier claim that West Berlin, located within East Germany's territory, fell under the East German government's authority. For Berliners the most important part of the Four-Power accord was that it guaranteed access rights for West Berliners to East Germany. The implementation of the accord was made dependent on the two Germanies and the Berlin city authorities regulating their relations and sorting out the detailed arrangements concerning Berlin.

The talks were not easy. EGON BAHR, Bonn's chief negotiator in

46

Moscow and East Berlin, has the following psychological explanation for the difficulties: 'It was much easier to negotiate with Mr Gromyko [the Soviet Foreign Minister] than with my East German fellow-countrymen,' he remembers. 'They were absolutely rigid, cold and hostile. And we knew that they acted like this not of their own will but because they were forced by the Soviets to do so. And it became interesting to find out if I could meet some people who were, say, 51 per cent German and only 49 per cent communist. That was our hope: to find such people.'

While negotiations with the East Germans were under way in 1972, Brandt's government came under sustained attack from the opposition and it lost its majority in parliament. Egon Bahr has vivid memories of those tense times: 'It was a terrible discussion. We were called traitors and were accused of spoiling the chances of German unification because we were saying that the GDR was a state and we had to treat it as a state. But we were convinced it was necessary to go on, that this was the right policy and, if we lost the elections, we would lose holding the banners high in our hands.' In fact, Brandt's governing coalition increased its majority in the elections, paving the way for the conclusion of the Basic Treaty between the two Germanies in December 1972, which ended 23 years of make-believe – the fiction that East Germany did not exist.

The debate in West Germany was mirrored on the other side of the intra-German border, though there – in the absence of a democratic system – the discussions took place behind closed doors. PETER FLORIN, by then first deputy Foreign Minister, was among those caught up in the controversy: 'Within the leadership of the SED, there was an intense debate about how relations towards the FRG should be shaped,' Florin remembers. 'There were those who feared that the FRG government, led by the Social Democrats, would somehow try to strangle the GDR by embracing it. On the other hand, quite a number of other personalities felt that it should be possible to use this favourable situation to normalize relations. This second group finally prevailed.' Ulbricht, by then 78, was among those who had reservations about the whole process. He was therefore retired as SED leader in 1971. His replacement was Erich Honecker, who had supervised the building of the Berlin Wall.

For Berliners the Four-Power accord and the Basic Treaty changed life for the better. The Wall stayed, but it became increasingly porous. West Berliners, who had for a decade been able to visit East Germany only on special occasions, like Christmas, could once again see their relatives and friends quite frequently. Road and rail access between West Germany and West Berlin was improved. The Bonn government was allowed to represent West Berlin internationally and extend diplomatic protection to the city's inhabitants. The presence of West German government agencies in the city was sanctioned: in fact, it had more West German civil servants than Bonn. For their part, the East German authorities agreed to permit their citizens to visit the West in cases of pressing need, such as illness, and family occasions like weddings and funerals.

The improvements that came in the wake of *Ostpolitik* made life much easier for KLAUS SCHÜTZ, who had become West Berlin's mayor in 1967: 'In the years before,' Schütz says, 'it was very difficult for me, as the mayor, to talk to people here when they came to see me with their problems – not being able to see their parents or their children. So the new agreements were very important for bringing people together.'

Berliners were not the only beneficiaries of *Ostpolitik*. The East German regime also gained a great deal. Mutual recognition by the two German states led to their admission to the United Nations in 1973; and East Germany, which, prior to the Basic Treaty of 1972, had maintained diplomatic relations with only nineteen states because of the West German-sponsored diplomatic boycott, had within three years increased its tally to 115.

East Germany's gains went well beyond the notions of international prestige. As contacts between the two Germanies multiplied in the 1970s, there was a huge increase in West German economic aid which had, in one way or another, sustained the poor relations in East Germany. Many forms of hidden subsidies dated back to Adenauer's years and the reasoning behind these was to make East Germany less dependent economically on the Soviet Union. Over the years East Germany had become the invisible member of the European Community because its goods could be exported without quota restrictions to West Germany. West Germany also undertook the task of financing the upkeep and improvement of the road and rail links between West Germany and Berlin.

East Germany had already introduced a more unorthodox business practice: that of the trade in human beings. Shortly after the Wall went up, East German officials offered to release political prisoners to the West in exchange for a fee. This trafficking in people began modestly in 1963, when the East Germans handed over eight prisoners. By the time the communist regime collapsed in 1989, it had 'sold' nearly 250,000 people – many of them not actually prisoners – for an estimated DM3.5 billion, most of it supplied in the form of goods, ranging from oil to bananas. EGON BAHR still feels embarrassed about the practice: 'I have to confess that I had all the time the feeling that it was morally bad to buy human beings,' says Bahr. 'But there was a tacit agreement between government and opposition in Bonn to continue, based on the conviction that if you can free people for money, you should do so. In the meantime, I think it had become part of the GDR's budget and, since prices were going up in all sectors of the economy, this included also the prices for human beings.'

Buying people's freedom was bad enough, but the system was open to further abuse because prisoners fetched a price that was 25 times as high as the fee charged for ordinary people who applied to emigrate simply to join their families in the West. The East German authorities, therefore, used to put many of these applicants in gaol on trumped-up charges so as to maximize their income.

There was a massive inflow of West German subsidies into the

49

East in the form of interest-free credit, duty-free access for East German goods and lump-sum payments to exempt West Germans travelling through East Germany from transit fees. This, as well as the psychological effect of the Wall, undoubtedly made the East German regime more stable economically than it would otherwise have been. One result of this was that the East German leadership – once the most insecure in Eastern Europe – became increasingly complacent. GREGOR GYSI, a lawyer who in late 1989 at the age of 41 became the East German communists' first and last genuinely reformist leader, considers this to have been one of the major flaws of the system: 'In practice the leadership of East Germany didn't change between 1945 and 1989', says Gysi. 'Apart from the odd new face, they quite simply grew old together. If at the beginning they were aged between 30 and 40, by the end they were between 70 and 80. And their view of the world remained unchanged and hence they had no point of contact with the new generations.'

The ageing East German leadership failed to realize the extent to which West Germany continued to be a source of fascination for East Germans – and the more so as the gap between the two Germanies began to widen once again in the late 1970s, when the communist economies in Europe started to grind to a halt. Meanwhile, Bonn had continued to pump huge subsidies into West Berlin to keep up its status as a showcase of the West. There was no way in which East Berlin could match the expensive shops of the West Berlin Kurfürstendamm or the personal freedoms and cultural diversity on the other side of the Wall.

Ostpolitik ushered in a vast increase in contacts between Germans on the two sides of the divide. Ideas and opinions could be exchanged, and this led to frequent comparisons being made between living standards and life-styles in the two Germanies. These rarely favoured the East. If the policy of accommodation and the accompanying subsidies temporarily shored up the East German regime, the longer-term impact of the ever-expanding contacts was to undermine East Germany. Its whole *raison d'être* was gradually fading away. The foundations of the Berlin Wall began to crumble well before the Wall itself was breached and even before Erich Honecker declared, at the beginning of 1989, that it would stand for 50, if not a hundred, years. Though Honecker's prediction seemed rash at the time, no one could have imagined then that by the end of the year the Wall would be lying in ruins.

ICBMs – the mainstay of Moscow's nuclear deterrent – trundle past the Lenin mausoleum on 7 November 1964, during the annual military parade marking the anniversary of the Bolshevik revolution.

3

IN THE SHADOW OF
THE BOMB

For all but a small group of scientists and politicians involved in the development of the atomic bomb, awareness of the nuclear age began on 6 August 1945, when a United States air force B-29 bomber dropped 'Little Boy', the first atomic bomb, on the Japanese city of Hiroshima, killing some 70,000 people on the day. But the nuclear arms race had begun well before the annihilation of Hiroshima. Although Nazi Germany never came near to producing a nuclear bomb, American fears that Hitler might acquire such a weapon played a major part in the establishment of the American nuclear research laboratories at Los Alamos in 1942. Work along similar lines got under way in the Soviet Union less than a year later. But the impetus for speeding up the Soviet research was the successful testing and employment of nuclear weapons by the United States in July and August 1945. Soon after that, Lavrenti Beria, the head of the security apparatus, was put in charge of the project.

ROALD SAGDEYEV, who started work a few years later as a young physicist in the top-secret establishment with the code-name 'Arzamas-16', where the Soviet nuclear programme was developed, heard from his more senior colleagues about the political pressure to produce a bomb. 'Stalin felt he was trailing behind the Americans after August 1945,' Sagdeyev says. 'There was a plan according to which the bomb had to be built by the end of 1949. Stalin's hangman,

Beria, was the chairman of a special committee to supervise the bomb programme – a hint that scientists might become an endangered species if they were unable to build the bomb. But my friends were very fortunate. They were able to explode the first design [in August 1949] a few months before the deadline. My teacher, Lev Artsimovich, remarked: "Imagine what would have happened if the bomb had not exploded. It would have been the bloodiest test of a nuclear bomb."'

Moscow's success in ending the Americans' nuclear monopoly prompted Truman in January 1950 to authorize the development of the even more powerful fusion weapon, the hydrogen bomb. Given the destructive power of fission bombs of the Hiroshima type, the increased explosive force of the H-bomb was perhaps of more psychological than military importance, although its much better yield-to-weight ratio did greatly facilitate the design of strategic missiles. The fear in Washington was that Moscow would get there first. EDWARD TELLER, the nuclear physicist who has come to be known as the father of the H-bomb, recalls these fears: 'Stalin had explicitly said in response to Hiroshima, "We are going to have the atomic bomb and we are going to have more." I then believed that the possibility of the hydrogen bomb was already there on the Soviet side and not to work on it would be dangerous.'

Indeed, the Soviet hydrogen bomb programme had started before the American one. A week after exploding their first atomic bomb in 1949, Igor Kurchatov's team switched their research to the fusion bomb. But, as so often during the Cold War, the Americans had the dubious distinction of winning that race. They exploded the first thermonuclear device in November 1952. Less than a year later the Soviet Union followed suit.

Back in late 1949 the Soviet atomic bomb was not the only development to worry Washington. In October Mao Tse-tung's communist forces triumphed in the Chinese civil war. Communism, though apparently contained in Europe, was on the march in Asia. The American administration initiated a thorough policy review to deal with the continuing dangers. The document completed in April 1950 became known after the initials of the National Security Council as NSC-68. Its assessment of Soviet military strength exceeded that of earlier reports. 'What we saw, particularly in Europe,' says PAUL NITZE, the main author of NSC-68, 'was a Soviet Union which had clearly superior conventional capabilities. The situation was quite desperate and you needed to do something.' Nitze, who was Director of the Policy Planning Staff at the State Department, went beyond assessing Soviet military capability to describe Soviet intentions and the ideology that motivated them. In the document, Nitze says, 'we emphasize the fundamental design of the Kremlin – those who control the Soviet Union – to retain and solidify their absolute power, first in the Soviet Union, and second in the areas now under their control. And we put third the ideal of communist expansion, the fulfilment of the Marxist-Leninist goal of a world dominated by socialism.'

NSC-68 concluded by calling for a massive, though unspecified, increase in American military expenditure, both nuclear and conventional. The nuclear build-up was already under way. However, President Truman did not accept the case for an extensive conventional rearmament programme until after North Korea's invasion of South Korea in June 1950, which led to a huge American military involvement to stop the spread of communism in the region. By the end of the Korean war in 1953 the American defence budget had more than trebled – to reach $50bn.

The 'New Look'

In June 1953, after three years of bitter fighting, a ceasefire was concluded in Korea. This made it possible for President Eisenhower to introduce a new defence strategy, more in tune with his thrifty approach to government finance. He believed that a strong economy was a fundamental precondition for strong defence; and the economy could be stable only if taxation was kept low. The military implications seemed obvious. One tonne of TNT cost at that time $1,700 to manufacture. Fissionable material could produce the same explosive impact for only $23. The cost of matching Soviet conventional strength would be prohibitive, so America – and the NATO alliance – should rely more on nuclear weapons. Eisenhower's 'New Look' strategy appeared to have been made more feasible by the deployment in 1953 of tactical nuclear weapons. How these short-range artillery shells or rockets equipped with nuclear warheads could be used without doing damage to those employing them or their immediate environment was never successfully explained.

The 'bomber gap' and the 'missile gap'

In its own terms, Eisenhower's 'New Look' was a triumph: he had the rare distinction among postwar American presidents of leaving office with a clearly balanced budget. But within a reduced overall military expenditure, spending on nuclear weapons increased more than the President would have liked. Much of that was due to exaggerated estimates of the Soviet Union's strategic force. These excessive estimates were based on poor information in the era before the arrival of spy satellites; were fuelled by the Kremlin's calculated acts of deception; and found fertile soil in the worst-case scenarios prepared by strategic planners. First came the 'bomber gap'. In 1955 the Soviet air force put on display its first long-range bomber, the B-4 *Bison*, for the benefit of foreign air attachés. To make up for the lack of numbers, 10 *Bison* made a wide circle and flew over the assembled guests for a second time. The trick worked; the world was impressed by Soviet strength. However, its unintended result was that Eisenhower had to give his air force more of the B-52 strategic bombers than he had planned.

The myth of the 'bomber gap' was followed by the equally fictitious 'missile gap'. That was, in part, a result of *Sputnik*, the first artificial satellite, which the Soviet Union launched in October 1957. Concern spread in the United States about the strength of the Soviet

Khrushchev thought he could bully the young American President, who was barely four months into office. (In the background, turning to his right between the two leaders, is Andrei Gromyko, that most durable of Cold War foreign ministers, who held his post from 1957 to 1985.)

missile forces. Khrushchev contributed much to reinforcing these fears by boasting at every point about Soviet military prowess. SERGEI KHRUSHCHEV, the late Soviet leader's son and a missile designer by profession, recalls a speech his father made in 1961 at a plant in Ukraine, where he 'told the workers, "Now you are really producing missiles like sausages" – a remark that was published in the press'. This was sheer invention. As late as the end of 1963, when the United States had over 550 intercontinental ballistic missiles (ICBMs), the Soviet Union had fewer than 100. Yet the alleged 'missile gap' became an important issue in the presidential election campaign of 1960. Eisenhower knew it was untrue because even before the launch of the CIA's first spy satellite, *Discoverer*, in the summer of 1960, the U-2 reconnaissance planes were providing reasonably reliable information. However, the American intelligence agencies were divided on this issue and Kennedy's Democrats made the most of the 'missile gap' scare in the run-up to the elections.

After the Kennedy administration assumed office, a thorough inquiry conducted by Robert McNamara, Secretary of Defence, concluded within weeks that the 'missile gap' was a fallacy. In spite of that, the administration did not feel it could go back on its pledge to boost the strategic missile force. Although the other side was lagging far behind, inertia in American policy-making led to a vast expansion in the missile force. The United States reached its target of over 1,000 ICBMs and 650 submarine-launched ballistic missiles (SLBMs) in 1967. This was a vast nuclear arsenal with a destructive potential well in excess of anything required simply to deter the Kremlin from aggression against the United States.

ALEXANDER BESSMERTNYKH, the former Soviet Foreign Minister, who spent three decades dealing with the United States before his retirement in 1991, was 'always curious about that mystical figure of 1,000 ICBMs. And there was no answer. If you tried to check it,' Bessmertnykh says, 'there was no document that would say that there was a specific calculation, say by the joint chiefs of staff, for anything that came to this 1,000. And only later, after several years, I met one of President Kennedy's assistants; and he told me the figure was taken just out of the blue – because it looked impressive. It was not a rational decision. And since that number was not actually warranted by any strategic calculations, it probably created an impetus to the arms race which the makers themselves did not expect.'

Decisions on the Soviet side were often a great deal more irrational. Whereas in the United States the president and his executive would often have to justify any new arms procurement initiative in the face of political opposition and in the full glare of publicity, in the Soviet Union the military-industrial complex worked in secret, unhindered by any checks or balances. Many Soviet weapons projects were either pointless or wasteful. One such project was the MiG-25 high-altitude interceptor, under development in the early 1960s to counter the planned American supersonic high-altitude bomber, the B-70. McNamara cancelled the B-70; nonetheless, the MiG-25 still went into production, now without a genuine target. In the early 1970s two similar ICBMs, the SS-18 and the SS-19, were being developed by different design bureaux. 'Both had their patrons in the Politburo,' says ALEXEI ARBATOV, Director of the Moscow Centre for Geopolitical and Military Forecasts, 'so in order not to defeat either of them, a decision was taken to employ both systems.' This was not the exception but the rule because, as Arbatov then adds, 'as recently as three or four years ago the Soviet Union was simultaneously developing and deploying 13 new offensive strategic weapons programmes in response to six by the Americans.'

In his farewell address, delivered in January 1961, President Eisenhower warned Americans about the excessive influence of the military-industrial complex. Arms manufacturers, the service chiefs and their congressional lobbyists had a shared interest in exaggerating the Soviet military threat. However, JACQUES GANSLER, who was in charge of weapons procurement at the United States Defence Department in the 1970s, in between periods of working for companies with defence-related business, puts it in a different way. 'In the national security regime', Gansler says, 'it's very hard not to err on the side of caution. You tend to emphasize; if we can do it – they should be able to do it – therefore they will do it – therefore we must do it. That's not a conspiracy, that's a sincere effort to try to do what you think is a necessary risk minimization. Clearly, the Soviets were doing the same thing. There's a mutuality of interest here because if the budgets are higher, the industry gains, the services gain and the Congress gains because they've got jobs and everybody's happy.'

Theories of deterrence

There were many reasons for the nuclear arms race: Moscow's eagerness to catch up with the Americans; exaggerated estimates in the United States about the strength of the Soviet strategic force; mutual fears, even paranoia, concerning the intentions of the other side; the need to cut – particularly in the West – spending on expensive conventional arms; and the influence of the pro-nuclear sections of the military-industrial complex. There was also a strong tradition in Washington that America's superiority in the nuclear sphere should be maintained. Meanwhile, Moscow was catching up to reach parity. In a sense both concepts, 'superiority' and 'parity', counted for little after Moscow had acquired a credible deterrent in the second half of the 1950s. By then the 'delicate balance of terror' had been established. But what use, if any, did strategic thinkers envisage for nuclear weapons? In the beginning it was all so simple. America had the bomb; it was still at war with Japan; an invasion of the Japanese islands would have cost many thousands of American lives (and quite likely more Japanese casualties, too, than the combined effect of the Hiroshima and Nagasaki bombs). Besides, by forcing Tokyo into a quick surrender, Truman managed to prevent Soviet troops from taking part in the occupation of Japan and helping Moscow pursue its own agenda, as it was doing in Germany and Eastern Europe. Whether it was intended or not, the use of the nuclear bombs also amounted to a warning to Stalin that he should not in future go too far in testing America's patience.

However, the immense destruction wrought by the use of these two bombs transformed nuclear weapons into a taboo. They were never used again during the Cold War. But the existence of nuclear weapons had a crucial bearing on the shaping of Soviet–American relations. Mutual fears about their possible use contributed perhaps more than anything else to the prevention of direct conflict between the two sides. It was a major factor in the development of the theory of peaceful coexistence espoused by Stalin's successors after his death in 1953. According to the new doctrine, in the nuclear age war between the opposing social systems was no longer inevitable, as Stalin had proclaimed. Khrushchev still believed that communism would triumph around the world, but this victory would come not through war but as a result of the ideological struggle coupled with the economic contest between the two blocs.

The notion of peaceful coexistence followed the development of a Soviet nuclear deterrent. For a time after the Hiroshima and Nagasaki bombs, the United States retained its nuclear monopoly. Already under Truman American nuclear weapons were regarded as a counterweight to what was seen as a vast Soviet superiority in conventional forces in Europe. Though the first Soviet nuclear explosion in 1949 caused immediate consternation in Washington, it was to be years before the Soviet nuclear force came anywhere near to posing a credible threat to the territory of the United States. It was not until the second half of the 1950s that Moscow gradually acquired the capability to deliver nuclear charges to America, first on its bombers and then, from the late 1950s, by means of its ICBMs. In any case, the United States continued to enjoy a huge superiority in nuclear strength until the late 1960s. However, superiority in the nuclear field mattered little in practice. Even though at the time of the Cuban missile crisis in 1962 the United States had a massive lead in nuclear weapons, that did not mean that the administration thought it had a first-strike capability. ROBERT MCNAMARA explains: 'President Kennedy and I believed that if we launched our 5,000 against their 300, we could not with certainty conclude we could destroy all of the 300. And if one or five or 10 or 50 remained and were launched against us in response to our strike against them, millions of US citizens would be killed. What president and what secretary of defence would ever expose their people to such a risk?' Credible deterrence therefore needed only a relatively small nuclear force.

Deterrence under Eisenhower was used in an all-embracing way. His defence strategy was linked to the threat that any act of aggression on the part of the Soviet Union might bring about massive nuclear retaliation. This was the price of the cost-cutting budgets under the policy of the 'New Look' which weakened America's conventional forces. Eisenhower backed up his policy by his celebrated remark at a news conference in March 1955, when he said that, used against military targets, nuclear weapons were, in effect, no different from ordinary bullets.

Kennedy criticized Eisenhower's doctrine of massive retaliation on the grounds that it was ineffective in small-scale local conflicts and that it restricted America's options to a choice of either initiating huge devastation or acquiescing in gains made by Soviet-backed countries. The 'New Look' was replaced by the notion of flexible response – meeting an aggressor on its own ground and using the means appropriate for the purpose. This led to an expansion in both conventional and nuclear forces, although much of the conventional build-up was diverted to the American war effort in Vietnam. Flexible response was adopted as NATO's strategy in 1967; however, the new military doctrine still assumed that in the event of a massive Soviet attack, NATO would have to use nuclear weapons to stave off defeat. It simply put back the clock to the stage at which Western forces would have to resort to a nuclear response.

It was during the early 1960s – a time of massive escalation in nuclear weapons first on the American and then also on the Soviet side – that the most well-known concepts of nuclear strategy were developed. Foremost among these was mutual assured destruction (MAD), which was to become the cornerstone of American thinking. THOMAS SCHELLING of Harvard University was one of its leading exponents. 'MAD originally was a very simple notion,' Schelling says. 'The key idea was that neither side, by attacking first, could deny the opponent the capability of virtually unlimited, punitive destruction.'

But hardly had the notion of MAD been developed when it came under threat from moves to deploy anti-ballistic missile (ABM) systems in America and the Soviet Union. A potential aggressor with an ABM fence might be tempted into launching a massive first strike against an opponent's missiles in the belief that its own defensive umbrella could protect it against most of the other side's expected retaliation, which would have been much weakened by the initial attack. The obvious response to developing ABMs would be to multiply the number of ICBMs to ensure mutual assured destruction. That was going to lead to the madness of yet another round in the nuclear arms race. At the Glasboro summit in 1967, ROBERT McNAMARA had serious problems trying to persuade Alexei Kosygin, the Soviet Prime Minister, to desist from deploying ABMs. 'I thought Kosygin was going to develop a heart attack,' McNamara recalls. 'The blood rushed to his neck, he became red in the face and said – and these were his exact words, "Defence is moral, offence is immoral; we are only defending Mother Russia." And I think he believed it.'

The 1972 treaty on banning the deployment of (almost all) ABMs was to be one of the triumphs of detente. But by then the deployment of missiles that could carry more than one nuclear warhead had got under way to reduce the effectiveness of a possible defensive shield. 'The multiple independently-targetable re-entry vehicles, or MIRVs, are the illegitimate child of ABMs,' says PAUL WARNKE, a senior American arms control negotiator in the 1970s. 'They were developed to make sure that the offence could overwhelm the defence.'

The issue of defence as a destabilizing force came back with a vengeance when President Reagan announced his Strategic Defence Initiative (SDI) in 1983. His plan, quickly dubbed 'Star Wars' because of its science-fiction-like qualities, envisaged the development of an impenetrable shield against strategic forces in which laser and particle beam weapons would knock out the opponent's ballistic missiles. Although there were serious doubts as to whether 'Star Wars' could ever work, wrangling over SDI did much to slow down the progress of disarmament talks in the mid-1980s, when Gorbachev regarded it as the main obstacle in the way of compromise on other issues.

Nuclear blackmail

During the Cold War strategic thinkers envisaged different scenarios for the possible use of nuclear weapons, ranging from limited strikes to all-out retaliation. The taboo on the actual use of the Bomb stayed, but on several occasions during periods of tension a threat

– or a hint – that nuclear weapons might be used was employed as a form of blackmail. Within days of the start of the Berlin blockade in June 1948, Truman sent to Germany two squadrons of B-29 bombers of the type used in dropping the Hiroshima and Nagasaki bombs. In reality, these planes had not been modified to carry atomic bombs, though this fact was concealed. Whether this episode made any difference to Stalin's tactics remains open to doubt.

Eisenhower and his supporters have claimed credit for stopping or preventing Chinese military action by threatening to use nuclear weapons on several occasions in the 1950s, most notably in forcing a ceasefire in the Korean war in 1953. 'The Korean conflict was settled as a result of the direct threat by Eisenhower to utilize nuclear weapons if a solution was not found,' says GENERAL ALEXANDER HAIG. 'That convinced the Soviets to impress upon their allies that this was the point where a negotiated settlement should be arrived at.' However, China's decision to yield may have been prompted by Stalin's death and its consequent concern over the level of Soviet support for Peking. Besides, China was also worried by the rising cost of the war.

Three years later it was Khrushchev's turn to brandish nuclear missiles in the face of the British and the French to persuade them to withdraw from Egypt at the time of the Suez crisis. SIR WILLIAM HAYTER was the British ambassador in Moscow at the time: 'I was woken up in the middle of the night and sent for by the then Foreign Minister, Dmitri Shepilov, who handed me a note. It was a letter [Prime Minister] Bulganin wrote nominally to [Prime Minister Sir Anthony] Eden – though, in fact, it was meant for publication and was published before Eden ever got it – and it contained rocket-rattling threats.' However, Khrushchev's move was very much in the nature of a publicity stunt. At that time Moscow barely had a nuclear deterrent against Washington's overwhelming strategic force which, according to expectations, would have been used to retaliate against the Soviet Union in the event of a Soviet attack on America's NATO allies.

Khrushchev's Cuban missile gamble

Using nuclear blackmail or pressure was a dangerous game, and this message was brought home to the world most clearly during the crisis which followed the deployment of Soviet medium-range nuclear missiles in Cuba in October 1962. Khrushchev had decided to send missiles to Cuba primarily to find a way to eliminate Moscow's inferior status to Washington in the nuclear arms league. The long-term Soviet objective – finally achieved under Brezhnev – was to achieve parity in the sphere of nuclear weapons. This goal was more political than military in inspiration because the Soviet Union possessed, by any standards, a credible deterrent even during the latter part of Khrushchev's rule. Since the Soviet Union was lagging far behind the United States in the arms race, the cheapest way to claim that a parity in the nuclear field had been established was to lie. Khrushchev used to brag about non-existent Soviet achievements. But his continued boasting sometimes proved counter-productive; in 1960 it reinforced the 'missile gap' scare in the United States, thus contributing to a huge nuclear build-up under Kennedy.

Next to Khrushchev's vivid imagination, the cheapest and quickest alternative to deploying more of the gigantic ICBMs was to instal intermediate-range missiles nearer the United States. The emergence of a communist regime under Fidel Castro in Cuba – an island barely 150 kilometres from the coast of Florida – provided a golden opportunity. Even the Soviet SS-4 missiles, with a range of 1,900 kilometres, could hit targets nearly as far away as Washington; the SS-5, with its longer range, would cover much of the United States. FYODOR BURLATSKY, one of Khrushchev's aides at the time, says: 'I edited Khrushchev's letter to Fidel Castro after the Cuban missile crisis in which he explained why he had decided to place the missiles on Cuba. And he wrote: "We were together with the Minister of Defence, Marshal Malinovsky, in Varna, Bulgaria. And we were walking on the beach of the Black Sea and Marshal Malinovsky told me," Khrushchev explained to Castro, "look, over on the other side of the Black Sea, in Turkey, there are American nuclear missiles which can destroy in six minutes all cities in the south of the Soviet Union. That's terrible. And then", Khrushchev continued, "I asked Malinovsky, why can't we do the same as the United States? Why couldn't we place arms, for example, on Cuba? Malinovsky answered that maybe it was a good idea."'

There was another reason for installing missiles in Cuba. In April 1961 Cuban anti-Castro émigrés, backed by the CIA, had launched an abortive landing raid in Cuba in the hope of starting an uprising against the authorities. The invading force was routed and the Bay of Pigs incident confirmed Fidel Castro's worst fears about Washington's intentions towards his regime. Its effect was to push Castro into Moscow's welcoming arms. Khrushchev was eager to protect Castro's revolutionary regime, which had adopted the communist system of its own will – unlike Moscow's East European allies, who had it foisted on them by Stalin. It was important to defend Cuba; and it was equally important to emphasize this to Castro in explaining the need for deploying nuclear missiles on Cuba. ALEXANDER ALEXEYEV, the *de facto* Soviet envoy to Cuba since 1959, when he arrived there under cover as a Tass news agency correspondent, returned to the island in June 1962 with Khrushchev's instructions: 'Just tell Fidel that we are ready to ensure the security of Cuba by all possible means. And tell him that for the sake of the Cuban revolution we are even prepared to install our nuclear missiles in Cuba – to frighten the Americans.'

Alexeyev had already struck up a friendship with Castro three years earlier, when he first visited the island. Knowing Castro well, he thought the Cuban leader would be reluctant to accept the stationing of Soviet nuclear missiles. After all, he had been arguing that Cuba must defend itself by its own efforts and with the help of public opinion in Latin America and throughout the world. In fact, Castro went along with Khrushchev's plan. 'Fidel's reaction was pretty interesting,' says Alexeyev. He plunged into thinking and said to us, "Yes, it's a very interesting idea, but not to save the Cuban revolution. I see it as important for the socialist camp in its struggle against American imperialism and that's why I see that you need it. If that is so, we are ready to accept it and to take part of the risk.'"

Following Castro's acceptance, a massive operation got under way. Between July and October a total of 43,000 Soviet servicemen were shipped to Cuba, along with hundreds of tanks, anti-aircraft missiles and other military equipment – all of it designed to service and, in the event of an American attack, defend the 42 SS-4 missiles delivered to the island. (The SS-5s never arrived.) What made the entire operation even more extraordinary was the fact that it was carried out in the utmost secrecy. Khrushchev had forbidden Alexeyev to communicate anything relating to the operation in writing; contact had to be kept through personal emissaries. The Soviet servicemen, dressed as ordinary holidaymakers, arrived in Cuba on cruisers. On arrival they were given Cuban army uniforms. Military equipment was unloaded under cover of darkness. Everything that had to be carried on deck was covered in tarpaulins, and nuclear warheads were surrounded with lead to prevent the detection of radioactive emissions.

The reason for the secrecy was Khrushchev's desire to present the Kennedy administration with a *fait accompli*, by announcing the completion of the deployment of intermediate-range missiles after the mid-term congressional elections in the United States in early November. Once the SS-4s and SS-5s were in place, there would be little the Americans could do about it; and, with elections out of the way, there would be less incentive for the administration to act. Khrushchev's cloak-and-dagger operation nearly paid off. Senior American officials – with one exception – were convinced that the Kremlin would not risk a confrontation with the United States by deploying offensive weapons in Cuba; and since Moscow at that time had not deployed nuclear missiles anywhere outside Soviet territory, it seemed unlikely that it would abandon that practice with regard to Cuba. As late as mid-September a national intelligence estimate concluded that the Soviet leaders would probably not deploy intermediate-range missiles in Cuba. RAYMOND GARTHOFF, who joined the State Department from the CIA a year before the Cuban crisis, says: 'That, of course, was a serious error, although one of the authors of that estimate argued later it wasn't really their mistake, it was Khrushchev's mistake!'

The one American official who did not share his colleagues' complacency towards Moscow's designs on Cuba was John McCone, Director of the CIA. He was struck by reports of the build-up of powerful SAM-2 anti-aircraft missile batteries in Cuba which – in spite of the all-encompassing secrecy – did filter out and he concluded, without any hard evidence, that the reason for their deployment was in all probability to protect nuclear missiles against attacks from the air. His conclusion, which was not backed by the CIA, was dismissed by the administration. But McCone's repeated warnings while on honeymoon in France in September led to the resumption of reconnaissance flights over Cuba.

On Sunday 14 October a U-2 spy plane flew over western Cuba; pictures it took over San Cristóbal, about 150 kilometres west of Havana, were carefully scrutinized the following day by CIA analysts, who concluded that they showed a medium-range nuclear missile site. Early in the morning of 16 October McGEORGE BUNDY, the National Security Adviser, went to the White House to break the news to Kennedy, who was having breakfast in his bedroom. Was the President shocked? According to Bundy, he was not: 'He was a strong man and a cool customer. And he was impressed by the importance of the information. But "shock" is too strong a word.' Kennedy summoned a meeting for later that morning of a group of military and civilian officials who became known as the 'ExComm' – the Executive Committee of the National Security Council. It was to remain in continuous session throughout the 13-day crisis.

To an outside observer, placing Soviet SS-4s in Cuba may have seemed simply a response to the earlier deployment of American Jupiter missiles in Turkey. McGeorge Bundy admits that 'we did understand that the Russians might see it as just tit for tat'. But for

68

the Americans there were two crucial differences. Bundy explains: 'The missiles in Turkey had not been placed there secretly. They were part of a reasonably well-recognized, if not exactly of a universally admired, arrangement, namely the NATO defence arrangements. And in thinking about Soviet missiles less than 100 miles from the United States, from the point of view of the American people that kind of deployment of armed force by a major power was exactly what the Monroe doctrine said must never happen.'

The Monroe doctrine – rooted in the idea that the American continent should be kept free from interference by non-American powers – was not particularly popular with the European powers during the nineteenth century and it was no more popular with the Soviet leadership. But it was deeply ingrained in the political consciousness of Americans. There was also another reason to stand up to Khrushchev over the siting of Soviet missiles in Cuba. It was a development which many American officials and Washington's foreign allies considered to be an attempt to shift the nuclear balance of power. ROBERT MCNAMARA was sceptical about that: 'Kennedy and I didn't believe it was a shift in the balance; our chiefs of staff and many others did believe it was. If we didn't respond there was a very great risk that our allies would lose confidence in our willingness to prevent the Soviets from carrying out aggression elsewhere in the world. Moreover, the Soviets would feel that they could get away with further steps of what appeared to be aggression under the cloak of deceit.' In any case, Kennedy had earlier painted himself into a corner by warning Moscow – at a time when he was not aware of the deployment of the medium-range missiles in Cuba – that any such event would lead to the gravest consequences.

Washington and Moscow eyeball to eyeball

ExComm faced a choice of three options. But the first of these – to do nothing – was unthinkable, the more so given Kennedy's earlier warning. To impose a naval blockade on Cuba and prevent the full deployment of all the Soviet missiles was another option, though at that time the Americans did not know for certain whether the nuclear warheads for these missiles had been delivered to Cuba. (In fact, they had been shipped to Cuba by the time the embargo was imposed and were available to be fired within a matter of hours if such an order came from Moscow.) The third choice was to launch an air attack on the missile sites – an operation that would probably have to be followed up by a full-scale invasion. GEORGE BALL, the deputy Secretary of State, was one of the handful of advisers on ExComm to be strongly opposed to military action. 'I thought we should not take any irremediable action,' Ball recalls, 'because we ought not to exhaust all the possibilities for working it out with the Soviet Union. For that reason the idea of an embargo seemed highly sensible.' United States officials began to make preparations for a blockade which, for reasons of international law, was to be described in less provocative terms as a 'quarantine'. But preparations also got under way to assemble an invasion force, a move that was to cause near panic in Cuba a few days later.

After a week's deliberations, Kennedy went public on 22 October and announced to a startled world the Soviet missile deployment in Cuba and the American response, with a naval quarantine due to start within 48 hours. Many feared this measure might lead to a direct confrontation between the two superpowers. What if the Soviet ships did not stop? In the event they did. But this was by no means the end of the crisis. Kennedy was insisting on the removal of Soviet offensive weapons from Cuba as the price of lifting the blockade around Cuba. To add weight to his words, American strategic forces around the world were put on alert – one of three occasions during the Cold War that this happened. On the day the blockade came into operation, 24 October, the Strategic Air Command (SAC) was moved, for the first and last time during the Cold War, to a state of alert known as Defence Condition 2 – just one stage away from combat deployment. To make sure that Moscow knew what was happening, the order for the alert, issued by General

Thomas Power, commander of the SAC, was not encoded. What made the situation more alarming was that Kennedy and his senior aides – who were often at odds with their more hawkish top brass – were not aware of this and similar instances of sabre-rattling by the military chiefs. However, the Soviet forces were never moved to an advanced state of readiness.

As Washington awaited a response from Khrushchev, days of excruciating tension followed. Then, on 25 October, Khrushchev sent a rambling and emotional letter in which he suggested that the Soviet missiles would be withdrawn if the United States pledged not to attack Cuba. But the sense of relief felt by the American leaders lasted only a few hours because next day, while ExComm was discussing Khrushchev's offer, a more toughly worded letter arrived from Moscow, demanding this time that the *Jupiter* missiles be pulled out of Turkey. Further bad news turned this day into 'Black Saturday' when it was reported that a U-2 had been shot down over Cuba and Washington assumed (wrongly) that the order must have come from Moscow. GEORGE BALL remembers those dangerous hours: 'I was absolutely scared to death. I told my wife there was a very serious problem going on and suggested that she go down and get the basement into some kind of shape and told her, "You and the black cook, go down there, and take a Bible for her and a case of Scotch and cigarettes for yourself" – which she did.'

The mood was no better among the Soviet leadership in Moscow – though ordinary Soviet citizens had no idea what was happening because of a media black-out until nearly the end of the crisis. SIR FRANK ROBERTS, the British ambassador in Moscow, was struck by the sudden collapse of confidence among Soviet officials after the Americans imposed the blockade. He says: 'I remember all the Russians I was meeting were almost gibbering, saying "You represent England, you are a naval power, this is an act of war."' As the days passed without an agreement, it appeared to the Moscow leadership that the danger of an American attack on Cuba was just around the corner. 'There was a feeling', says SERGO MIKOYAN, whose father Anastas was one of Khrushchev's closest colleagues, 'that we were just on the eve of a Third World War, especially on 27–28 October. There was confusion and, in the very last hours, even panic. Khrushchev actually became very much afraid that he had led the country into a catastrophe.'

Khrushchev's fear was based on the expectation of an immediate American assault on Cuba, directed primarily against the Soviet missile bases and their defenders. Although the Soviet troops had been ordered to fight to the death, to wage war against the United States in the Caribbean – regarded as an American lake – would have been disastrous for Moscow. For Khrushchev to contemplate the destruction of a sizeable Soviet force on Cuba with equanimity might have been too much to expect. For that reason Washington was concerned that he might retaliate in other regions where Moscow enjoyed superiority, by attempting to destroy the *Jupiter* missiles in Turkey or by pushing the Western allies out of West Berlin.

There was another potential danger that the American administration was not aware of at the time. Thirty years after the crisis General Anatoli Gribkov, who had visited Cuba during the crisis to supervise the construction of the missile sites, disclosed that in addition to the SS-4 missiles there had been nine *Frog* tactical missiles, equipped with nuclear warheads, in Cuba in 1962. He also sent belated shivers down the spines of surviving former ExComm members by claiming that, unlike the SS-4s, which could only have been launched following an order from Moscow, it would have been within the authority of the local Soviet commander to fire these missiles had American forces invaded Cuba. If the *Frog* missiles had been used against American forces, Washington would have been under intense pressure to retaliate with a massive nuclear strike.

This doomsday scenario appears somewhat less likely when challenged by the testimony of Major-General Leonid Garbuz, deputy commander of the Soviet forces in Cuba, who says that Khrushchev 'personally instructed' the six senior officers before their departure for Cuba that 'all the decisions to use the nuclear missiles would come from Moscow and Moscow only'. During the crisis itself, Garbuz adds, 'all the missiles, including the tactical missiles, were in the lowest stage of alert, which was set by Moscow. And we didn't have the right to move it from one stage of alert to another, except by order from Moscow.' On the day Kennedy announced the blockade, Moscow's instructions were repeated. Garbuz says: 'On 22 October, at 21.35 hours, we received the order allowing us to use conventional weapons but prohibiting under any circumstances the use of any nuclear weapons.'

Pulling back from the brink

At the time ExComm's members were blissfully unaware of whatever dangers the presence of *Frog* missiles in Cuba may have posed. But for much of 'Black Saturday', 26 October, they were wrestling with the problem of how to deal with the different demands contained in Khrushchev's two letters. Finally, a stern reply was drafted: Washington would not negotiate unless the Soviet missiles in Cuba were dismantled and removed. But a message communicated separately conceded Khrushchev's two demands. It pledged that America would not invade Cuba if the Soviet missiles were pulled out; and Kennedy promised to remove the *Jupiter* missiles from Turkey once the Cuban crisis was settled.

The world awaited Khrushchev's response – but no one more eagerly than those in Cuba, the island that would have been the battlefield for the first Soviet–American war. AMBASSADOR ALEXEYEV was asleep when his phone rang early on Sunday morning. 'It was [Cuban] President Dorticós', Alexeyev recalls, 'and he asked me, "Alejandro, what are you doing?" I answered, "Well, I'm sleeping." He asked me why I was sleeping, the radio had just announced that the Soviet government was withdrawing its missiles from Cuba. I answered him that American radio was always ready to invent any *canard*. But he told me that it wasn't American radio, it was Radio

Moscow. I was really shocked because there had not been any signal from Moscow that this was going to happen.'

Khrushchev's gamble had failed to pay off. He had hoped to boost Moscow's superpower status by increasing its nuclear threat to the United States. Now the Soviet missile units had to face the humiliation of a withdrawal from Cuba, supervised by American forces. As for the informal undertakings contained in Kennedy's message to Khrushchev, these were hardly important. Kennedy had wanted to remove from Turkey the obsolete *Jupiter* missiles – which Khrushchev so feared – even before the Cuban missile crisis. What was more important to Kennedy was that he should not be seen to be losing face by withdrawing the *Jupiter* under duress. So his undertaking was kept secret.

Nor was Kennedy's pledge to refrain from invading Cuba very significant given the fact that after the Bay of Pigs disaster of the previous year a United States invasion of Cuba was not on the cards, although Washington continued to encourage plots against Fidel Castro. Khrushchev, on the other hand, was widely considered to have let down a Third World ally. What made the bitter pill more difficult for Castro to swallow was that it was Khrushchev who had first persuaded him to accept the missiles, yet the decision to remove them had been made without even consulting him.

Anastas Mikoyan arrived in Havana in early November to pacify the Cuban leader. It was a difficult task. 'Castro was very angry and there were difficult moments when he even stopped the talks for three days,' says SERGO MIKOYAN, a fluent Spanish speaker who accompanied his father on the trip to Cuba. The deadlock was finally broken by an unexpected event. Mikoyan's wife died in Moscow and he decided not to return to the funeral but to devote himself to the task of persuading Castro to go along with the deal. AMBASSADOR ALEXEYEV was present at the negotiations: 'This actually played a most important part in sorting out our relations with Cuba,' Alexeyev explains. 'Cubans are a very sentimental people; all members of the Cuban government came to express their condolences to Mikoyan,

Nikita Khrushchev and Cuban President Fidel Castro on the Lenin mausoleum, May Day, 1963. Behind the smiles, not all was well; Castro felt betrayed by Khrushchev's decision six months earlier to pull out the Soviet missiles from Cuba. During his visit Castro insisted on inspecting Soviet nuclear missile facilities before accepting Khrushchev's claim that Moscow could protect Cuba from Soviet territory.

who became a very important person. And that actually saved the situation.'

Although there were other dangerous times in the Cold War when the superpowers were at daggers drawn – notably during the repeated Berlin crises of 1958–61 and at the time of the Middle East wars of 1967 and 1973 – the Cuban missile crisis was, perhaps, the occasion when the world came closest to a nuclear confrontation. 'John Foster Dulles, when he was Secretary of State [under Eisenhower], used to say that the leaders of the world should be able to reach the brink and look into the abyss to conduct foreign policy,' says OLEG TROYANOVSKY, who was Khrushchev's foreign policy aide at the time of the Cuban missile crisis. 'But when Kennedy and Khrushchev did reach the brink and looked into the abyss, I think both sides got really and truly scared. And both of them handled it quite well. Kennedy, in that he was always leaving the door open for Khrushchev, and Khrushchev in realizing after a few days of the confrontation that political means should be sought out of the crisis. In the long run there was something positive in it, in that both sides realized the danger of nuclear war, not theoretically but in practical terms.'

ROBERT MCNAMARA considers this bleak fact to have been the crucial message for the nuclear age. 'The greatest contribution of the missile crisis', says McNamara, 'was the degree to which it heightened an understanding of the danger of nuclear war – the danger of continuing indefinitely the combination of human fallibility and nuclear warheads. Khrushchev and Kennedy were determined to put the crisis behind them and move forward on a more cooperative basis.'

The new spirit of cooperation bore fruit in 1963 with the establishment of the 'hot line' between Moscow and Washington, which aimed to provide an instant and well-established means of communication in times of crisis via teleprinter instead of the frequent improvised contacts during the crisis. Moreover, after years of fruitless negotiations, the two sides also signed a partial nuclear test-ban treaty by which they undertook to refrain from testing nuclear devices in the atmosphere. More ambitious plans for a total ban foundered on Moscow's reluctance to allow on-site inspections, which would have been required to monitor small underground nuclear explosions. (Britain signed the treaty: the other two emerging nuclear powers, France and China, refused.) However, the test-ban treaty was the first modest step towards regulating the nuclear arms race and it reduced atmospheric pollution from radioactive fall-out.

The humiliating withdrawal of Soviet missiles from Cuba reinforced Moscow's determination to build up its nuclear capability to a level where it matched that of the United States, which was also expanding rapidly at the time. The 1960s witnessed a huge increase in the number of nuclear missiles on both sides, leading to a massive 'over-kill capacity', with the theoretical power to destroy the world. A more immediate concern focused on the destabilizing effect of this build-up and this strengthened the calls for arms control. Through its positive and negative effects, the Cuban missile crisis created the momentum for measures that would eventually lead towards the policy of detente.

'Phrases ... and bases.' While the American general places the Stars and Stripes on the map to mark yet another US military base, this time in Greece, the man in his back pocket is shouting 'peace', 'defence' and 'disarmament' into the microphone. (Soviet poster 1952.)

4

THE WAR OF WORDS

'Naturally many of us felt somewhat uncomfortable at times,' begins BORIS BELITSKY, the veteran Soviet broadcaster who joined Radio Moscow's English-language service in 1946. 'On the other hand, as the Cold War developed and as, say, the Voice of America also began to hand out obvious propaganda, this gave rise to a certain spirit of competition, an athletic competition, if you like, between broadcasters. And inevitably there was an element of competition, of outdoing the other chap.'

Journalists were in the forefront of the war of words that raged throughout the Cold War. During periods of thaw in East–West relations the shrill voices were toned down, but in this war there was no ceasefire. Much of this had to do with the different attitudes to journalism in Soviet-style and democratic societies. GÜNTER SCHABOWSKI, who in the early 1980s was editor of *Neues Deutschland*, the East German Communist Party's newspaper, points out the main difference: 'Journalists in socialist countries were not the conscious or unconscious force that can have a destabilizing function – as it does in democratic public life – to counter the arrogance of power. Their role was that of being the apologists of the authorities. Their overriding function was not the provision of information but propaganda and indoctrination. We had a slogan "agitation through facts". There was much direct falsification of facts but that was not the case at all times and in all situations. The socialist media's most devastating effect was its consistent ignoring of reality, which was crying out more and more for change.'

Journalists in the West could afford to take sides in the East–West confrontation. Their colleagues in the East had no choice. They either supported the authorities' policies or had to suffer the consequences. Alternatively, if they managed to escape to the West, they could join the other side and broadcast back to their own countries.

International broadcasting was the most explicit attempt by the Cold War adversaries to win the hearts and minds of people on the other side of the Iron Curtain. However, the Soviet Union had got off to a flying start. The ideological struggle, based on the teachings of what soon became known as Marxism-Leninism, was part of the Soviet government's practice from the time of the Bolshevik revolution. As the technology became available, Radio Moscow launched its foreign-language service in 1929 with broadcasts in German, soon followed by programmes in English and French. Until the outbreak of the war, the service was officially called 'the sector for broadcasts to foreign workers in the USSR' so as to avoid the charge from other governments that the Kremlin was trying to spread communist propaganda round the world – which is what it was doing.

The pattern did not change after the war. 'With the start of the Cold War, our broadcasting became even tougher politically,' says BORIS BELITSKY. 'I would describe it as something like a messianic spirit, an attempt to instruct the whole world how it should go about shaping its life. This was partly a reflection of domestic propaganda, which could count on a certain measure of success because it had to do with a captive audience at that stage. But the attempt to inject the same messianic spirit into foreign broadcasting was futile. And the emphasis on "Stalin the Great", "Stalin the Immortal" and so on could not but antagonize many listeners because it went against the democratic spirit in which they had been brought up.'

For the United States (and Britain) foreign-language broadcasts began with the immediate prewar and wartime emergency. They were designed to counter German and Japanese propaganda. The Voice of America (VOA) barely survived attempts to dismantle it in the immediate postwar period, on the grounds that it was no longer needed, and it was only in 1947 that it launched its Russian-language transmissions. (The BBC had started a year earlier.)

Although slow to start engaging in the battle of the airwaves, the Americans did come up with one very significant innovation in the propaganda war. This was the creation of two 'surrogate' stations, Radio Free Europe (RFE), which went on the air in 1950 and was soon broadcasting to six East European countries (though its Albanian service closed down after a few years); and Radio Liberation (RL), which followed suit in 1953 with its programmes aimed at the Soviet Union. The purpose of these stations was not so much to represent the policies of the United States administration and report on matters as seen from Washington – which was left to VOA – but to try to reflect the concerns and interests of the people in the countries to which they were broadcasting.

GEORGE URBAN, who became RFE's director in 1983, after a long career at both RFE and the BBC, explains the thinking behind surrogate broadcasting. 'After the occupation of Eastern and Central Europe by Soviet forces and the installation of communist governments in these countries,' says Urban, 'there was a feeling that these nations should be given a forum because under one-party rule in those countries different views could no longer be voiced. And the Americans in their wisdom and foresight decided that this forum should be RFE and RL, and their task was to provide a whole mix of opinions that would normally have been heard and printed in an independent Poland, or Czechoslovakia, or Hungary. They were to replace the non-existing democratic life of these countries, but from the outside because there was no other way of doing it.'

The American administration did not want to be associated in the public mind with RFE and RL, so the stations – based in Munich – were portrayed as independent, privately supported organizations. In fact, they were secretly funded by the CIA to avoid congressional oversight because details of the CIA's budget did not have to be disclosed. In practical terms the stations were an extension of American foreign policy. 'RFE was a product of the Cold War', says JAN NOWAK, who became the first head of RFE's Polish service in 1951. 'It was George Kennan, the creator of the containment policy, who understood the need for RFE. And the idea was, well, let's contain the Soviet Union, and the internal contradictions within the Soviet system will sooner or later bring it down.'

The task of RFE and RL was to get through the thick cobwebs of censorship under communist rule. The two new stations had a successful model to follow: this was West Berlin's Radio in the American Sector (RIAS), set up in 1946, to counter the broadcasts coming from Berlin Radio, which was under Soviet control. Throughout their rule East Germany's communist authorities laboured under a disadvantage that their comrades elsewhere in the Soviet bloc did not have to face. RIAS, together with West German radio and later television stations, made nonsense of any attempt by the East German authorities to maintain a monopoly over information.

STEFAN HEYM, the left-wing German émigré writer who had escaped from Hitler's rule to the United States, settled in East Germany in 1952, only to find himself in trouble with the censors. 'The East German situation was different,' says Heym, 'because if they didn't print me, the West Germans would – so I made money in any case. But the East German government tried to prevent my words from reaching the ears of the East German people. But again you had this strange situation that in Germany the Wall was only three yards high and radio and television could easily cross the Wall. In the age of electronics, you can't exercise censorship. And even at the time of the old East German regime I was one of the most popular writers in this country.'

Elsewhere in the Soviet bloc, it was easier to maintain a monopoly over information. Censorship took many forms. At the most basic level it involved censors going through every text destined for publication or broadcast. In the Soviet Union itself, censorship was in the hands of Glavlit, the Main Administration for Safeguarding Secrets in the Press, established in 1922. BORIS BELITSKY recalls the way the Glavlit officials worked: 'In Stalin's time the mechanics were appalling. Every page of script had to be vetted by a censor, and our relations with the censors were at times very strained, since they felt that nothing in their view questionable should go on the air. I recall instances of censors doing ridiculous things even under Khrushchev, crossing out points Khrushchev made in his speeches during his tour of the United States [in 1959]. And our attempts to point out, "Look, he said this," were of no avail. The censor would say: "Yes, but it hasn't been published inside this country," and that was it. So it was censorship *ad absurdum.*'

During the decades of communist rule censorship was not imposed with the same severity in all the Soviet bloc countries. Moreover, in the world of information, as elsewhere, periods of thaw alternated with times of freeze. In less repressive times enterprising journalists managed on occasion to find a way around the confines of the official line. JIŘÍ DIENSTBIER, Czechoslovakia's Foreign Minister after the collapse of communism in 1989, worked as a journalist in Prague in the 1960s, when there were opportunities for freer broadcasts. 'With the programmes on medium wave', says Dienstbier, 'you were cautious. But on FM, at midnight when nobody listened from among the apparatchiks, we were almost completely open. We had one very nice experience. Foreign Minister Václav David, who was one of the worst hardliners, once by chance listened to our programme on FM from 11 p.m. to 12 p.m. Well, next day they phoned the radio from the ministry to send them immediately a transcript of this programme. I got to the radio within an hour, deleted lots of sentences, the technicians cut the tape accordingly, and both transcript and tape were sent to the ministry.'

Suitably censored?

'Yes, of course, but after the broadcast.'

Although Radio Free Europe was set up to counter the rigid

censorship of the media in the communist countries, it was not itself entirely free from a milder form of censorship. GEORGE URBAN says: 'It's hard to believe, but at the time of detente there were certain managers at RFE who would discourage certain Western articulations because they thought it might hurt the Russians' feelings or damage East–West relations too much. In the 1970s and early 1980s [the British journalist] Bernard Levin was on what amounted to a blacklist because he was too anti-communist, his articles were too vehement and some of his judgments were thought to be too confrontational. One of the first things I did in 1983 was to stop all that. I removed the whole idea of black-listing. Anything that's printed has to be used – within reason. That was the ruling. It all had to be verified and our people did that from a factual point of view. But there was no list.'

With Western radios broadcasting to the East, censorship proved to be counterproductive. JAN NOWAK says: 'Censorship was our ally because when censorship was tightened, more people were listening to us. One move of the knob on the receiver and people would learn everything the censors were trying to suppress.' Nowak's point was well illustrated by listener surveys in Czechoslovakia in 1968. When Dubček's administration lifted censorship, RFE's audience dropped substantially. When the Warsaw Pact crushed the Prague Spring and reliable information in the domestic media once again became a scarce commodity, the number of people listening to RFE in Czech and Slovak doubled.

Although RFE thrived on censorship in Eastern Europe, it was also the target of attempted full-scale censorship in the form of jamming. Jan Nowak says: 'Jamming was our great adversary. But it was never 100 per cent effective. And it was terribly expensive. Only local jamming was effective. They could cover Warsaw, but people could go out into the countryside to have pretty good reception for listening. And the revolution of the transistor radio helped us immensely. You could manipulate a transistor radio; in one position or another you could get better reception. And jamming was counterproductive for the regime. It was a sign that the regime didn't want the truth. It was something that created a forbidden fruit and, in effect, was a way of helping us.'

The incidence of jamming was an indicator of the state of East–West relations and worries over the domestic situation. The Soviet authorities suspended the jamming of the Russian-language broadcasts of the BBC and VOA in 1963 as the peaceful resolution of the Cuban missile crisis ushered in a period of international thaw. That lasted until the invasion of Czechoslovakia in 1968, when jamming restarted. Then, with detente in full flow, jamming was stopped again in September 1973 – 10 days before an international conference in Geneva which was scheduled to discuss the free flow of information. The rise of Solidarity in Poland in 1980 – and fear of its possible impact on the Soviet people – led to the shutters coming down again. It was not until 1987 that the Soviet authorities finally ended jamming the BBC and VOA. RL was always considered much more dangerous by Moscow, and its broadcasts had been continuously jammed since it first went on the air. It was not until December 1988, three years after the launch of *glasnost*, that its broadcasts could finally reach their destination unhindered by deliberate interference.

Jamming was the clearest possible signal that the communist authorities considered Western broadcasts to be effective in undermining their monopoly over information. But what kind of impact did it have? RFE played its most controversial part in 1956 during the Hungarian uprising. MIKLÓS VÁSÁRHELYI, who was press secretary of Prime Minister Imre Nagy at the time, is a historian who has studied American policy towards Hungary during the uprising. 'I worked two years ago for three months in the National Archives in Washington and saw all the instructions Charles Bohlen, the American ambassador in Moscow, got from the State Department at the time. As early as 25 October [two days after fighting began] he got instructions from Secretary of State Dulles that he must personally assure Mr Khrushchev and [Prime Minister Nikolai] Bulganin that the United States had no vital interests in Central Europe. This meant that the Soviets practically had the right and opportunity to crush the Hungarian revolution from the beginning. RFE's propaganda made the impression here in Hungary that in our struggle for liberation – and liberation of the slave peoples was the American slogan at the time – we had the full support of the United States.'

How important was RFE in maintaining the Hungarian people's resolve to fight?

'It was decisive. Absolutely decisive. Everybody, including myself, we were all sitting in hallways listening to the radio. We had no television in Hungary then and RFE was the most important radio. And it was very important in fomenting the illusion in the Hungarian public that this was a struggle in which we had some chance because the big powers, first and foremost the United States, were fully with us. We could have imagined much stronger and more resolute political and diplomatic action. [Henry] Cabot Lodge, the United States representative in the UN, only called on the Security Council to put the Hungarian question on its agenda after Hungary was occupied, when it was too late. Then, of course, the big propaganda machine began to work against Soviet oppression and so on.'

In 1956 GEORGE URBAN was not yet working for RFE, but he was an avid listener. 'I can testify that incitement as such coming from the radio did not occur. What did happen was that RFE – as was its duty – gave a truthful picture of all press opinions in the West as well as all political opinions as given by President Eisenhower and others. I remember very well the critical day of Sunday 3 November – the day before the Russians came back – when *The Observer* in London printed an editorial which stated that the Hungarian people were putting up a magnificent fight for liberty and it was high time the West gave them armed support – or words to that effect. That and similar articulations were rebroadcast in Hungarian as a quotation from the press, but people sitting in cellars in Budapest with guns, waiting for the Russian tanks, would not make that fine distinction. People just "heard" that the radio had said Western aid was coming.'

In the years after the Hungarian uprising the style of RFE's broadcasts was toned down. This reflected the Eisenhower administration's move away from the idea of 'liberation' and rolling back communism and a return to containment. Significantly, Radio Liberation was renamed Radio Liberty in 1963. But the importance of external broadcasting did not diminish. JAN NOWAK, whose Polish service at the RFE adopted a far more cautious approach in 1956 to report the upheavals in Poland that coincided with the Hungarian uprising, believes that 'in times of crisis 80 per cent of people in Poland' used to listen to Western broadcasts. Meanwhile, both the United States and the Soviet Union quadrupled their efforts, in terms of hours broadcast abroad, during the two decades that followed the launch of RFE. Their weekly output was almost identical: 500 hours each a week in 1950, rising to 1,900 hours in 1970.

The task of stations broadcasting to the Soviet bloc was made easier by the communist authorities' treatment of information as a precious commodity that could not be distributed in large quantities. Apart from brief periods of liberalization, as in Hungary in 1956 and Czechoslovakia in 1968, many topics remained taboo until well after Mikhail Gorbachev's policy of *glasnost* emerged in 1985. The successive terminal illnesses suffered by Brezhnev, Andropov and Chernenko were not reported until after their deaths. There was a long-standing ban on reporting a whole range of social problems, including drug addiction, prostitution and crime, which were not supposed to exist under 'developed socialism', the official term for Soviet society during the Brezhnev era.

Speed of reporting was another journalistic quality that was not appreciated by Soviet officialdom. With a science degree from Moscow university, BORIS BELITSKY was the natural choice for presenting Moscow Radio's science and technology programmes for its listeners around the world. 'It was also my duty sometimes', says Belitsky, 'to interpret at news conferences given by our space-men. And I remember one occasion when I interpreted for one of our cosmonauts – I think it was Leonov, the first man to perform a walk in space in 1965. I returned to the radio in a rush and wrote something up – only to have it rejected by Glavlit. The reason was that it hadn't been published yet. So I argued with the chap, saying, "How could it have possibly been published when the man only said this half an hour ago and I rushed here to put it on the air as soon as I could?" And the answer was, "Until I see it in black and white, such sensitive information cannot go on the air."'

Delays in reporting news – if it was embarrassing – remained long. In September 1983 it took six days for the Soviet media to admit Soviet responsibility for shooting down a Korean airliner. Even as late as April 1986, the accident at the Chernobyl nuclear power station was not reported until nearly three days later.

Western broadcasters were also helped by the dull menu put on display by the state-controlled media on the other side of the Iron Curtain. Much of the news consisted of endless speeches by commu-nist officials – delivered in a jargon that was completely divorced from everyday speech – interspersed with tributes to economic and social achievements at home and denunciations of the wicked plans of Western imperialist conspirators abroad. 'I was once asked by [the West German] *Stern* magazine to write a story about East German television,' says STEFAN HEYM. 'And I did the following for four weeks solid: I looked and listened to only East German TV news – and I watched what would happen to my mind and to myself, and I wrote that down. And I found out that this East German TV was written according to certain patterns which kept on being repeated.'

Did you find it excruciatingly boring having to watch East German television?

'Well, I only knew that I couldn't have done it much longer without going insane.'

The staple diet of praise for domestic achievements and blacken-ing the reputation of the other side remained the main dish served up by communist broadcasting to the world. Distortion was an essential ingredient. BORIS BELITSKY recalls one example from the reporting of the Soviet space programme: 'Unfortunately, some of the facts were, let us say, embellished to produce a bigger impression. There was Gagarin's flight [in 1961], for example, when it was officially claimed that he had come down inside his space capsule, which was untrue. This was a risk the Soviet space experts were not prepared to take at that moment and he ejected at a certain height above the earth and parachuted down. This was a typical example of embellishment – absolutely unnecessary at that time – in which we were all deceived.'

'Western propaganda was better than Eastern propaganda', says CHARLIE COUTTS, a Scottish communist who was always impatient to improve the way the communist message was communicated. 'In the late 1940s there was a period when the revived British fascist party staged a procession in London and the police banned all processions on May Day. And what the labour organizations did was to walk on the pavement with their banners. There were some scuffles and a few arrests. That night by accident I heard Radio Budapest and it said that throughout the world workers had been celebrating May Day, with all these wonderful demonstrations in Moscow and Bucharest and so on. But in Britain workers had been put in the Tower of London for demonstrating on May Day. "If I ever get near that place, I'll hang them all," I thought at the time. "If that's going to win any support for socialism, they must be daft."' But a few years later Charlie Coutts went to Hungary and later joined Radio Budapest, starting a career that took him beyond the Cold War era.

BORIS BELITSKY believes that there was much heavy-handed propaganda on both sides; however, he singles out the BBC for praise. 'What made the BBC so powerful as an instrument of news dissemination', Belitsky says, 'was the fact that it never hesitated to present different points of view. There were even difficulties over this during the Suez crisis when the BBC insisted on presenting the

Labour point of view along with the Conservative view, which supported the invasion of Egypt. Here in the Soviet Union we were never able to present such a pluralistic spectrum of opinion. We had to present only the official view.'

Broadcasters were engaged in a mighty battle to further the cause of East or West. GEORGE URBAN played a prominent part in this, but he does not accept that RFE was a propaganda station. 'If you are opposed to illness,' says Urban, 'are you a doctor or are you a propagandist against sickness? I could never make sense of the idea that this was propaganda, although I agree that in some Western countries this was viewed among the public as propaganda. But it was propaganda only in the sense that the truth had to be spoken. Now, of course, if you speak the truth 10 times a day, it has a certain resonance that's larger than the truth spoken once a day.'

CHARLIE COUTTS saw his role as a broadcaster with a clear mission, albeit one that underwent a perceptible change as the role of ideology declined: 'I wanted to communicate on a number of levels. I communicated with a desire to defeat the West and win the Cold War. Yes, I communicated with a desire to convince people that there were worthwhile things in a socialist society. But later on I tried to avoid – which I would not have tried earlier – setting about convincing people that their capitalist government was about to be overthrown forthwith.'

There is no doubt about which side won the war of words that erupted between East and West with full force in the late 1940s. By any standards – the quality of its broadcasting, the truthfulness of its contents, the speed of its reporting – the West came out on top. Audience figures underline this. Whereas in the Soviet bloc countries, depending on the situation, between one-third and three-quarters of the adult population regularly listened to Western broadcasts, in the West there was only a very limited audience, consisting mainly of the politically converted and short-wave enthusiasts, who tuned in to Moscow Radio and its subsidiaries.

(Moscow's message had a much larger audience in the Third World, where the benefits of Soviet assistance, combined with yearning for a better life and lack of information about conditions in the Soviet Union, made people more receptive.)

Trying to gauge the full significance of broadcasting during the Cold War is a tricky task. But well before the Iron Curtain rusted – let alone was dismantled – its metal had been perforated by the sounds on the airwaves. 'How can you measure the impact of radio?' wonders JAN NOWAK, with more than four decades of experience in broadcasting. 'Our measurement is what the Poles in Poland say now. I returned to Poland in September 1989 – a critical moment – when the Mazowiecki government was formed. It was the first non-communist government in the communist orbit. And I had a wonderful welcome at the airport. There were crowds of people because RFE – without telling me – had broadcast the time of my arrival. The whole Solidarity leadership was there. It was all on television. Next day I went to see my native city for the first time in 45 years. I stopped a taxi and the driver said, "I recognize who you are because I saw you on television." And when we reached my destination I said, "How much?" And he said, "Nothing." I said, "Why?" He said, "Well, I've been listening to RFE, free of charge, for so many years; I can at least offer you a free drive." And this was the biggest reward to me and my colleagues for all that we'd done.'

Hungarian insurgents during a lull in the fighting against Soviet troops in Budapest during the uprising of October–November 1956.

5

EASTERN EUROPE: THE RELUCTANT SATELLITES

As the Cold War intensified and the international political climate turned decidedly chilly in 1947, Stalin began to speed up the Sovietization of Eastern Europe. He was no longer prepared to settle for a belt of friendly countries on the Soviet Union's western borders, but wanted to create states that were in all important respects identical to the Soviet system. This gave rise to one of the crucial differences between the Eastern and Western blocs because the United States did not expect its allies to duplicate slavishly its form of government.

By early 1948 Stalin had accomplished his main objectives. Throughout Eastern Europe the communist parties had seized complete control over government. In Poland, Czechoslovakia, Bulgaria and (after its foundation in 1949) East Germany, this situation was masked by the survival of other political parties, but their role was restricted to acting as cheer-leaders for their communist counterparts. Elsewhere, the local leaders proved to be less hypocritical and established one-party regimes.

Eastern Europe's communist leaders received their orders directly from Moscow. But Stalin wanted to impose an all-pervasive Soviet presence in his new empire, and thousands of advisers were dispatched to oversee the transformation of all East European institutions along communist lines. Special attention was given to the security forces. GENERAL BÉLA KIRÁLY, commander of Hungary's infantry forces at the time, recalls how the Hungarian army was brought under complete Soviet control: 'First there arrived eight or nine persons in October 1948. They were absolutely diplomatic. They emphasized this by saying, "Look, we are only advising this and you do out of it what you think is proper." Then in early 1949 a new wave of advisers came – thousands this time – and a Soviet adviser was attached to every command or supply institution down to regimental level. This coincided with the replacement of experienced officers in key positions with workers' cadres. You saw many a new officer looking awkward in his uniform. Two weeks before he was a yokel; now he was a colonel. He didn't know anything about the army, but beside him there was a Soviet adviser who would give the Hungarian a piece of paper and told him, "Here you will sign it." It was a Soviet text translated into Hungarian. In other words, the second wave of Soviet advisers came not to advise but to command.'

The unequal relationship between Moscow and its East European allies extended also to the sphere of the economy. Stalin exacted huge reparations from his defeated enemies, transferring whole factories to the Soviet Union. Many prisoners of war – a term that included thousands of non-combatants – were rounded up and spent up to 10 years working in Soviet labour camps. Joint companies were formed in crucial areas of the economy, such as transport and energy, to keep them under Moscow's control.

The establishment of the Council for Mutual Economic Assistance (Comecon) in 1949 was another means for tying the East European states closer to the Soviet Union. One of its initial tasks was to help enforce the economic blockade that Stalin had imposed on Yugoslavia after his excommunication of Tito in 1948. It also represented a response to the Marshall Plan's encouragement of European economic integration from which Stalin was determined to shield his allies.

Eastern Europe also embraced the Soviet model in politics and public life. The communists created artificial electoral coalitions with other organizations, which were variously called patriotic, democratic or national 'fronts' – reflecting, even in their names, the Cold War mentality of the age. Voters were faced with a 'choice' of one candidate, already endorsed by the communist-dominated electoral coalition. (It was not until 1970 that Hungary began a cautious experiment with multi-candidate, but single-programme, elections.) Nonetheless, the authorities enforced a high level of participation in these electoral charades, claiming a 99.99 per cent turn-out as a matter of routine. Staunchly Stalinist Albania managed to beat that figure with a 100 per cent turn-out in the 1987 election.

Compulsory participation in elections followed the totalitarian pattern in the Soviet Union, where it was not enough for citizens to refrain from criticizing the regime; they had actively to demonstrate their loyalty to it as well. (This prompted East Europeans to compare Soviet rule unfavourably with the centuries of Ottoman Turkish occupation, because at least in those days they had not been forced to go on May Day parades and chant, 'Long live the glorious Turkish army!')

East European leaders aped the Soviet example in every possible way. They forced through a policy of massive industrialization. The emphasis on investment in heavy industry reduced the supply of consumer goods. The forced collectivization of land created food shortages. In almost every country the standard of living dropped

Meeting of the 9th Congress of the Czechoslovak Communist Party, 1949. The giant portrait of Klement Gottwald, the leader of the Party, is flanked by those of Marx, Engels, Lenin and Stalin. The slogan reads: 'With Comrade Gottwald, forward to socialism.'

below the prewar level which, with the exception of Czechoslovakia and East Germany, had been relatively low in any case. Political opponents and the Churches were persecuted. The media were transformed into the mouthpiece of the communist regime. Leading communists were tried on a variety of bizarre trumped-up charges that ranged from collaboration with the Nazis during the war to working for the Western and Yugoslav intelligence services.

Khrushchev's thaw

By the time of Stalin's death in 1953 Eastern Europe, with the exception of Yugoslavia, had been integrated fully into the Soviet system. But the resulting combination of repression, loss of national independence and economic hardship created an unstable situation. Aware of the potentially explosive situation, Stalin's successors started to encourage East European leaders to adopt a 'new course' of reforms.

There was a change in style in relations between the Kremlin and its satellites. 'Our ambassadors in the East European countries, especially in Stalin's time, were like governors,' says FYODOR BURLATSKY, one of Khrushchev's aides. 'They gave so-called "advice", and the leaders of these countries followed the advice very carefully. This included advice about everything, from the *kolkhozes* to the KGB. But when the big turn in relations between the Soviet Union and Yugoslavia started, the style of relations changed and the ambassadors really did become more like advisers than governors.'

Khrushchev's reconciliation with Tito in 1955 coincided with his acceptance of the Austrian State Treaty – an agreement that ended Austria's occupation by the four wartime allies. These developments were viewed with high expectations in Eastern Europe. Moscow's acceptance of Yugoslavia's right to follow a different path towards socialism indicated that the other communist countries, too, might have greater scope to pursue their own policies. The troop withdrawal from Austria – in exchange for Austria's neutrality –

was another good sign to East Europeans who were hoping that Soviet forces might one day also be withdrawn from their countries.

However, these hopes received a rebuff with the foundation of the Warsaw Pact, the political and military alliance of the Soviet bloc, in May 1955. The new organization came into being a week after West Germany's accession to NATO which, with West German rearmament, boosted the military strength of the Western alliance. Yet Hungarian Prime Minister ANDRÁS HEGEDÜS, one of the signatories of the Warsaw Pact's foundation document, saw that event in a relatively favourable light. 'The Warsaw Pact was not a Cold War product,' Hegedüs says. 'Its text was relatively moderate in tone. At that time there were Soviet troops on the territory of Hungary, East Germany, Poland and Romania. The Warsaw Pact gave, at least in theory, an opportunity for these countries' leaderships to take control over their armies. Before the Warsaw Pact they had no such control. For example, control over the Hungarian army and the Soviet troops in Hungary was in the hands of the general staff in Moscow and, of course, of the Soviet Communist Party leadership. But, of course, the Warsaw Pact only represented a change in theory, not in practice, because we were not an independent country. We were strongly dependent on Moscow.'

Although the Kremlin's more conciliatory policies had been pursued since 1953, Stalin's heirs remained divided over the pace and extent of change. It was not until Khrushchev's denunciation of Stalin's crimes at the 20th Congress of the Soviet Communist Party in February 1956 that the reforms accelerated and the general political mood really began to change.

The thaw engendered by Khrushchev's secret speech led to unforeseen consequences throughout the Soviet bloc. The problem with Khrushchev's programme of de-Stalinization was that it undermined the position of many East European leaders, who had slavishly imitated their Big Brother in Moscow. After all, if Stalin had been a criminal – and on a massive scale – then his East European associates were no better, except that their victims were fewer in number. In one respect they were regarded as even worse than Stalin because they had subordinated all vestiges of national independence to the Kremlin.

No leader in Eastern Europe was in more danger than Mátyás Rákosi, the Hungarian Communist Party leader, who used to pride himself on being Stalin's greatest Hungarian disciple. His vulnerability was all the greater because he had a rival, Imre Nagy, who had a clear alternative programme. Nagy had already gained popularity in 1953 when, following Stalin's death, the new Soviet leadership insisted on his appointment as Hungary's Prime Minister – sharing power with a disgruntled Rákosi – and encouraged him to put into practice his reformist policies. As a result of Nagy's 'new course', living conditions improved and the extent of repression was scaled down.

However, following one of the periodic power struggles in Moscow, Nagy and other reformers came under attack from Stalinists in Hungary. At the beginning of 1955 he was removed from the post of Prime Minister. His replacement was András Hegedüs, who at the age of 32, to his own surprise, became Europe's youngest Prime Minister. The following year, in June 1956, as the Soviet leadership became more aware of Rákosi's growing unpopularity in Hungary, Hegedüs was to have an even bigger surprise when one of Khrushchev's closest colleagues, Anastas Mikoyan, arrived in Hungary. 'Mikoyan arrived without an invitation', Hegedüs recalls, 'and he told Rákosi and me that in the opinion of the Soviet leaders it was time for Rákosi to become a pensioner and I should become the First Secretary of the Hungarian Communist Party. I declined very sharply because I was a realistic young man, not an adventurer. And I think that in Hungary at the time only an adventurer would have wanted to be the leader.' Rákosi was then succeeded by his long-time deputy, Ernő Gerő, another dyed-in-the-wool Stalinist, who was both unable and unwilling to introduce any genuine reforms.

The Hungarian uprising

Meanwhile, pressure for change was building up. Under the impact of Khrushchev's thaw, the fear of repression had faded away. But the increasingly vociferous calls for new policies met a brick wall of resistance. Mounting public frustration found an outlet in early October at the reburial of several prominent victims of the Stalinist show-trials. A few weeks later students began to call for democratic reforms and the withdrawal of Soviet troops from Hungary. They decided to march through Budapest on 23 October to show their solidarity for Poland, where the national communist Władysław Gomułka had just been elected Party leader in the face of strong pressure from Moscow.

The authorities banned the demonstration. SÁNDOR KOPÁCSI, Chief of the Budapest Police, was expected to enforce the ban. He was summoned to the ministry of the interior on 23 October to discuss with officials, including the new Soviet adviser, how the police should deal with the planned demonstration. 'I explained', Kopácsi recalls, 'that we did not have the means available to Western police forces – truncheons, water cannon or mounted police. We had only guns: and I asked, who was going to take the political responsibility for resorting to firearms straight away? No one wanted to take the blame for the decision and the minister phoned Party leader Gerő who agreed that the ban on the demonstration should, after all, be lifted.'

This conciliatory mood did not meet with the Soviet adviser's approval. And he was no ordinary police officer. Kopácsi describes the scene: 'This rather German-looking adviser – he had blue eyes and fair hair – got up and expressed his surprise that a fascist demonstration was taking place in Budapest and the Hungarian police was hesitating whether or not to disperse it. I replied in a very restrained tone that the comrade adviser must have just arrived from Moscow and was not familiar with the situation in Hungary. Had I realized that I was addressing Army General [Ivan] Serov, the head of the KGB, frankly, I wouldn't have dared say this.' The demonstration went ahead. Hundreds of thousands of people marched through the centre of Budapest, and in the evening many of them went to Hungarian radio to have their demands broadcast on the air. The radio's management refused; the demonstrators refused to budge; tension increased; the security police in the radio building began to fire on the crowds; the demonstrators got hold of weapons from the soldiers, who were sent to defend the radio; and the armed revolution got under way.

Hungary's leaders were panic-stricken. While the siege of Hungarian radio was going on, senior officials, meeting in a late-night session, decided to meet some of the demonstrators' demands, including the call to appoint the popular Imre Nagy Prime Minister again. Pending Nagy's confirmation the following day, ANDRÁS HEGEDÜS was still Prime Minister that evening. He recalls the tense meeting: '[Yuri] Andropov, the Soviet ambassador, phoned Gerő and asked him if the Hungarian leadership would agree to receive help from Soviet troops. Nobody said anything. Andropov was still on the phone and Gerő answered that the Hungarian leadership agreed. We had spent just one minute on that question. That was enough.'

Hegedüs, who three days after the decision signed an official request for Soviet military assistance to provide Moscow with a post-dated invitation, recalls his reasoning at the time: 'I thought that if Soviet troops went into Budapest, order would be restored more rapidly and without bloodshed. I thought that it would be a show of strength, as in East Berlin in June 1953. But I was wrong. In reality it was pouring oil on the fire.'

In fact, Soviet units were already on their way to Budapest from their barracks near the Hungarian capital at the time the Hungarian leadership approved their intervention. Their appearance on the streets of Budapest provoked more fighting, since many of the revolutionaries' grievances had to do with Hungary's subservience to the Soviet Union. Nor did the insurgents realize that the Soviet troops had not, at that stage, received the order to open fire. In any

100

case, the entire Soviet operation was a shambles. COLONEL VITALI FOMIN, who was one of the Soviet military advisers stationed in Hungary at the time, points out the difficulties: 'It was wrong to deploy tanks in Budapest without sufficient infantry support. What's the point in tanks shooting at a few armed men? And if you deploy an army, you have to explain to the soldiers why you are doing it. But even I, with my experience in Hungary, didn't understand what was happening. I also remember that our street maps of Budapest dated back to 1945 and since that time many streets had been renamed. Our troops couldn't find their way around until I got a new map of Budapest from the Hungarian general staff, and that's how I became a guide.'

The Soviet troops were bewildered as they were fired on by Hungarian insurgents for whom they, along with the hated security police, became the main target. By contrast, the Hungarian army and the ordinary police were rarely attacked; and in any case, many soldiers joined the uprising even before Imre Nagy changed course and embraced the revolutionaries' cause on 28 October.

The revolution triumphs

Nagy's decision to take the side of the insurgents was made possible by the defeat of the Stalinists in the leadership, several of whom – including András Hegedüs – were smuggled out of Budapest in Soviet armoured cars. The revolution had triumphed. On that day Imre Nagy ordered an immediate ceasefire; declared that the uprising was not a counter-revolution; and announced that the government would start negotiations with Moscow on the withdrawal of Soviet troops from the country.

Nagy was not acting on his own. Khrushchev's political firefighter, Anastas Mikoyan, along with another Soviet leader, Mikhail Suslov, had earlier spent two days in Budapest. They had already persuaded the Hungarian Communist Party Politburo to replace the Stalinist Gerő with the more flexible János Kádár as party leader.

They were to return to Budapest later to give their apparent blessing to Nagy's more wide-ranging reforms. Meanwhile, Nagy was in constant touch with Ambassador Yuri Andropov. A few days later GENERAL BÉLA KIRÁLY, the Commander of the National Guard – the revolution's new law and order force – gained an insight into the close proximity between Moscow and the Hungarian leadership. One day he went to the Soviet embassy, from where Andropov asked him to ring Prime Minister Nagy and find out whether he had received a Soviet memorandum about talks on the withdrawal of Soviet troops. Király was intrigued: 'Interestingly enough, the Hungarian government's internal secret telephone service, the so-called "K" system, was hooked up to the Soviet embassy. Dial 1, and the Prime Minister will pick up the phone without a secretary. And I dialled 1 and Imre Nagy picked up the phone to tell me that the memorandum had been received.'

Mikoyan's and Suslov's second visit to Hungary during the uprising coincided with Imre Nagy's declaration on 30 October of the restoration of multi-party democracy and the formation of a coalition government. Two days later he declared Hungary's neutrality and announced that Hungary was leaving the Warsaw Pact. Was Nagy carried away by the enthusiasm of the crowds? Or did he try to put his own ideas into practice? MIKLÓS VÁSÁRHELYI, who was Nagy's press secretary during the revolution, believes it was a combination of the two. 'There was certainly big pressure on him from the people,' Vásárhelyi recalls, 'but he had already elaborated this point in 1955 when, citing the example of Yugoslavia, he declared that a socialist country does not have to be a member of a military pact led by the Soviet Union. His aim was to see a neutral, independent and socialist Hungary. But he had no plan to restore democracy in the Western sense of the term.'

Nagy's declaration of Hungary's neutrality and its withdrawal from the Warsaw Pact have been seen as the reason for the Soviet invasion on 4 November that toppled his government. With the benefit of hindsight, it seems that Nagy must have been naive to believe that Moscow would tolerate Hungary's moves towards independence. But at the time the situation appeared very different. Moscow was keen to have better relations with the West and it seemed that there was a group in the Soviet leadership that was ready to make serious concessions. Miklós Vásárhelyi explains: 'Before Mikoyan and Suslov left Hungary, they personally told Nagy, "Comrade Nagy, all our confidence is in you. You can do anything you see acceptable. There's only one thing you have to save, and that's socialism in Hungary." So in a way he got a blank cheque. They agreed to a multi-party system – though one that in their thinking would remain under the Communist Party's control. They didn't expressly declare that Hungary could become neutral, but that was understood to be included in their statement that the only important thing was for Hungary to remain a socialist country – like Yugoslavia.'

Nagy had spent many years in exile in Moscow before and during the Second World War. He knew the Soviet leadership well and must have felt that the Kremlin had, through Mikoyan and Suslov, endorsed his reforms. Moreover, their visit to Budapest coincided with a Soviet government declaration which stated unequivocally that the Kremlin would not interfere in the affairs of other communist countries. But Nagy was probably not aware of the deep divisions in the Soviet leadership. SERGO MIKOYAN, Anastas Mikoyan's son, remembers the events: 'After his talks with Imre Nagy, my father decided that we could do a deal with the Hungarian government and ordered our troops to leave the city. Then he flew back to Moscow and from the airport he went straight to the Kremlin to tell Khrushchev that everything was O.K., that we'd done a deal with the new government and we don't need to intervene. But Khrushchev interrupted him and said, "You are too late: while you were on the plane, two hours ago, we gave the order to our troops to crush the uprising." My father was shocked and he wanted to resign.'

The Soviet leadership's decision to intervene – and this time

103

decisively – was taken on 31 October. Fresh Soviet troops poured into Hungary to build up sufficient strength for the crack-down. When the anxious Hungarian leaders asked for an explanation, the Kremlin reassured them by saying that the Soviet forces were being regrouped prior to their withdrawal. It was in the wake of these troop movements that Imre Nagy declared Hungary's neutrality and withdrawal from the Warsaw Pact in the hope that by so doing he could remove any legal basis for Soviet military intervention in Hungary.

Meanwhile, Moscow kept up the pretence of planning to pull out its troops. On 3 November talks opened between the two sides on working out the details of the Soviet withdrawal. After an adjournment, a second round of negotiations was held that evening at the Soviet forces' headquarters just outside Budapest. COLONEL VITALI FOMIN was there as an interpreter. 'The talks were quickly concluded,' Fomin says. 'Then a waitress brought in some wine and we all had a drink while the Hungarians were waiting for their cars to arrive. Suddenly, three KGB officers came into the room and stood behind the chairs where the Hungarians were sitting. They were followed by Army General Serov, head of the KGB, wearing his full dress uniform. He threw his white gloves on the table. That was the sign. The Hungarians were immediately disarmed and placed under arrest.'

Moscow crushes the uprising

Next morning the Soviet attack began. The scale of the operation was considerable. The Red Army had massed 2,000 tanks in Hungary – the same number Hitler had used during 1940 in his conquest of France, one of Europe's three strongest military powers. They were backed by 60,000 soldiers from fresh contingents that had not been infected by the virus of contact with Hungarians during the previous two weeks. MARIA GOMORI, who worked as a civil servant in Budapest, recalls her encounter with the occupiers: 'After the

Russian troops came in on 4 November, the soldiers were sitting in their tanks and we were very much afraid of them. Whenever we went out into the streets, they were shooting at us. Some days later when the shooting stopped and they came out of their tanks, they said they wanted to go to the ocean. We said, "But we have no ocean." And they said, "So where are we?" And we said, "You are in Hungary." And they really had a hard time believing it because they were told they were fighting the British in Suez.'

The Soviet troops fought some bitter street battles with groups of insurgents, but there was little organized resistance. That would have been suicidal in any case, but it was made virtually impossible with the KGB's arrest of the Hungarian defence minister and the army chief of staff at the talks held on the eve of the attack. Only the National Guard, a lightly armed force, still had its command structure intact. Its commander, General Király, and his deputy, Sándor Kopácsi, were at a loss what to do.

Nagy and many of his closest associates sought refuge at the Yugoslav embassy. General Király, who was not aware of that, took several hundred of his men to the Buda hills to wait for instructions from the government. SÁNDOR KOPÁCSI took a detachment of police to the parliament building, which was protected by a ring of Hungarian army tanks. 'The Soviet units arrived,' Kopácsi recalls, 'and they told us that we could all leave freely – the officers with their sidearms – if we surrendered. Minister of State Zoltán Tildy told us there was no point in resistance: parliament would be reduced to rubble burying all of us inside. We gave this order to the soldiers, who leapt out of their tanks and protested that they would fight back. We pleaded with them and managed to persuade them to surrender. It was a harrowing scene: everyone was weeping. When the Soviet soldiers took away even the officers' arms, we protested that this was not part of the deal. They replied: "You'll be able to discuss all that in the Soviet Union."'

Fighting between small groups of Hungarians and the Soviet troops continued for days. General Király's unit was harried by

Soviet forces from Budapest into western Hungary. After 10 days on the run, most of them escaped across the Austrian border.

Kopácsi was less lucky. He was arrested the day after the Soviet attack and taken to one of the Soviet barracks, where the unknown Soviet adviser he had met two weeks earlier now turned out to be the KGB's boss, Army General Serov. 'Ringed by a group of Soviet generals, Serov in a theatrical gesture pointed a Mauser gun at me and said: "You are a cursed counter-revolutionary and for that I will have you hanged from the tallest tree. Do you remember how you told me off at that meeting?" I most certainly did. I was sure I was about to be executed. I handed him my ID card, to prove that I was an MP, and protested, saying: "I am a member of the Hungarian parliament with immunity from arrest." He grabbed my ID card, threw it on the floor, stamped on it and kicked it into the corner.'

Kopácsi escaped death to tell his story. He was sentenced to life imprisonment at the trial of Imre Nagy and his leading associates, in which the former Prime Minister and three others were sentenced to death. That was in June 1958, the trial having been repeatedly postponed at the Kremlin's request to avoid the bad publicity Nagy's execution would create during a number of international gatherings scheduled for late 1957 and early 1958.

The repeated delays of the trial were only one example of Moscow's control over Hungarian policy-making. Although the Kádár regime that was installed by Moscow after the uprising brought to an end some of the worst excesses of the former Stalinist leaders, its dependence on Moscow was no less humiliating for Hungary. KÁROLY GRÓSZ, Hungary's last communist leader and a local party official in 1956, explains: 'I considered the Soviet intervention the natural solution at the time. Its advantage was that there was less bloodshed than there would have been with a long and bloody civil war. But it left its own indelible mark on Hungary's historical development. Had Hungarian forces tackled the events, Kádár's later policy could have become far more assertive and

106

Hungary would have had more scope for independent political moves.'

The idea that the second and final Soviet intervention reduced bloodshed is shared by few Hungarians; after the revolution triumphed, there appeared to be no prospect of a civil war in Hungary. Nagy's government had managed to unite the nation. Whether retribution against Stalinist officials would have followed – there were very few atrocities against them during the uprising – is another matter.

Kádár managed gradually to establish a degree of autonomy for Hungary, particularly from the late 1960s onwards when he introduced a number of market-oriented economic reforms. Hungary with its 'goulash communism' was not the only country to take advantage of the opportunities provided under Stalin's successors for pursuing policies that differed from Moscow's. Part of that degree of freedom was due to the Kremlin's realization that creating carbon-copies of the Soviet model made communism in Eastern Europe less attractive to the people. Some latitude in allowing these countries to experiment with mild reforms or continue certain national traditions was expected to make membership of the Soviet alliance system more palatable to the East Europeans.

In fact, throughout the post-Stalin era, the Kremlin's dilemma in its policy towards the satellites was to reconcile the competing claims of viability and cohesion. To make the East European regimes more viable – and their peoples less likely to revolt – they were to enjoy greater scope for pursuing their own policies. However, if that autonomy of action threatened to go too far, the Kremlin stepped in to put an end to a process that threatened to undermine the cohesion of the Soviet bloc.

From the West's point of view, the dilemma over Eastern Europe concerned justice versus stability. It was regrettable that the peoples of Eastern Europe were denied the freedoms and prosperity enjoyed in the West. But Moscow's firm grip over Eastern Europe did ensure a high degree of stability in a region notorious for national rivalries. Eisenhower's administration talked a great deal about going beyond containment and rolling back communism. 'Our first opportunity to do exactly that was in Hungary in 1956,' says WILLIAM COLBY, Director of the CIA in the 1970s, who was involved in covert operations in Europe in the 1950s. 'President Eisenhower decided that it was tough on the Hungarians, but they weren't worth World War Three.'

If Moscow's problems in Eastern Europe became more difficult after the late 1950s, that was due not to Western pressure but to the emerging Sino-Soviet split. Tiny Albania sided with Peking after 1961. Its success in moving away from the Soviet bloc had been made possible by the same reasons that had contributed to Tito's break with Stalin in 1948; neither Yugoslavia nor Albania shared a border with the Soviet Union and they had no strategic importance for the Kremlin. Romania, having successfully got rid of the Soviet troops stationed on its territory in 1958, gradually adopted a semi-independent foreign policy under President Nicolae Ceauşescu. It took a neutral stance in the dispute between the two communist giants and forged close links with the West until President Ceauşescu's megalomaniac policies became an increasing embarrassment for his Western friends in the 1980s.

The Prague Spring

However, for the rest of Eastern Europe the lesson to be learnt from the crushing of the Hungarian uprising was that Moscow would not tolerate any of its allies trying to break away from the Warsaw Pact or establishing a multi-party democracy. So when communist reformers took control of the Czechoslovak leadership at the beginning of 1968, they went out of their way to assure the Kremlin that nothing like that would happen. Their aims were more limited, as ZDENĚK MLYNÁŘ, one of the prominent reformers in the Party leadership, explains: 'The aim of the Prague Spring was to bring together the socialist principles in the economy with political democracy. That could happen in Czechoslovakia – and only in Czechoslovakia – because we had had traditions of democratic socialism that stretched way back many years. The Soviet model of the one-party system and authoritarian rule was imposed on Czechoslovakia in 1948 and we wanted to go back to the pre-1948 years.'

Initially, there were many reasons to assume that the prospects for the reform programme associated with the 'Prague Spring' were good. Following intense consultations with the Czechoslovak Party Presidium in December 1967, Brezhnev had allowed them to make their own choice in replacing the discredited Antonín Novotný, a Stalinist survivor, as their leader. Alexander Dubček, who emerged as the new leader, had been brought up and educated in the Soviet Union and was initially considered completely reliable by the Kremlin. In the broader historical context there was little comparison between the hostility that Hungarians felt towards the Soviet Union before (and after) the 1956 uprising and the sentiments of most Czechs and Slovaks. Nor were there Soviet troops stationed in Czechoslovakia whose presence would have become a focus for popular resentment.

Above all, developments in Czechoslovakia proceeded in a peaceful manner. The communist leadership enjoyed unprecedented public support as it began to implement its policy of 'socialism with a human face'. Censorship was removed, victims of the show-trials were rehabilitated and wide-ranging economic reforms were actively considered. JIří HÁJEK, who was Czechoslovakia's Foreign Minister at the time, contrasts the situation in 1968 with that of 1956: 'In Hungary there were quite strong anti-Soviet and anti-socialist views. There were people who were fighting the communists. In our country there was no phenomenon of this kind. And we were trying to persuade our Soviet colleagues that in practice there was no such danger. But we didn't understand that their thinking was quite different: it identified the cause of socialism with the position of the conservative, dogmatic elements. They considered any democratic opening a mortal danger.'

In Moscow and some of the other Warsaw Pact capitals the situation was seen in a completely different light. The wave of reforms sweeping through Czechoslovakia – as well as the freedom of public debate that accompanied it – was seen as a threat for two reasons. At the very least it could become contagious, spreading to the neighbouring communist countries and encouraging their citizens to demand changes that the old-fashioned rulers in charge were not prepared to grant. Moreover, even though the Czechoslovak leaders reiterated their commitment to the Soviet alliance, there was no guarantee – once freedom of speech was granted – that more far-reaching demands for a genuine democracy with competing political parties might not lead to a situation where Czechoslovak citizens would opt for a Western orientation for their country. ANDREI ALEXANDROV-AGENTOV, who served as Brezhnev's foreign policy adviser throughout his years in power, remembers those fears: 'The main reason for the decision to go into Czechoslovakia with troops in August 1968 was not ideological but an understanding by our leadership of the Soviet Union's interests as a great power. It was a fear that Czechoslovakia would leave the Warsaw Pact and that will start the beginning of its dissolution. Already in 1953 in Berlin, and still more in 1956 in Hungary, we could see how everything was fragile. And here in the case of Czechoslovakia there was a very noisy and very active instigation from the West. Once during a session of the Politburo Brezhnev went up to our ambassador in Prague, Stepan Chervonenko, and said to him, just privately, "If we lose Czechoslovakia, I will retire as General Secretary."'

As Moscow's concern over the situation in Czechoslovakia grew, the Kremlin launched a war of nerves against the Prague leadership. Throughout the spring and early summer of 1968 the Soviet media denounced developments in Czechoslovakia, accusing the Prague leadership of paralysis in the face of Western attempts to bring about a counter-revolution in the country. 'We were getting all those signals and we were quite aware of them', says ZDENĚK MLYNÁŘ. 'And psychologically it was very difficult to pursue the policy of reforms and, on the other hand, to be afraid of the Soviet tanks. We actually thought those tanks would never come. We could have stopped the reforms and we could have suppressed the freedom of the press, but that would have meant suppressing them with our own hands.'

In late July and early August two summit meetings were held: one between the Czechoslovak and Soviet leaderships at Čierná nad Tisou on the Slovak–Ukrainian border; and a Warsaw Pact summit in Bratislava. But Dubček's repeated assurances to his allies that his reforms would not endanger communism failed to convince the Kremlin. On the night of 20–21 August troops from the Soviet Union and smaller units from Bulgaria, East Germany, Hungary and Poland moved into Czechoslovakia to begin a process that was to end in the crushing of the 'Prague Spring'. ANDREI ALEXANDROV-AGENTOV recalls that time: 'I knew about the moment when Brezhnev came one night into his cabinet and said that he, [Prime Minister] Kosygin and [President] Podgorny would spend the night with the general staff at the ministry of defence. There was never a thought about war action in Czechoslovakia. The mass of the troops that went into it, about 500,000 in one night – which amazed the NATO specialists – is in itself a proof of the fact that it was to have a psychological effect. Not a drop of blood was shed. Of course, a great help in that was the direct contact established with a very good personal friend of Leonid Brezhnev, President Ludvík Svoboda, a couple of hours before the troops began arriving. Svoboda understood the situation and gave the command that there would be no resistance.'

Although there was no armed resistance, there was massive public opposition to the invaders. 'The population reacted in every possible non-violent way; some of these were very imaginative and have probably entered the textbooks of non-violent resistance,' says

KAREL KOVANDA, who was a student leader at the time. 'I remember at one moment the clandestine radio station issued a call that all the street name-plates be taken down. And two hours later there wasn't a street name-plate virtually anywhere in the country. And the Soviet troops would be trying to figure out their way around town, getting hopelessly confused.'

The occupation was not as bloodless as its supporters claim. Scores of people were killed during or in the aftermath of the invasion. However, that was a much smaller figure than the number of victims of Soviet military action in Hungary in 1956 which, together with the retribution that followed, caused nearly 4,000 deaths, 700 of them Soviet soldiers.

Apart from the scale of the casualties, there were other differences between 1956 and 1968. The Soviet crack-down in Hungary was a response to an explosive situation; the move into Czechoslovakia was a form of preventive police action. In 1956 Moscow brushed aside a Romanian suggestion to join the Soviet military action in Hungary, fearing that this would rekindle age-old Hungarian–Romanian ethnic enmities. By 1968 Moscow wanted to share the responsibility for the invasion of Czechoslovakia by making it a joint Warsaw Pact action. In fact, this occupation of one of its members turned out to be the only military operation ever carried out by the Warsaw Pact.

The invasion of Czechoslovakia prompted Romania's President Ceaușescu, whose troops did not take part in the operation, to reduce military cooperation with the rest of the Warsaw Pact to a minimum. Albania, which had been pursuing a pro-Chinese policy since 1961, formally left the Warsaw Pact in the wake of the invasion. But the rest of Moscow's Warsaw Pact allies were reminded of the limits to their freedom of action. The Brezhnev doctrine declared that all members of the Soviet bloc had a responsibility to intervene in another communist country if there was a threat to what were termed the 'achievements of socialism'.

EASTERN EUROPE: THE RELUCTANT SATELLITES

The Solidarity challenge

The third major test for communism in Eastern Europe came in Poland in 1980. This was hardly surprising, since the communist regime in Poland had proved more vulnerable to public pressure than any other in the region. Alone among East European countries, Poland had an institution independent of the regime: the Catholic Church, which retained its influence throughout the communist era. It was revitalized by the election of the Polish archbishop, Karol Wojtyła, as Pope John Paul II, in 1978. Much of the land remained in the hands of the Polish peasantry, which jealously defended its independence from the state. Traditional anti-Russian and anti-Soviet sentiments – made more acute by the German–Soviet occupation of Poland in 1939 – were barely affected by Moscow's backing for Poland's postwar western borders, which West Germany refused to recognize even *de facto* until 1970. These circumstances made Poles perhaps even more resentful of their place within the Soviet bloc than their neighbours.

GENERAL WOJCIECH JARUZELSKI, who was Poland's leader in 1981–9, sees his country's postwar position in terms of *realpolitik*: 'There are marriages in which the two sides love each other – the ideal state of affairs. There are, on the other hand, marriages where there are differing opinions, even clashes. Reason persuades us that this marriage should continue. Our remaining in the Warsaw Pact derived from the division of the world at the time. We, after all, hadn't invented Teheran, Yalta and Potsdam. So we had to function within those realities. For us there was an additional element – namely, the Soviets guaranteeing our western border. So I would say it was a marriage based on calculation rather than emotion.'

Poland's communist regime also had a tradition of accommodating public unrest by sacking leaders who had attracted too much unpopularity. In 1956 Gomułka returned to the political scene and in 1970 he finally left it – each time on a wave of workers' riots. Ten years later it was the turn of his successor, Edward Gierek, to go into retirement, when shipyard workers in Gdańsk began a sit-in strike

Solidarity leader Lech Wałęsa flashes a V-victory sign at the Lenin shipyard in Gdańsk, Poland, where thousands of workers began a strike in May 1988. The shipyard was the birthplace of Solidarity during the strikes that started in the summer of 1980.

against price rises that led to the emergence of the independent trade union, Solidarity. Under Lech Wałęsa's leadership, Solidarity gradually metamorphosed into a broad social movement that eventually emerged as an alternative force to the Communist Party. In the process the communist regime's control over the media and other organizations gradually broke down, and Solidarity managed to extract a whole range of concessions without the authorities being able or willing to put in place a coherent programme of reform. The communist leadership's refusal to share power with Solidarity paralysed the administration. As Poland was sliding into anarchy, General Jaruzelski, who by then combined the offices of Communist Party First Secretary, Prime Minister and Defence Minister, imposed martial law on the country on 13 December 1981.

On three occasions within 15 years, in East Berlin, Hungary and Czechoslovakia, Soviet troops had intervened to protect the Kremlin's interests in Eastern Europe. In Poland during 1980–81 they stayed out of the conflict. ANDREI ALEXANDROV-AGENTOV maintains that Moscow had no intention to intervene in Poland. 'As far as I know – and I should know – Jaruzelski never asked us for troops,' Alexandrov-Agentov says. 'Nobody asked us for troops and nobody wanted to send them. Brezhnev had a great trust in Jaruzelski and he relied upon his ability to solve that question. Brezhnev never blamed him for martial law, he probably thought that it was necessary, but he never advised it and never demanded something like that.'

However, Soviet pressure on Poland in the form of public warnings, media criticism and hastily summoned meetings was a frequent occurrence. One such occasion was an unscheduled summit of the Warsaw Pact in Moscow in December 1980 which coincided with a concentration of Soviet forces on Poland's northeastern border. ZBIGNIEW BRZEZINSKI, who was President Carter's National Security Adviser, believes the United States should take some of the credit for deterring the Kremlin from using force in Poland. 'When the Soviets threatened to invade Poland in December 1980,' Brzezinski says, 'the United States took unprecedented actions to discourage the Soviets from so doing. I believe that our engagement in Afghanistan was a further factor which enhanced the credibility of our warnings to Moscow not to invade Poland because by then the Soviets knew that if there is resistance the United States will not merely be a spectator. It is conceivable that a guerrilla war in Poland would not have lasted that long because Poland is not Afghanistan. But the Soviets had to anticipate, in the light of what happened before, that we would not be passive.'

The American warning was something of a challenge to Yalta and the postwar division of Europe. The Americans had not provided arms to East European resistance fighters since the beginning of the 1950s, the last and most notable case being (in a joint venture with the British) the sending of armed Albanian émigrés back to their country in an attempt to bring down the communist regime. However, the Polish leadership's determination that it alone should deal with the situation was probably even more important. Warsaw had managed to diffuse earlier crises on its own, and having to rely on Soviet military assistance would have destroyed even the little credibility the regime still enjoyed. GENERAL JARUZELSKI, who was one of the members of the Polish delegation at the Moscow talks, believes there were several reasons why the Kremlin was dissuaded from using force at the end of 1980. 'First, there was still a chance that Solidarity could be held within the broadly understood framework of a trade union. Second, the conservative grouping in the Communist Party that was ready to turn to Moscow for help had not yet consolidated itself. Finally, the position adopted by our delegation headed by [Party First Secretary] Stanisław Kania gave our allies the feeling that this was our own internal matter and that we were able to resolve it using our own resources, without undermining the security of the Warsaw Pact as a whole. All these factors, including, no doubt, the American warnings, ensured that no intervention occurred at that time.'

There was another reason why the Kremlin was eager to keep its forces out of Poland. Soviet troops were already bogged down in a guerrilla war in Afghanistan, and an invasion of Poland, a country with nearly four times the population of Hungary, would have led to losses on a much larger scale than in Hungary in 1956.

Eventually, General Jaruzelski's crack-down saved Brezhnev the embarrassment of having to send in his own troops. Nor did Washington have to put into practice whatever contingency plans it may have prepared for a Soviet intervention in Poland. But the United States did impose trade sanctions on Poland and on the Soviet Union, which it held responsible for inspiring martial law. The impact of the American response was stronger than at the time of Hungary in 1956 and Czechoslovakia in 1968, when much of it had been confined to propaganda. That the effect of the sanctions – though only partially applied by the West Europeans – was now considerable was due to the policy of detente in the 1970s, which had greatly increased Poland's (and the Soviet bloc's) dependence on

116

Western trade and credit. It was ironic that President Reagan, a strident critic of detente, could now exploit the fruits of this policy by withholding some of the substantial benefits that detente had earlier extended to the Soviet bloc.

The political landscape that emerged in Eastern Europe after the suppression of the Solidarity movement looked distinctly bleak. Although the Kremlin had successfully maintained its domination of most of the region in the face of repeated challenges, it was confronted with a group of countries whose peoples continued to resent Soviet control. That control had been relaxed in some areas, but in others it remained as strong as ever. When NATO began its deployment of cruise and *Pershing-2* missiles in Western Europe at the end of 1983, after four years of intense public debate, the response from Moscow was quick. 'We got a note from the Soviet embassy, with no more than 50 words on it, saying that medium-range missiles would be deployed on the territory of Czechoslovakia and the GDR,' says BOHUSLAV CHŇOUPEK, who was Czechoslovakia's Foreign Minister at the time. 'I called Prime Minister Štrougal to ask if he knew anything about it. He said, "No, that's the first information I've had on it." I called Berlin and an official there answered that the same message had been received there. The deployment had not been discussed with us during any of the previous consultations.'

However, in the age of nuclear missiles, the military rationale for keeping Eastern Europe as a large buffer-zone on the Soviet Union's western borders had largely lost its purpose. In many other ways the countries of Eastern Europe gradually began to appear to be more of a liability than an asset to Moscow. Politically they were an embarrassment; economically they were of little use; their peoples harboured a mixture of fear, hate and contempt towards the Soviet Union. But the idea that Moscow would be better off without its reluctant East European satellites was too revolutionary for the geriatric leadership that had taken over power from Khrushchev two decades earlier. That idea had to await Mikhail Gorbachev's 'new thinking'.

The countryside around the Siberian city of Novokuznetsk, covered by mountains of toxic waste. Every year one million tons of poison is pumped into the air in the region – two tons for every inhabitant. Life expectancy for men in the area is around 54 years.

6

THE COMMAND ECONOMY THAT WOULDN'T OBEY

The Cold War was fought on many fronts: the arms race, many regional conflicts and the propaganda war were all part of a permanent state of conflict between East and West. But in the absence of a war between the superpowers, one of the ways in which the struggle between the first and second worlds was likely to be determined was by economic strength. The system that could prove itself to be more viable was expected to emerge as the victor from the Cold War.

For a time the contest seemed to be open. Khrushchev was certainly confident that the communist system would triumph over capitalism – a point he reiterated frequently but never as succinctly as on the occasion of a reception at the Polish embassy in Moscow at the end of 1956. SIR WILLIAM HAYTER, the British ambassador to the Kremlin, was among the Western diplomats at the reception for whose ears Khrushchev's remarks were meant. 'It was after these terrible things, Suez and Hungary,' Sir William recalls, 'and these two events between them had been a very great setback for Khrushchev's policy of detente with the West. He got very angry and overexcited and said, "We shall bury you." I don't remember what the exact Russian words were, but I think he probably meant, "We shall be at your funeral," rather than "We shall dig your grave." He meant that in this competition between us "We are going to win."'

Confidence in the worldwide victory of the communist system

119

was part and parcel of the ideology that Lenin and the Bolsheviks created on the basis of Marx's view of history. The replacement of the private ownership of the means of production with state ownership would not only end the exploitation of workers by their capitalist employers; it would also allow for rational planning of the economy in place of the anarchy of the market-place. This, in turn, would bring about increased efficiency in the use of economic resources, leading to much greater prosperity for all.

During the 1930s foreign sympathizers who visited the Soviet Union were so impressed by the apparent success of Stalin's economic policies that their praise knew no bounds; some even described Soviet communism as 'a new civilization'. The Soviet achievement seemed all the more remarkable because the capitalist world economy was going through one of its periodic slumps. Yet, the 'Soviet success story' of the 1930s was based, in great measure, on false statistics and on the deliberate deception of foreign visitors whose access was limited to a few model institutions.

The economic contest

However, by the 1950s the Soviet Union had made great strides, having emerged from the Second World War as one of the two strongest powers in the world. It had also succeeded in rapidly rebuilding and strengthening its war-ravaged economy. In the West, Soviet economic might was no longer just an object of worship for communists and fellow-travellers; it was now recognized by reputable economists and increasingly feared by governments. JIM NOREN, who worked for over three decades for the CIA analysing Soviet economic performance, recalls the prevailing mood at the time he joined the CIA's office of Soviet intelligence in 1959: 'People were drawing graphs,' Noren says, 'here is the GNP of the United States and here is the GNP of the Soviet Union, far below that of the United States but growing so rapidly that at some point in the not-too-distant future the USSR would overtake and surpass it. In fact, those graphs stayed on in American economic textbooks into the early 70s.' Even those who remained sceptical about the Soviet Union moving ahead of the United States were impressed by the achievements of the planned economy. JOHN KENNETH GALBRAITH, the American economist, recalls his feelings when he visited the Soviet Union: 'I spent some weeks there in the 1950s and I was impressed by the exuberance, the enthusiasm and the development one saw of heavy industry. But I never expected that system to outstrip ours.'

Khrushchev himself became the chief propagator of the idea that the Soviet Union would surpass the United States in its economic strength. But as ALEXEI ADZHUBEY, Khrushchev's son-in-law and one-time close aide explains, the idea went back much further: 'The idea of overtaking America started straight after the [October] revolution. Even children were called "Dogonyat-Peregonyat" – catch up and overtake – which became a popular boy's name.' Where Khrushchev went beyond this long-standing but vague declaration of intent was in specifying that the Soviet Union would overtake the United States in per capita GNP by 1970.

The Kremlin's optimism and Western concerns over the apparent success of the Soviet economy were motivated by two developments. Soviet economic growth in the 1950s, officially reported at about 7 per cent per annum, was consistently well ahead of the American growth rate. Besides, Soviet science, particularly in the field of rocket technology, scored a number of successes. With the launch of *Sputnik* in 1957, the Soviet Union became the first country to put an artificial satellite into space. Four years later Moscow won another round in the space race, when Yuri Gagarin became the first man to orbit the earth.

However, in the postwar years rapid economic growth was not unique to the command economies. West Germany's economic miracle was even more spectacular. In fact, countries that were severely devastated by the war moved ahead faster than those that suffered relatively less damage. Nevertheless, the planned economy

121

can work reasonably well when the main objective is to concentrate on fast growth in some key areas of the economy. 'When the economy is relatively basic,' says STEPAN SITARYAN, who was first deputy chairman of the State Planning Committee, Gosplan, between 1986 and 1989, 'and the task is to mobilize resources and direct those resources to certain priority areas, then the centralized system can work. It can mobilize extensive factors, getting more people to be employed and more capital invested.'

There was another reason for the rapid economic growth registered by the Soviet Union in that period. After the war the Kremlin plundered much of eastern Germany and other occupied countries, removing production facilities in the form of reparations. Many prisoners of war joined the millions of Soviet citizens subjected to forced labour. The economic exploitation of Eastern Europe continued well into the 1950s, with much of the region's resources geared to the needs of the Soviet Union.

Lies, damned lies, and statistics

However, economic growth, though substantial until the early 1960s, was overstated in official statistics – a practice that continued until the collapse of the Soviet Union. Much of the distortion was due to the methodology employed. Inflation, which officially did not exist but amounted to 2–3 per cent per annum, was not taken into account; so the value of production was a lot less than it appeared. The service sector, which in the periods of the highest industrial growth was actually contracting, was left out of the statistics.

There were also cases of deliberate falsification of results reported by enterprise managers to the authorities. 'When you have plans that enterprise managers have to fulfil, there's always an incentive for them to make the situation look better than it is,' says NIKOLAI BELOV, who became first deputy Chairman of the Central Statistical Office in 1985. 'It was quite natural for those directors who couldn't fulfil their plans to distort the data, because getting incentives from the government in the form of decorations and medals depended on that.' However, fear of punishment dampened the enthusiasm of managers who might otherwise have thought of cooking the books. As Belov says, 'deliberate – that's to say, criminal – distortions of the data were disclosed in only 5–7 per cent of the 150,000 inspection checks carried out annually.'

Given the shortcomings of Soviet statistical reporting, Kremlin leaders from Yuri Andropov onwards increasingly turned to the alternative, and much lower, estimates of Soviet growth provided by the CIA. But for several years access to that information was severely restricted within the Soviet Union. GENNADI ZOTEYEV, a research economist at Gosplan, was astonished when in 1983 he read the CIA's *Green Book* on the Soviet economy, noting that sometimes the CIA's estimates were half of the official Soviet figures. 'This had a dramatic influence on me, and I decided to check the calculations. I stole this book from the Gosplan library and spent several months trying to understand if these statistics were correct, and I found that in some cases even the CIA overestimated Soviet economic growth.'

Although Soviet statistics consistently exaggerated economic results, they did reflect the decline in growth over the years. When the statisticians' reports became embarrassing for the leadership, the results were simply suppressed. By the early 1980s the Central Statistical Office was sending what NIKOLAI BELOV calls 'very alarming reports to the highest authorities. It's no coincidence that our openly published statistical year-book became much smaller in volume. Not all the material relating to the standard of living and the macroeconomic situation was included in them.' However, silencing the harbinger of bad news did nothing to improve conditions.

As the rate of growth tailed off, stagnation and decline set in. Far from overtaking the United States in per capita GNP by 1970, as Khrushchev had promised barely 10 years earlier, even according to official Soviet figures the Soviet Union never got beyond half that of America. Meanwhile, no serious efforts were made to tackle the deep-seated problems of the Soviet economy, even though senior

Communist Party leaders were fully aware of the gravity of the situation. YEGOR LIGACHEV, who was to become Mikhail Gorbachev's deputy after 1985, remembers the catalogue of difficulties in the early 1980s: 'Reading the statistics and seeing what was going on, I came to the conclusion that the rate of growth was getting slower and slower, the quality of things that were produced left much to be desired, we were lagging more and more behind in scientific and technical progress, and we were lagging behind the West in the production of consumer goods.'

The shortage economy

But why had the state of the Soviet economy deteriorated so much by the early 1980s? The system of planning established under Stalin had worked reasonably well – though at a huge cost in human suffering – during the initial phase of industrialization in the 1930s, in the Second World War and in the subsequent process of postwar reconstruction. In or out of war, much of this effort had been organized along military lines. In its Stalinist form the command economy involved giving the state near-total control over the production and distribution of goods; allocating a huge portion of resources to heavy industry, much of it for military purposes; mobilizing workers, which, at its most extreme, led to the establishment of forced labour camps; and isolating the economy from the international markets. With such a self-contained economy established, foreign capitalist encroachments had to be kept at bay. When the United States offered aid to the Soviet Union under the Marshall Plan in 1947, Stalin turned it down and forced Czechoslovakia to follow suit.

However, as the process of industrialization and postwar reconstruction was completed, the economy expanded and became more diverse. Soviet-style planning turned into an increasingly cumbersome instrument to manage the economy. By the early 1980s, when the Soviet economy was turning out nearly 25 million different types of goods, the complexity of the operation had gone beyond the

124

capability of even a computerized planning system. Besides, in this more advanced phase of economic development, as STEPAN SITAR-YAN says, 'the problem is not the distribution of resources but the motivation of production and the very fast adaptation of production to changes in the situation. That's where the centralized system becomes incapable of responding to the changed conditions.'

At the heart of the system was Gosplan, which had a staff of 3,000 in the mid-1980s. But how did Gosplan operate? 'Gosplan didn't, of course, determine the colour of every T-shirt or every pair of shoes produced in the country,' says Sitaryan. 'But it did determine the overall quantity and volume of their production. It set the general figure for each ministry and each republic. Then these figures were given straight to the individual enterprises. When Gosplan was trying to control the whole economy under a bureaucratic machinery of 20 million officials this was, of course, totally ineffective.'

The result of this form of central planning, or administration, was the creation and maintenance of a shortage economy. (This prompted a joke about whether it was preferable to go to the capitalist or the communist hell. It went like this: 'So what was it like in the capitalist hell?' asks a man who opted for the communist hell. 'Oh, it was terrible,' his friend replies. 'We suffered the most appalling pain, being burnt, boiled and otherwise tortured by devils. But what was it like in communist hell?' 'Splendid,' his friend replies. 'We never suffered in the least. You see, when there was firewood, there was no coal; when they occasionally managed to get both firewood and coal, they ran out of matches to light the fires; and when finally they succeeded in getting firewood, coal and matches all at the same time, the devils were all summoned to attend a meeting of the local communist party cell.') The shortages were not simply a question of not having enough goods; even when there were sufficient quantities of a particular product, their quality, appearance or the range of choice was strictly limited.

Besides, there were never enough shops, restaurants or other outlets in the service sector, and this made standing in queues part and parcel of the Soviet way of life. 'It could be one hour, two hours or more,' says TATIANA ZHUK, a translator. 'And I remember when I was 13 or 14 and wanted a pair of jeans and heard they had them in a shop not far from our house. I was five hours in the queue – and I didn't get them. It was a great disappointment.'

The system of planning was not merely an economic device. Its purpose was also to help establish and maintain the communist authorities' control over the population's economic needs. 'Throughout its whole history our state struggled against a rational monetary system,' says GEORGI MATYUKHIN, governor of the Russian Central Bank in 1991–2, 'because people who have money are independent of the state. The more money they have, the more power they have. The totalitarian regime tries to destroy all rivals – and money is a source of power. Stalin started the strategic work towards eliminating all elements of the market. Money was given the role of ration cards. People were given very limited amounts of money – just enough to buy essential commodities. But there were no possibilities to accumulate money, to buy property or start a business.'

The role of money was completely distorted by the fact that incomes and prices were all centrally fixed. Wages and salaries were kept very low, and the lack of incentives discouraged any effort, a situation best described by the oft-quoted remark that 'They pretend to pay us and we pretend to work.' Since most goods were heavily subsidized, there was much waste. Farmers fed bread to their pigs because it was cheaper than animal feed; people living on housing estates, which were centrally heated from a power plant, would keep their windows open in the harsh Russian winter because their apartments had no individual heating controls and, in any case, the cost of heating was included in the rent. Irrationality was rampant. Georgi Matyukhin recalls a celebrated case: 'Before the war our scientists worked out the purchasing power of the rouble comparative to the dollar and said that the rate must be 11 roubles to one dollar. Stalin looked at the figures and said: "Five roubles is enough for the Americans. It's enough."'

The militarized state

The combination of rampant bureaucracy, all-pervasive inefficiency and lack of incentives – together with the abolition of the market, except for its black, grey and under-the-counter varieties – did much to weaken the Soviet economy and create constant bottle-necks in the supply of goods. However, there was another crucial factor that seriously distorted economic development: that was the military-industrial complex, a Frankenstein's monster created under Stalin that expanded and took over the Soviet economy. 'One of the main reasons for the defeat of the Soviet economy was the overkill in the military budget,' says PROFESSOR ROALD SAGDEYEV, who was head of the Soviet Space Institute in Moscow for 15 years until 1988. 'Between 20 and 25 per cent of our GNP was spent on the military build-up. I don't think even a flourishing capitalist economy would have survived for such a long time with such a huge proportion of the budget spent on the military.'

The size of the Soviet military-industrial complex was, indeed, stupendous. Because of the secrecy that enveloped the Soviet military machine and the hidden subsidies that were fed to satiate its appetite, no one knows for certain how much of the Soviet economy was devoted to military or related purposes, such as space exploration. Estimates vary between 14 and 50 per cent of the GNP. By comparison, military spending in the Cold War era in the United States reached a record 13.8 per cent of GNP in 1953 at the height of the Korean war and the American postwar rearmament effort, after which it steadily declined, remaining in the 4–6 per cent range in the 1970–80s. Yet many American economists argue that even that level of expenditure, combined with employment opportunities and powerful lobbying, gave the defence-related industries in the United States too much influence. 'The military-industrial complex in the United States developed a certain power of its own,' says JOHN KENNETH GALBRAITH. 'It decided what weapons should be produced and in what quantity. And it had the influence in Congress to get the money for those weapons – and it has it even now, in spite of the end of the Cold War.'

127

If the American military-industrial complex was powerful within the state, its Soviet counterpart constituted a large part of the state. Its importance was infinitely greater. Although Soviet propaganda regularly intoned the peace-loving nature of Soviet policies, the figures – where they can be established with any degree of certainty – tell a different story: that of the Soviet Union as a militarized state. During the Cold War the strength of the Soviet armed forces varied between 1.5 and 2.5 times the size of the United States forces. Nine ministries, one out of every seven, were completely devoted to military production, research or development and many others concentrated at least part of their effort on the same purposes.

The Cold War meant full order books for the giant military sector of the Soviet economy. 'All our major orders came from the military-industrial complex,' says MARK VINEBERG, Chief Designer of the *Mil* helicopter design bureau. 'We were never short of investment, never short of funds. Not more than 30 per cent of the 25,000 helicopters we've produced since 1947 were made for civilian purposes, the rest were for the military – or maybe, it's even 25 against 75 per cent. To keep the Cold War going meant for both sides – us and the West – the continuation of the money flow.'

The person who came to embody most the influence of the Soviet military-industrial complex was Dmitri Ustinov who was, at the age of 33, appointed people's commissar for the armaments industry at the time of the Nazi invasion of the Soviet Union in 1941. Thereafter, in a career that spanned much of the Cold War, he served under every Soviet leader from Stalin to Chernenko until his death in 1984. Unusually in Soviet practice, he was given the defence portfolio in 1976 (the first civilian to hold that position since Trotsky) and was promoted to the rank of a marshal. Ustinov was, by any standards, a prodigious consumer of military hardware. 'Even if certain weapons were not required for the needs of the army,' says COLONEL-GENERAL NIKOLAI CHERVOV, who served on the Soviet General Staff in the 1970–80s, 'Ustinov would accept them. Sometimes it happened that newly manufactured weapons were immediately taken to stores where they were quickly forgotten about.'

The enormous cost of this arms bonanza remained hidden. 'The budget contained the expenditure of the ministry of defence,' STEPAN SITARYAN says, 'but the prices charged for weapons were set at a very low level. This artificially lowered the defence ministry's spending.' In fact, it has been estimated that through this piece of creative accounting, each rouble spent, according to official figures, in the defence industry had actually cost 8–10 roubles if the prices prevailing in the civilian sector had been applied. Unlike the American military-industrial complex which, though powerful, remained open to public scrutiny and had to lobby for government contracts against other pressure groups, its Soviet counterpart was, in practical terms, part of a militarized state. The civilian sector had to take second place. Did this enormous military expenditure, sustained over several decades, break the back of the Soviet economy? For a country whose economy was less than half that of the United States, it was a tremendous burden. ALEXEI ARBATOV, Director of the Centre for Geopolitical and Military Forecasts in Moscow, sees the issue in a different light. He argues that the economy and society Stalin created in the 1930s was built on military lines and one of its strongest pillars was, in effect, a gigantic military machine, built for 'permanent mobilization and readiness for war'. Arbatov says: 'The Soviet Union was built for the Cold War and for hot wars. Without hostile surroundings, without an enemy, the state probably could not have existed for long. The Cold War served to legitimate, support and sustain the existence of the enormous military-industrial complex that was created before the war, that was expanding during the war and that was preserved on a very large scale after the war.'

In fact, the Soviet economy functioned well as a military machine. It was churning out vast quantities of weaponry and, thanks to the concentration of resources on it, the military sector – along with space exploration – was the only area in which the Soviet Union managed to keep up with the most advanced Western technology. If the main goal of Stalin and his successors was to build a military superpower, then the

129

command economy fulfilled its purpose. What this system failed to achieve was to produce guns and butter in equal measure.

The food deficit

With so much of the Soviet economy's resources poured into the insatiable defence sector, almost everyone else, the consumers, workers, pensioners, the civilian industries and the service sector had to suffer. However, there was one major exception. Agriculture, for long described as the Achilles heel of the Soviet economy, began to attract enormous investment, especially under Brezhnev. By the 1980s about one-quarter of all investment was earmarked for this sector. Yet a huge labour force working on the land, double that of Western Europe and North America put together, still failed to produce enough to feed the Soviet population. Year after year Moscow had to rely on imports of American grain and purchases, at knock-down prices, of surplus dairy produce from the European Community's butter and cheese mountains. For a Soviet leadership that regularly reiterated the superiority of its economic system over the capitalist adversary, this remained a humiliating issue.

Soviet agriculture had been ruined by Stalin, whose collectiviza- tion of land, starting in the late 1920s, was designed to herd the peasants together in *kolkhozes*, where their labour could be fully exploited to pay for industrialization. The immediate result of collectivization was a famine that caused millions of deaths. In the longer term it created an agricultural labour force that, like its industrial counterpart, had no incentive to work hard. Khrushchev tried to remedy the permanent shortfall in food production by opening up vast new areas for cultivation, the 'virgin lands' of Kazakhstan. Brezhnev followed that up with pouring investment into fertilizers and agricultural machinery – but to no avail.

The crucial issue of providing a real incentive for peasants by allowing a degree of private ownership of land was not allowed onto the political agenda until the end of the Soviet regime. Yet, the tiny plots of land that village-dwellers were allowed to have around their houses were estimated to produce one-third of the country's output of vegetables. PROFESSOR ABEL AGANBEGYAN, an economist whose ideas had considerable influence on Mikhail Gorbachev's plans for restructuring, or *perestroika*, believes that Gorbachev missed a chance by not starting his reforms in agriculture. 'Gorbachev was a specialist in agriculture,' says Aganbegyan; 'he had seen the Chinese experience when agricultural output doubled within four years as a result of agrarian reform. There were a lot of specialists, including myself, who tried to explain to him that we must begin our reforms in agriculture because agriculture gives the fastest results. He agreed in principle – but did nothing.'

Successive Soviet leaders, Gorbachev included, were reluctant to introduce far-reaching reforms in agriculture. So much of the money invested in boosting food production went to waste. Yet Brezhnev was committed to a continuous increase in meat consumption as a bench-mark for the rising standard of living. The problem was that meat production could be increased only if there was a corresponding growth in grain yields to provide animal feed for livestock. 'In 1972 there was a harvest failure,' says JIM NOREN, 'and then the decision was made: rather than let the meat programme go, they would import grain on a massive scale. Thereafter they were hooked. Whenever they didn't have enough domestic grain for the meat, they'd import the difference. The leadership wasn't just single-mindedly oriented towards military production; to maintain themselves in power they had to get growth in consumption and in living standards. They spent plenty of money on agriculture. The problem was that the way it was organized, the money went down a sink-hole.'

Resistance to reform

Although economic problems were mounting from the end of Khrushchev's rule onwards, until Mikhail Gorbachev launched

131

perestroika, there was a marked reluctance to initiate or sustain any far-reaching reforms. Why? Inertia was one reason. The system, as it was established under Stalin, created a huge bureaucracy of party and local government officials, working side by side with enterprise managers who were political appointees. After Stalin's death they enjoyed a quiet life where initiative was not required and job security was guaranteed. At the same time a whole range of privileges – not available to ordinary citizens – was provided, particularly for the higher echelons of this group, known as the *nomenklatura*. These privileges ranged from access to special shops with better-quality goods, to chauffeur-driven cars and summer-houses or *dachas* in the country.

Any changes that would rock the boat were anathema to the *nomenklatura* and to the bloated and much-militarized heavy industry sector. Impatient reformers like Khrushchev and Gorbachev met considerable opposition; the former was ousted from the leadership in 1964 for what were described as his 'hare-brained schemes', while the latter became the target of an unsuccessful coup attempt in 1991. Meanwhile, a cautious and conservative figure like Brezhnev stayed in office for 18 years until his death in 1982.

True, Brezhnev did not appear to be completely opposed to reforms at the beginning of his term. Within a year of Khrushchev's dismissal, Prime Minister Alexei Kosygin launched a range of reforms, granting more independence for enterprises from the central bureaucracy and providing greater incentives to managers. Few of these measures were implemented and even fewer survived for any length of time.

The backlash against economic reforms was particularly strong after the crushing of the Prague Spring, when the Czechoslovak leaders' combination of political liberalization with a socialist market economy was denounced as anti-socialist. 'Our intervention in Czechoslovakia was more than just a crime,' says KAREN BRUTENTS, a former Soviet central committee official. 'It was also a great mistake because the first – and maybe not so brave – reforms were then abandoned. They were followed by 15 years of political frost in the Soviet Union itself.' As the Kosygin reforms fizzled out, the years of stagnation set in. Growth rates continued their downward spiral. Even more importantly, the Soviet economy missed out on the latest advances in computer technology and information science. The gap between the developed Western countries and the Soviet Union, which had narrowed in the 1950s, began to widen again in the 1970s.

However, for a time the Soviet economy was shielded from the full impact of its own inefficiency by an unexpected windfall. The Soviet Union was a major exporter of oil. 'We received a gift in the shape of the energy crisis of 1973,' says GENNADI ZOTEYEV. 'With the energy price increase the Soviet economy got about $200 billion between 1973 and 1985. That helped save the old Soviet economic system and it helped the Brezhnev regime survive.'

Comecon failure

In fact, Moscow could probably have made more money out of its oil exports. However, a large proportion of its oil deliveries was supplied to its East European neighbours at prices that were based on the average of the preceding five years on the world market. For a period of nearly 15 years, the price of Soviet oil sold to Moscow's partners in the Comecon trading bloc was lagging behind the world market price. This system of pricing, which also applied to other commodities, was portrayed by Comecon officials as one of the triumphs of planned trade because it cancelled out sudden sharp price fluctuations common to the capitalist economies. Yet its effects turned out to be as harmful for the East European countries as the windfall oil income was for the Soviet Union. Protected from the shock administered to most Western economies by the oil price explosion after 1973, they had little incentive to restructure their production. Economic decline in Eastern Europe mirrored similar developments in the Soviet Union under Brezhnev and subsequent leaders. So by the time the communist regimes collapsed in 1989,

133

these countries were in a much poorer shape than a decade earlier to face the challenge of transition to a market economy.

Of course, when Comecon was established in 1949 by Moscow and its European allies (East Germany joined in 1950), the market economy was a term of abuse in Eastern Europe. Even Comecon's full name – Council for Mutual Economic Assistance – was designed to demonstrate that trade relations between its members would be based on reciprocal benefits and common advantage – unlike the world markets where, as the communists argued, the stronger exploited the weaker side.

The establishment of Comecon followed Stalin's rejection of the Marshall Plan, and one of its purposes was to insulate the East European countries from their traditional Western trading partners. The reorientation of these countries' trade towards each other over the next 40 years was another reason for their economic woes in the 1980s. With each of the Comecon countries conducting between 60 and 90 per cent of its trade with fellow-members (the exception was Romania under President Ceauşescu in the 1970s, when he loosened his country's links with Moscow), Eastern Europe missed out on many technological innovations and high-quality goods from the West. That trend was exacerbated by Western controls over the exports of sensitive military-related technology. When trade with the West opened up on a larger scale during the period of detente in the 1970s, lack of hard currency forced the East European countries (apart from Czechoslovakia, which pursued a more prudent policy) to take out large foreign credits. Each of them paid a heavy price for this in the 1980s, when they emerged from the higher interest-rate regime of the time with debt-ridden economies.

Within Comecon itself very little progress was made towards economic integration. Initially, Comecon remained a façade behind which trade continued, as before, on a bilateral basis. From the second half of the 1950s the coordination of plans got under way. But as VYACHESLAV SYCHEV, the last Secretary of Comecon, says, 'Only the terminology of plan coordination was multilateral. Its practical realization was on a bilateral level. And this remained so until the end of Comecon.'

Khrushchev's attempts beginning in the late 1950s to introduce a division of labour within Comecon led to political divisions among its members. Plans to assign each country a different role were fiercely resisted by Romania which, under Comecon's blueprint, was to remain a food producer. Romania's determination to become an industrialized country was one of the reasons that led to its distancing itself from dependence on Comecon.

The trade pattern established between the Soviet Union and the East Europeans was peculiar by the normal standards of a dominant power and its satellites. Traditionally the European colonial powers bought raw materials from their colonies in exchange for manufactured goods. In the case of Comecon the reverse of that was true. The Soviet Union supplied large quantities of fuel and other raw materials to the East Europeans in exchange for engineering products, consumer goods and food. This pattern became particularly controversial after the oil-price hikes of the 1970s, which made fuel a more precious commodity on the world markets. STEPAN SITARYAN explains the situation: 'I am not offending anyone by saying that we were delivering hard-currency goods and we were buying outdated machinery while we could have bought the same products – but more up-to-date – in the West for our oil and gas. This was the price we paid for being in an alliance, the Warsaw Pact.'

Moscow did not have such a bad bargain. If it had tried to offload all its oil in the West for hard currency, that would have pushed down the world market price of oil. Converting to hard-currency trading within the bloc – as finally happened in 1991 – was considered to be ideologically beyond the pale and would have ruined the rouble. In any case, Moscow was also buying valuable food from Eastern Europe at reasonable prices. Nonetheless, for much of the 1970–80s, it was subsidizing its Comecon allies, and this led to increasing friction. KÁROLY GRÓSZ, Communist Party leader in Budapest, remembers meeting his opposite number in the Soviet capital. 'I remember the time when I visited Boris Yeltsin in Moscow in 1985,' says Grósz, 'and we had a quarrel – but in the literal sense of the word – because Yeltsin, in his usual blunt and even ill-mannered way, told me that we Hungarians should no longer treat them as a milch-cow, living off them.'

Squabbles inside Comecon multiplied after 1987 as Soviet oil became more expensive than oil sold on the world markets. The tables were now turned and the East Europeans had more reason to complain about being overcharged. Meanwhile, Comecon's long-term structural weaknesses and the absence of a convertible currency became an increasing hindrance to economic cooperation. Goods were exchanged largely on the basis of barter and this put a brake on expanding or even maintaining the volume of trade.

The Hungarian and Czechoslovak models

Hungary, whose market-oriented policies starting in 1968 turned it into a show-case of relative prosperity within the Soviet bloc, had long been arguing for similar reforms across the whole of Comecon. But during the Brezhnev era the Soviet leadership remained opposed to restructuring economic institutions within the Soviet bloc. Only small-scale tinkering with the established system was permitted. In the early 1970s the Kremlin even turned against Hungary's domestic reforms, which were based on the idea of giving the managers of state-owned enterprises a degree of independence from the planners. Moscow forced Budapest to put these policies into reverse and dismiss the leaders of the reformist wing.

One of the victims of this political purge was REZSŐ NYERS, the architect of Hungary's economic reforms, who was first demoted and then sacked from the Politburo in 1975. Nyers thinks there were several reasons why Moscow opposed these policies. 'The Soviet leaders objected to the independence we gave our enterprises', says Nyers. 'They said we had to choose between anarchy and the system of planning. Their second concern was that Hungary's economy would open up to the Western countries and East–West contacts would be an alternative to relations with the Soviet Union. Third, they feared – rightly – that if our reforms were allowed to go ahead, they would produce a reform epidemic in Eastern Europe. Finally, they feared on political grounds that these changes would go hand-in-hand with the freer flow of Western ideas, and this would loosen discipline among the East European countries and would have a damaging effect on the Warsaw Pact.'

The heavy hand of the Kremlin stifled the boldest of the Hungarian reforms and slowed down even the cautious innovations. The Hungarian reforms were further undermined by the half-hearted commitment of the Budapest leadership and the lack of similar developments within Comecon. By the mid-1980s – when further measures had been introduced to boost private enterprise – the Hungarian experiment was beginning to lose its shine as Hungary became the largest per capita debtor in Eastern Europe.

Many of Mikhail Gorbachev's reforms of the late 1980s were based on the economic experiments that Hungarians (and others) had introduced over the preceding two decades. The problem was that by the time Gorbachev introduced full-scale *perestroika*, or restructuring, precious time had been lost. Years of stagnation had led to a widening of the technological gap in favour of the market economies; and people, especially in Eastern Europe with easier access to the West than the Soviet population, had become disillusioned with the idea that the Soviet-style economy could be reformed. By the time Gorbachev was trying to persuade the more conservative East European leaders to follow in the steps of his *perestroika*, the peoples of their countries were far more eager to adopt the full-scale capitalism of the West.

But could market socialism have worked if it had been espoused more widely and much earlier within Comecon? At the time of the Prague Spring, which coincided with the introduction of Hungary's economic reforms, many East European economists, Nyers among them, believed so. Now he is more ambivalent, seeing the whole experiment as, at best, a transitional phase towards a market economy, albeit one with a high level of social ownership and welfare: 'In the late 1960s there was still a real hope for market socialism. If adopted successively in the other East European countries, it could have led, perhaps, to a transition to a modern social-democratic system of the Swedish style. But by the 1980s it was too late; the economic problems had become too big; Gorbachev came too late and he changed things too slowly.'

The economic contest fought out during the years of the Cold War ended in defeat for the Soviet bloc. In a sense it was always an unfair competition because the Soviet Union and its allies had started out with the handicap of having much more backward economies than the West. However, there was one major exception, Czechoslovakia, which before the Second World War was one of Europe's economically most developed states.

The former Czechoslovakia is, perhaps, the best case for testing the efficiency of the command economy against its capitalist competitors. After all, unlike the other Soviet-bloc countries, it started from a roughly comparable position with most West European countries after the war. Moreover, apart from a brief period in the mid-1960s, it refrained from introducing Hungarian-style reforms, pursuing instead traditional Soviet-style policies. So how did Czechoslovakia fare under the conditions of the command economy? Not well, according to PROFESSOR VALTR KOMÁREK, who was director of the Institute of Economic Forecasting in Prague during the 1980s, a think-tank whose frustrated economic reformers emerged to lead Czechoslovakia after the Velvet Revolution of 1989. 'Our starting conditions after the war were much better than those of most West European countries,' Komárek explains. 'We were a developed country; our GDP was roughly $200 per capita; the Japanese was about $79 per capita; the Italian about $135. We hadn't suffered much through the war – as opposed to, for example, West Germany which had been nearly completely destroyed. And yet when we prepared an analysis in 1985–7, we concluded that our GDP per employee was only about 60 per cent that of the developed Western countries. The problem was that our entire economic strategy was based on arbitrary political decisions communicated through Gosplan and was coordinated through a kind of military strategy.'

Czechoslovakia's previously high level of economic development was no help in counteracting the damaging effects of bureaucratic central management. The former diversity of its production structure was stifled by a surplus of old-fashioned heavy industry geared to the Soviet market. The prospects for improvement received a further blow in the wake of the crushing of the Prague Spring, when reform-minded politicians, managers and economists – who were often the best-qualified for their jobs – were dismissed from their posts *en masse*. This has had a far-reaching effect on the standard of living. 'If Czechoslovakia had enjoyed the same conditions as Austria,' Valtr Komárek says, 'then we would be better off today than Austria. The adoption of the planned economy wasn't altogether a catastrophe; but it was certainly a piece of bad luck.'

If Czechoslovakia's misfortune was its relative economic decline vis-à-vis its capitalist neighbours, that of the other Soviet-bloc countries was their failure to come near to catching up with the West. Most of them shared the mounting problems created in the Soviet Union by the dictatorship of the bureaucracy over the economy. The results were stagnation, a wasteful use of resources, low efficiency in production and constant shortages (which sustained thriving black and grey markets). There was also environmental degradation on a huge scale and a deterioration in public services.

Mikhail Gorbachev's reaction to this catalogue of horrors was to try to reform the system. His attempt failed and, as communism collapsed, the Soviet-bloc countries began to adopt the market system – ironically at a time when most capitalist economies were also experiencing problems, particularly with high unemployment. But to provide better conditions for his attempted reforms, Gorbachev had linked his endeavours at home to improving relations with the West. The outcome of that policy was to end the Cold War.

The Vietnam Veterans Memorial in Washington. The names of more than 58,000 American soldiers killed or missing in action in Vietnam are engraved on its black granite slabs. Since its inauguration in 1982, the Monument has become a shrine to the dead. In its first 10 years, over 30,000 objects were left there, including wedding rings, family albums, purple hearts and cowboy boots. (Designed by Maya Ying Lin.)

7

TRIALS OF STRENGTH:
VIETNAM AND
AFGHANISTAN

'A lot of officers used to compare our war in Afghanistan more and more with the war in Vietnam,' says TIMUR KANUKOV, who served in the Soviet army in Afghanistan in the mid-1980s. 'This view was very widespread among officers because the parallels were too transparent – a great power in a small country, fighting and failing, with many casualties. And even though it was prohibited to make any comparisons with Vietnam, it was a commonplace in our conversations.'

Vietnam and Afghanistan have been compared on many occasions as the two wars that tested the strength of the superpowers more than any other regional conflicts during the Cold War. America's involvement in Vietnam required the largest and longest military commitment by Washington during that period; more than a decade later Afghanistan posed the same challenge to Moscow. Each side spent huge resources on maintaining its allies in power – yet they both failed in the end. The communist victory in Vietnam contributed to a weakening of American power around the world for a decade; the Soviet Union itself collapsed even before its allies were finally driven from power in Kabul.

America's road to Vietnam

The initial American involvement in Vietnam was a response to the communist victory in China. At the end of the Second World War, Washington was looking forward to the dismantling of the British and French colonial empires; by the early 1950s, it was financing the French in Indo-China in their fight with the communist-dominated Viet Minh forces, who were led by Ho Chi Minh.

'The Americans were paying for our war, supplying equipment and giving credit,' says CLAUDE CHEYSSON, who was in Saigon in 1952–4 as an adviser to the pro-French Prime Minister of Vietnam. 'But it was only later, at the Geneva peace conference convened [in 1954] to end the French war in Vietnam, that I realized that for the Americans it was a kind of crusade against communism. They were anxious to use the domino effect and crush Vietnamese communism in order to impress the other communist states, in particular China.'

The Geneva conference followed the French defeat by the Viet Minh forces at the siege of Dien Bien Phu. At the conference a ceasefire was agreed. To separate the warring sides, it was decided that the Viet Minh forces would move north of the 17th parallel while the French and the Vietnamese fighting under their command would go to the south. Elections throughout Vietnam were to be held in 1956 under international supervision. However, Ngo Dinh Diem, the South Vietnamese strongman, refused to allow southern participation in the scheduled elections, having held a referendum in 1955 that abolished the monarchy and proclaimed South Vietnam a republic.

President Diem's authoritarian policies and his reliance on his minority fellow-Catholics in government created a fertile ground for opposition to his rule. Some of the Viet Minh supporters who had moved north after the Geneva conference returned south to join a guerrilla war against the unpopular Diem regime. American financial and military support for Diem gradually increased in the Eisenhower years. Communism had to be contained in Vietnam just as much as it had been successfully resisted only a few years earlier

142

in Korea. GENERAL ALEXANDER HAIG, who fought in both wars, has no doubts that Vietnam was a textbook example for the policy of containment. 'The North Vietnamese were ideological advocates of Marxism-Leninism, they believed in their cause and no nation could have fought more valiantly or courageously to have that cause prevail. But the basic issue was the imperialist Marxist, Soviet-driven threat. Now had it been something different from that, I would never have been a proponent of the United States entering that conflict.'

However, not everyone among American policy-makers was convinced that the struggle in Vietnam was a clear case of communist aggression directed from Moscow. GEORGE BALL, deputy Secretary of State under Presidents Kennedy and Johnson, was one of the sceptics. 'I did not believe at all that this was a kind of surrogate attack by the Soviet Union and the Chinese,' says Ball. 'It was nationalism. I don't think it was part of the Cold War because what's emerging from the Soviet, or Russian, side these days is that they didn't plan it themselves to the extent that the United States should be embarrassed by some kind of local problem. They were very reluctant to pour any substantial resources into it. And I think the Chinese felt the same way. It was part of the general obsession with the Soviet threat – an obsession which from our point of view was very well founded at that time, except that this particular case was falsely assumed to be an aspect of it.'

However, the general trend was towards increased American involvement in Vietnam. Under Kennedy, American assistance to South Vietnam was considerably stepped up and thousands of military advisers were dispatched to help the authorities in the war against the insurgents. The first phase of the escalation was partly in response to the establishment in December 1960 of the communist-controlled National Front for the Liberation of Vietnam (NLF) to coordinate the struggle against Diem.

'It was the Kennedy administration which really started the major involvement,' says HENRY KISSINGER, National Security

143

Adviser in the Nixon administration, which inherited the burden of American involvement in Vietnam. 'What they thought was that they and their predecessors knew how to stop general war and limited war. They thought that the opening that existed was for a guerrilla war and they thought Vietnam was a test case in which they could demonstrate that a guerrilla war would also not succeed. And, of course, they knew that a guerrilla war would not be fought in Southeast Asia by the Soviets themselves.'

A counter-insurgency campaign, backed by American weapons and advisers, might have worked if the South Vietnamese government had enjoyed popular support. However, Diem's corrupt regime had alienated much of South Vietnamese society. Nor did his overthrow and assassination in a military coup in 1963, which was followed by the fall of several governments in quick succession, improve the standing of the Saigon authorities. America was faced with the choice of acquiescing in the victory of the NLF or taking over much of the fighting itself. Many among the American military were dubious about large-scale, direct military involvement in Vietnam. ADMIRAL ELMO ZUMWALT JR, who was to become commander of United States naval forces in Vietnam in 1968, was among those who advised against an escalation in the American military presence. 'My own view was that I strongly supported our containment strategy,' says Zumwalt, 'but that Vietnam was the wrong place to draw the line because it was a country that was not really a viable national entity; that the place to take a stand was in Thailand, Indonesia, Malaysia and the Philippines. My advice was overruled.'

The problem for the United States was that the conflict was taking place in Vietnam. 'We didn't pick on Vietnam; it came up,' says MCGEORGE BUNDY, who was National Security Adviser to Kennedy and Johnson. 'We had by 1961 a prolonged engagement in support of the South Vietnamese people and that was simply one of the existing positions on the Cold War map when the Kennedy administration came in. And it would not have occurred to us to withdraw. What happened, of course, was that the contest intensified and the requirements to sustain the South Vietnamese against military defeat went up. Through the Kennedy administration we had no belief that we needed to change from a policy of military and financial support and the supplies of equipment and advisers. In the Johnson administration it became pretty clear in 1964 and early 1965 that either we would have to do more or accept the defeat of the South Vietnamese government.'

President Johnson was not prepared to see South Vietnam in communist hands. The massive escalation of American military involvement followed an incident in the Gulf of Tonkin, when North Vietnamese patrol boats reportedly fired on the American destroyer *Maddox* in August 1964. The United States retaliated with bombing raids on North Vietnam, and Congress passed, almost unanimously, a resolution authorizing the President to use all necessary means to prevent further aggression. In March 1965 American combat forces landed in South Vietnam to join the 23,000 advisers already stationed there; within three years the number of United States forces in the country had increased to 550,000.

GEORGE BALL remained firmly opposed to raising the stakes in Vietnam. 'Beginning right after the Gulf of Tonkin incident – shooting at flying fish or whatever – I bombarded the President with memoranda, saying, "Cut your losses and get out of there." First, I wrote a 60- or 70-page memorandum, but I didn't send it immediately to the President; I waited two or three months, while he was in the middle of campaigning for the elections, and when I sent it to him he called me the next morning and said: "Why haven't I had this before? I spent all night reading it twice. Meet me as soon as you can." So I went over to the White House and he had assembled [Secretary of State Dean] Rusk and [Defence Secretary] McNamara and said, "On page 25 you say this, on page 37 you say this. Now, how do you reconcile this or how do you defend that," and so on.

'I mention this only because he clearly had read it very carefully and was deeply disturbed by it. But then McNamara immediately shot me down in flames and Rusk joined in and so did Bundy. I was very much alone in the room – except for the President, the one person who stayed cool and who had a feeling that there was a very big question about this because I challenged every one of the assumptions we had. And I was influenced by the fact that I had been working with the French during their agony in Indo-China. So I had a sense of what the Viet Cong, the North Vietnamese, were like and I had a feeling that these people weren't going to be easy to overcome.'

In any case, George Ball's cautionary words against actively entering the war in Vietnam remained a minority view. The escalation began and it was not until the presidential elections of 1968 that leading American politicians switched to the policy of reducing or ending the military involvement in Vietnam.

The Soviet Union's road to Afghanistan

Success has a thousand parents; failure is an orphan. The Soviet invasion of Afghanistan was as much of an ignominious failure as the American intervention in Vietnam, and those who were at or near the pinnacle of Soviet power in 1979 have since then tried to blame others for the decision to send Soviet troops into Afghanistan. In any case, it appears to have been an agonizing choice to make and one that was resisted for a long time by the Soviet leadership. ANDREI ALEXANDROV-AGENTOV, Brezhnev's foreign policy adviser, recalls the circumstances: 'Almost from the first day, the three leaders of the Kabul revolution literally implored some form of Soviet military support. And the question of whether to do it or not was on the agenda of the Politburo almost as long as that concerning Czechoslovakia. At the beginning everyone was against, especially Brezhnev; he would not hear about the troops going into Afghanistan. "What have we lost there and what have we to find there?" he asked.

'But then the strength of the *mujahidin* [resistance fighters], equipped with modern American weapons, with support coming from Saudi Arabia and Iran, led to a real internationalization of the conflict. The large-scale interference of the United States, Pakistan and China created a fear in Moscow that Afghanistan would be turned into a new American military base instead of Iran, which America had lost. The last and decisive impulse was the coming to power of that sinister figure, [Hafizullah] Amin, who killed the leader of the revolution, [Nur Mohammad] Taraki, and wanted to accelerate the building of socialism in Afghanistan by killing thousands of peasants and priests, not to mention the petty bourgeoisie. That secured the solid resistance of almost all the people against the new power.'

The reports of foreign involvement were grossly exaggerated, partly by the Afghan government itself, which used this as a pretext for demanding more aid from Moscow. The communist regime which had come to power in April 1978 – and was under the control of the radical *Khalq* (or masses) faction – was so universally hated that resistance was widespread without any large-scale outside encouragement. Opposition had been engendered by the government's ruthless attempts to centralize and modernize a traditional, rural and, in part, nomadic society. The tenets of Marxism-Leninism were to replace age-old Islamic values. The redistribution of larger estates alienated the landowners without attracting the support of the peasants who were given the land, because without access to the tools required to work the land, the new smallholdings remained largely worthless.

The presence of several thousand Soviet military advisers was also an irritant to many independent-minded Afghans. Still, it fell well short of the kind of occupation which was now being contemplated. Moscow had traditionally enjoyed close relations with Kabul, even in the days of the Afghan monarchy when Soviet aid was flooding into the country in return for a broadly pro-Soviet foreign policy. The Kremlin was now concerned that Amin's violent revolution would undo decades of investment in Afghanistan by creating so much resistance that it would end in the overthrow of the communist regime. Moreover, a great deal of the hatred engendered by the communist government was being deflected onto the Soviet Union, and the fall of the Kabul regime might deliver Afghanistan into the hands of the Americans.

Whatever the nature of the Kremlin's concerns, the Soviet military were somewhat reluctant to invade. COLONEL-GENERAL NIKOLAI CHERVOV was on the general staff of the Soviet army at the time. 'I know for sure that the general staff and the high-level officers were against sending troops into Afghanistan. And especially Marshal Ogarkov, Chief of the General Staff, and Marshal Akhromeyev, his first deputy, were against this idea and actually advised the political leadership not to do this because it would be a big mistake. Marshal Ogarkov was trying to persuade the Politburo not to take this decision to invade, giving the example of Great Britain's history and saying it would cause great losses in manpower and money. But unfortunately his influence was not strong enough compared with that of Defence Minister Ustinov, who was in the Politburo.'

The Soviet top brass may have had its doubts about the benefits of a full-scale invasion; however, they were concerned about providing protection for Soviet advisers already based in Afghanistan, some of whom had been massacred by the resistance. But whatever the exact position of the general staff – and its members may have been divided – important decisions were made by the *troika* of Yuri Andropov, Chairman of the KGB, Foreign Minister Andrei Gromyko and Ustinov, with the ailing Brezhnev usually approving them.

ALEXANDER BESSMERTNYKH, who was at one time Gromyko's personal assistant, says: 'Knowing Gromyko, I am surprised that he was part of the decision that was taken to introduce troops into Afghanistan. The Cold War produced the most cautious foreign ministers in the history of the world. I think he participated in that decision not just because he was a hardliner. Maybe there was a lot of information that made us misjudge the situation. I think there was a deliberate emphasis on the threat to Soviet interests in Afghanistan, and the role of the United States was presented in a very exaggerated way by some of the services in our government.'

Many of the alarmist reports from Kabul originated from the KGB. Although KGB Chairman Andropov shared the Soviet leadership's initial reluctance to send troops into Afghanistan, as one of the members of the executive *troika* he bore much of the responsibility for the final decision to go ahead with the invasion, which was taken by the Politburo in mid-December. It was top secret; even ANDREI ALEXANDROV-AGENTOV says he had been kept in the dark about it. 'One night in December 1979 I read a telegram from our ambassador in Kabul in which he enumerated all the variations proposed by Amin as motives for the entry of our troops. And I phoned Andropov who was then in the KGB and asked him: "Well, what are you going to say in answer to Amin's proposals?" "What Amin?" he said. "There is no Amin there. There is Karmal and our troops are already in Kabul." That shows how that decision was made: there were no official sessions, no set protocol.'

Babrak Karmal of the more moderate – and for Moscow more predictable – *Parcham* (flag) faction of the communist movement was installed in power by the Soviet army. Amin was killed on 27 December in the assault on the presidential palace outside Kabul. For the Soviet soldiers, whose numbers were soon to rise to 115,000, the reasons for moving into Afghanistan were explained in the stark terms of the Cold War. 'What the political officers were telling the soldiers', says the journalist ARTYOM BOROVIK, who paid several visits to Afghanistan, 'was that they were not fighting with the *mujahidin*, rather they were fighting basically with America. I remember one officer telling me that it's better to fight a war with America here in Afghanistan than in the streets of Moscow or Leningrad. We should stop imperialism here and not in Russia. Later on I found out that the same things had been told to American soldiers in Vietnam, "We should stop that bloody communism here in Vietnam and not on Broadway or Park Avenue." These stereotypes were the same.'

As with the American military presence in Vietnam in its earlier phase, the Soviet build-up in Afghanistan was designed to serve a

149

limited purpose – but it was soon followed by an almost inevitable military escalation. 'The initial idea was one or two divisions, no more, just to put them in garrisons and let Babrak Karmal know that he could always fall back on their support,' says LEONID SHEBAR-SHIN, who became head of the KGB's foreign intelligence in 1989 after tours of duty in Afghanistan, Pakistan and Iran. 'And the troops had been told not to get in touch with the local population, to avoid any contact and to be as little visible as possible – but it did not happen that way. The columns were shot at, they didn't know who was shooting at them, but they disregarded the orders and shot back and were shot at again. So that was a natural escalation.'

The superpowers get bogged down

From the beginning of their involvement in Vietnam and Afghanistan, the campaign to win the hearts and minds of the local people became a feature of both the American and the Soviet war efforts. 'We would bring doctors and provide medical assistance, we would distribute clothes and food for children and we would hold sessions with the respected elders who were the heads of Afghan villages,' says LIEUTENANT YEVGENI KHRUSHCHEV, who served in Afghanistan in the mid-1980s.

But the charm offensive went hand in hand with harsh tactics. 'The most outrageous experience that I had in Afghanistan', says Yevgeni Khrushchev, 'was when I first witnessed a rocket attack on a village from where we had just come back after distributing food and clothes. Despite all my arguments that we could trust people in the vicinity of our camp, the commander still ordered an artillery barrage, just to intimidate the population, to prevent a possible night attack on the army's position. And that was the first time I realized that what I and my service, the psych-ops service, were trying to accomplish in Afghanistan looked futile compared with the merciless blood-bath we were drawn into by the stupidity of the Kremlin rulers and the *mujahidin* fanatics from Pakistan.'

Trying to enlist the support of the local population was not an easy task. PETER MAHONEY went to Vietnam as a lieutenant in 1970. 'Part of my job as an adviser was to train what were called people's self-defence forces, PSDF – civilians whom we would train to defend their hamlets so that the soldiers could be taken for other jobs. Generally, these PSDF consisted of kids, 14–16 years old, too young to be drafted. And there was a group of 29 of them from three hamlets that were closely located to one another. My team put them through a six-week training course. At the end of the six weeks there was a big graduation ceremony and the province's chief came down and gave them each a little neckerchief to wear. About a month and a half later two Viet Cong cadres came to the village, gave a small speech and all 29 of them walked off and joined the NLF – taking all their weapons and their training with them. They made their choice to oppose the Americans and my feeling at the time was, well, who am I to tell them that they are wrong.'

In spite of their overwhelming military superiority, Soviet troops in Afghanistan likewise encountered unexpectedly stiff and relentless resistance. As the war dragged on, the views of many Soviet soldiers began to change. 'After a year in Afghanistan', says ALEXEI CHIKISHEV, who served in Afghanistan in the mid-1980s, 'I began to consider the *mujahidin* guerrillas exactly the same as the guerrillas who fought here in the Soviet Union against the Nazi German army – and although they were our enemies, their war was just. The people of Afghanistan didn't invite the Soviet army into their country.'

More than a decade earlier the war in Vietnam had changed the thinking of a whole generation of young Americans, including many of the servicemen who fought there. 'I remember precisely thinking at the beginning', says WAYNE SMITH, a combat medic who served in Vietnam in the early 1970s, 'that the fight was against the communists in North Vietnam who were attempting to take over the so-called "free Vietnamese" in the southern part of the country. The change was pretty abrupt once I got into combat because combat tends to distil reality; you live or you die. And the fight in Vietnam was about survival, not about winning the war.'

'Discipline had collapsed in the American armed services,' says GEORGE 'SKIP' ROBERTS, who arrived in Vietnam with the marines in 1969. 'I think in 1970 there were 350 court martials going on for murder or attempted murder of officers. Everyone knew the war had no purpose and to die there meant you were a fool. You had a calendar with 365 days and you crossed it off day by day. And that was your goal, to stay alive, reach day one and get on the freedom bird to get you out of there. But my best friends weren't rotating that day because we weren't sent as units but as individuals. So every month one-twelfth of your friends left. Other armies have studied that and it's considered a great mistake because it breaks unit cohesion in the field and creates great costs in psychological problems.'

Meanwhile, on the home front in the United States, opposition to the war increased, particularly in the wake of the NLF's *Tet*, or lunar New Year, offensive in early 1968, when the Viet Cong emerged from their rural bases and briefly occupied several cities. Vietnam was the first war to be televised, bringing images of the horrors of fighting into people's homes. The media magnified the impact the war was already having on Americans. 'The cohort of young men who were being drafted to go into that war', says the American broadcaster JOHN CHANCELLOR, 'was relatively small. It must have been 6–7 million young men of draftable age. The casualty figures were rising every week, and if you were the member of a small group like that, you would have been terrified that Uncle Sam would come and send you off to the war.

'The media didn't have anything to do with the reactions of those young fellows. The war was seen to be unwinnable in the letters sent home by a lot of the soldiers. And these young men would go back to every little town in the United States and say, "this thing is terrible". The media itself – the anti-war columnists and commentators – had an effect only in that they amplified the social change that was going on. The pictures made a very unpopular war even more unpopular. So, did we have something to do with bringing it to an end? Yes, but we only brought it to an end a little more quickly.'

In terms of media coverage, the contrast with the secretiveness surrounding the Soviet war in Afghanistan could not have been greater. ARTYOM BOROVIK was among the first Soviet journalists to be allowed to write the truth about that war. 'Until 1986 nothing could be written about the war in Afghanistan,' says Borovik. 'If you thumb through Soviet newspapers and magazines of the early 1980s and read reports from Soviet correspondents, you would get the impression that Soviet soldiers in Afghanistan were picking flowers and doing nothing else. By the mid-1980s this terrible official lie started to contradict what people were hearing from the Afghan vets, and by then every cemetery in Russia already had a fresh grave or two. And the only thing written on the grave was, for example, "Sasha Ivanov, died, fulfilling his internationalist duty." Where and why, you could never know.'

As the human and economic cost of American involvement in Vietnam mounted, a strong anti-war movement took shape. A large section of the political establishment joined the crusade to bring the war to an end. SENATOR WILLIAM FULBRIGHT, Chairman of the Senate Foreign Relations Committee, became a vociferous critic of the war. 'We had no business there,' says Fulbright; 'it was a civil war and, I'm afraid, we made it much worse than it would have been without us. We had the idea that we were all-important, all-powerful and we could do anything. I guess since the atomic bomb we'd thought that since we could destroy everything we could do anything. We had a bad case of egotism.'

As the anti-war movement gathered momentum, President Johnson decided against a further escalation of the conflict in the wake of the *Tet* offensive. Instead, he sought to find a political solution. The bombing of North Vietnam was first restricted and then halted in October 1968 while informal talks between Washington and Hanoi got under way. Richard Nixon was elected president in November, having pledged to pull out of Vietnam with dignity.

American troop withdrawals began in 1969 as a peace conference bringing together the United States, North and South Vietnam, and the NLF opened in Paris.

Washington's concern that the North Vietnamese would exploit the American withdrawal led to the invasion of Cambodia by United States and South Vietnamese forces in 1970. The purpose of the incursion was to cut off the Ho Chi Minh trail through which North Vietnam was sending reinforcements and supplies to the South. This move provoked a further wave of anti-war protests in America. 'The division in public opinion', says HENRY KISSINGER, 'made it very difficult to negotiate or conduct a strategy because whatever we did was immediately second-guessed by a large percentage, at least, of leadership opinion.' By March 1972, when the number of American troops stationed in South Vietnam had dropped below 100,000, a major offensive by the North Vietnamese led to the renewal of American bombing raids on the North and to the mining of Haiphong and other northern harbours.

However, it was not until after another particularly intensive display of America's destructive air power – the Christmas bombing of North Vietnam in 1972 – that an agreement was finally concluded in Paris in January 1973. The accords declared a ceasefire; required all American forces to be withdrawn from South Vietnam; an international peacekeeping force was to be deployed; and North Vietnamese troops already based in the South were allowed to stay there but were not to be reinforced.

The American withdrawal completed the process of 'Vietnamization' whereby South Vietnam took on the full burden of defending itself. But South Vietnam's resistance did not last long. The government of President Nguyen Van Thieu gradually lost ground to the combined North Vietnamese and NLF forces and was finally defeated at the end of April 1975 when, amid chaotic scenes, Saigon fell to the communists. Containment had failed and fears about the domino effect appeared to come true when the communist victory in Vietnam produced a similar outcome in Cambodia and Laos.

The reasons for failure

But why did America, a superpower, fail to achieve its goals in Vietnam? It was, of course, fighting not just a small country but one that was equipped with sophisticated weapons supplied in huge quantities by Moscow and Peking. 'I was in charge of the 3,300 Soviet military specialists in Vietnam,' says COLONEL-GENERAL VLADIMIR ABRAMOV, who arrived in Hanoi in 1967. 'Our task was to teach the Vietnamese how to use the equipment, including the aircraft and the anti-aircraft defence system, supplied by the USSR. Before, in 1965–6, Soviet specialists in anti-aircraft units had participated in the first few battles and, as part of anti-aircraft defence systems, each with 20–25 people, they had been responsible for shooting down American aircraft.'

Although America poured huge resources into its military effort in Vietnam, it was still fighting a limited war. An invasion of North Vietnam by land or sea, for instance, was out of the question. 'I was on Robert McNamara's staff in the Pentagon when the conflict really blossomed into a full-blown war,' says GENERAL ALEXANDER HAIG, who later served in Vietnam. 'I said at the time that if we Americans are going to risk the lives of our young people, it must be with a dedication to win – and that meant we had to mobilize all the resources of this country. I am convinced that had we done that back in 1965, Hanoi and Moscow would have recoiled from calling our bluff. But we did tie both hands behind our back, and by the time President Nixon began to apply a fuller range of American national power it was too late because the American people did not support that effort.'

General Haig believes that lack of American aid for South Vietnam in the wake of the Paris agreement was also the reason for Saigon's subsequent collapse. 'What the advocates of the agreement believed was that there was a fighting chance for Saigon to survive. But that required two preconditions: the first was the commitment of the United States to support Saigon with the same level of military and economic support that we had earlier. What we did instead was

155

immediately to begin to dry that up and terminate it. Second was the obligation to police international agreements and to insist that the obligations incurred formally by treaty were abided by. Well, they were not – but a few months after the accords were signed the American Congress [in June 1973] voted away the power of the president to conduct any military operations in Southeast Asia. Unbelievable; and I label the people who were involved as having blood on their hands.'

Others believe that the reasons for America's failure in Vietnam were more deep-seated than merely a lack of commitment in resources. 'My main concern was not to get involved,' says DENIS HEALEY, who was Britain's Defence Secretary between 1964 and 1970. 'Johnson was nagging [British Prime Minister Harold] Wilson the whole time and McNamara was nagging me to provide even a token force in Vietnam. And I used to say to Bob [McNamara], "Look, it's the wrong war, you can't win it and the way you're fighting it makes your defeat certain" – because the Americans were plastering Vietnam with napalm and defoliant and killing millions, including innocent civilians, without really affecting the course of the conflict. Now I was fighting a war in Borneo at that time against Indonesia and I wouldn't let a single British bomb be dropped from a British aircraft on Indonesian territory, even in Borneo, because I thought it would mobilize local support against us. We won the Borneo war before the Americans were defeated in Vietnam simply by keeping the support of the local population. But my problem was to avoid the Americans involving us directly in Vietnam. It was simply to have a partner in crime.'

Washington's problem was that it was fighting a war in Vietnam on an immeasurably larger scale than the British were doing in Borneo. In addition, success or failure in Vietnam was not just a question of military tactics. PAUL WARNKE, who became Assistant Secretary of Defence in 1967, did not support the American intervention in Vietnam. 'The difficulty was that the war wasn't an invasion from the North solely; there was very substantial, maybe majority, support in the South for the reunion of Vietnam. The fact is that the government in Saigon was an American creation. It did not have the allegiance of the Vietnamese themselves. So we were engaged in nation-building but didn't know what kind of a nation the local people would tolerate. Our motives were entirely commendable; we were trying genuinely to bring democracy to Vietnam but unfortunately it can't be imposed from the outside; it has to arise internally.'

If Washington found the war in Vietnam unwinnable, Moscow had no easier task in Afghanistan a decade later. The difficulties were obvious to virtually all those who saw the fighting in Afghanistan. 'People couldn't understand', says ARTYOM BOROVIK, 'how come you would go to the same place to fight and each time you would win a battle but still it wasn't under your control, you had to go and fight in the same place over and over again and it demoralized the army. We basically controlled the territory that was under our tanks. By the end of the war it was a sort of nervous breakdown of the whole army. Soldiers and officers were frightened even of little kids. I remember a helicopter was trying to land at Bagram air base and a little kid ran close to the place where it wanted to land and the pilot thought he was throwing a Molotov cocktail. So he pushed a button, a rocket went down and just destroyed the little guy, leaving nothing of him. When the helicopter landed they found his hand, not with a Molotov cocktail but with a rock.'

It took Washington more than four years from Nixon's election promise in 1968 to effect the withdrawal of American troops from Vietnam. The Soviet leaders became aware of the mistake they had made with regard to Afghanistan at an even earlier stage, but trying to get out was no less difficult. ANDREI ALEXANDROV-AGENTOV says: 'Rather soon our leaders understood the graveness of their misjudgment and began to think how to escape. Brezhnev was too ill to manage that, although he talked about it. Andropov died too soon. Chernenko could not do anything at all, he was half dead even when he was in his study in the Kremlin. Gorbachev began where Andropov finished. He immediately gave orders to make plans for finishing our war in Afghanistan.'

The KGB, whose intelligence reports had urged a Soviet intervention in 1979, was also coming to realize that its proposals had landed the Soviet Union in a quagmire. LEONID SHEBARSHIN made 25 trips to Afghanistan between 1984 and 1991. 'By 1984 it had become clear that the war could not be won. It took some more time to come to the conclusion that the only way out was the policy of national reconciliation. In 1985 the Soviet leadership changed and the period of *perestroika* started. The war had no place in the new thinking in foreign policy. We had to leave Afghanistan but we hoped it would be possible to leave Afghanistan as a friendly and stable state – which did not happen, unfortunately.'

For the new policy of national reconciliation to work, it was necessary to get rid of the discredited figure of Karmal. Shebarshin says: 'Kryuchkov [the head of the KGB's foreign intelligence] and I took part in the effort to persuade Karmal that it would be better for himself and for the country if he stepped down. The decision had already been taken by his colleagues and former followers – with our consent, of course, but it was not our initiative. So we managed to show Karmal the light, so to say. We helped to persuade Karmal by peaceful means.'

You didn't need to use anything other than peaceful persuasion?

'Definitely not. There was a very long and very frank and very difficult talk, but finally, next day, Karmal decided that he could not stay.'

To make Karmal's departure easier, he had been invited to the Soviet Union for medical treatment in April 1986. In May he was replaced by Mohammed Najibullah, the head of the much-feared KHAD security police. Moscow was hoping that through a combination of tough action against the hardline resistance and concessions to the waverers, the new Afghan leader would be able to cement his government's support. This would then allow Soviet forces to prepare their withdrawal from Afghanistan – a policy that the Soviet Politburo finally approved in November 1986, setting a two-year deadline for the pull-out.

The Kremlin's decision had not been prompted by the kind of intense public pressure that had persuaded the Nixon administration to withdraw American forces from Vietnam. The Soviet media had maintained a black-out on all truthful reporting of the war in Afghanistan. Yet people still knew through the accounts of returning soldiers and foreign radio broadcasts what was happening there. Opposition to the war could not be expressed in public; however, public opinion of a sort did play a part in persuading Gorbachev that Afghanistan was a bleeding wound for the Soviet Union that could be healed only through a withdrawal. ANDREI ALEXANDROV-AGENTOV, who stayed on as foreign policy adviser during Gorbachev's first year in power, recalls: 'There came tens of thousands of letters, saying, "Why are our boys losing their lives there?" It made a very strong impression on the new leader who understood that if he wanted to stay in power and be popular, he would have to put an end to it.'

Meanwhile, *glasnost*, openness in the media, was beginning to gain ground. 'The major breakthrough', says ARTYOM BOROVIK, 'was in 1987 when [the weekly] *Ogonyok* published my dispatches from Afghanistan. It was very difficult to publish it because first you had to give the manuscript to the military censorship and then to Glavlit, the civilian censorship. I had given them 150 pages and they were returned with 300 remarks and corrections. But we were able to show what was really going on; Soviet soldiers dying, Afghan people dying – before that you couldn't even do that. And even though I didn't say in 1987 that we should stop the war, because it would never have been published, and I didn't say that it was bad, I did try to show that it was bad.'

With the Soviet media kept on a tight leash until after the Kremlin's decision to withdraw, the role of public opinion was limited. What was more important in persuading the Soviet leadership to attempt its version of 'Vietnamization' was the increasing realization that, in the absence of a massive escalation, the war was unwinnable. A combination of Afghanistan's rugged terrain, together with the fierce sense of independence, warlike traditions and the strong Islamic faith of its people, proved too much of a challenge. The United States also played a crucial role. 'When the Soviets entered Afghanistan, my point of view was accepted', says ZBIGNIEW BRZEZINSKI, President Carter's National Security Adviser, 'and we engaged ourselves, for the first time ever in the entire history of the Cold War, in actively supporting military resistance against the Soviets, which means lethality directed against the Red Army. And we became engaged in that very actively and that was an unprecedented step, the result of which was to bog the Soviets down in their equivalent of Vietnam. If we hadn't committed ourselves to support the *mujahidin*, the Soviets might well have worn them down at some point.'

A Soviet army convoy leaves Kabul along the Salang highway, heading back to the Soviet Union during the final phase of the withdrawal from Afghanistan in February 1989.

160

American assistance to the *mujahidin*, channelled mainly through the CIA, was stepped up under President Reagan. From the mid-1980s the Afghan resistance groups were supplied with sophisticated anti-aircraft missiles which put an end to the Soviet air force's mastery of the skies. Washington's aid to the *mujahidin* was very important in frustrating Moscow's attempts to overcome the Afghan resistance. Similarly, Soviet supplies to North Vietnam had earlier contributed significantly to America's failure in Vietnam. Even when they stayed in the background, the superpowers' role in determining the outcome of these two conflicts was crucial.

The withdrawal of Soviet forces from Afghanistan began in 1988 and was completed in February 1989. Moscow continued to supply military and economic aid on a large scale to the Najibullah regime. The Kabul government's survival for the next three years was also helped by the fractious nature of the Afghan resistance. There were two separate, loosely knit alliances, with seven Sunni Muslim groups based in Pakistan and eight Shi'a Muslim groups in Iran. In contrast, the Americans in Vietnam had faced a highly disciplined North Vietnamese army and the NLF guerrillas, who were under tight communist control.

What the superpowers shared was a formidable adversary in each case. The Vietnamese communist forces and the *mujahidin* were prepared to wage a long war. They also fought for their own countries and on terrain that was familiar to them but difficult for the outsiders: the jungle in Vietnam and mountains in Afghanistan. When aid was cut off, the ramshackle regimes in both Saigon and Kabul quickly collapsed. Moscow's assistance to Najibullah was halted in January 1992 following the collapse of the Soviet Union; four months later the *mujahidin* were in control of Kabul.

The cost of defeat

Of the many regional conflicts fought during the Cold War, Vietnam for America and Afghanistan for the Soviet Union proved to be the toughest. America lost over 58,000 servicemen in Vietnam. The more limited Soviet involvement in Afghanistan – the number of Soviet troops there never exceeded one-fifth of the American military presence in Vietnam at its peak – resulted in 14,000 Soviet deaths.

Apart from the terrible waste of human life, the superpowers also suffered humiliation, financial losses and a reduction in their influence and power around the globe. 'The consequence of Vietnam was that we greatly weakened our ability to withstand the Soviet Union elsewhere,' says ADMIRAL ELMO ZUMWALT JR. 'For over 10 years we put most of our budget into bombs and bullets and aircraft rather than modernizing our forces. And that meant that we went through a period of great weakness, particularly in the Ford and Carter years. Even earlier, during the years that I served as Navy Chief from 1970 to 1974, each year I had to report to the President that the odds were that we would lose in a conventional naval war with the Soviet Navy.'

Fears over Soviet superiority in conventional weapons were a serious concern to the American service chiefs, although a direct military confrontation between the superpowers remained a hypothetical scenario. But America's apparent loss of will to assert its foreign policy interests had a more immediate impact around the world. 'Vietnam was a general setback for the US in terms of its global foreign policy', says LAWRENCE EAGLEBURGER, Secretary of State under President Bush, 'and was so painful that even today it raises questions about our willingness to use force. And there was a time with the ending of the war in Vietnam when it would have been very difficult for us to contemplate the use of force had it been necessary.' In Washington the legislature reflected the widespread belief among the American public that the United States should not be acting as the world's policeman. Congress voted in 1973 to ban further American military involvement in Indo-China; less than three years later it followed that up by prohibiting the use of funds for covert action in Angola.

ROBERT MCNAMARA was Defence Secretary in the period when America's engagement in Vietnam turned into a full-scale war. He remains reluctant to discuss the merits of the American intervention. 'As a participant in the decision-making process relating to Vietnam,' says McNamara, 'I don't wish to comment publicly on it until the scholars complete their analyses of that decision-making process. I have followed a strict policy of not commenting on Vietnam since I left the [Defence] Department – with the single exception of the time when I appeared in court voluntarily in support of General Westmoreland [who commanded the US forces in Vietnam].'

> *But would you be prepared to make a few remarks about how you view the war now?*

'To this day many who supported the war believed that it prevented the spread of communism across Southeast Asia, that it contributed to the break-up of the Soviet Union and hastened the end of the Cold War. I am not going to pass judgment on whether their views are correct or incorrect, I can only say that whether they are right or wrong, that war exacted a fearful price both in terms of lives lost and in terms of political divisions in our country. We continue to suffer from those divisions; and that price was far greater than those of us in power at the time had foreseen.'

In view of the subsequent collapse of the Soviet Union, it can be argued that the American policy in Vietnam – though a failure at the time – did, perhaps, slow down the communist advance around the world. However, the opposite point can be made with much greater conviction. Washington's role in Southeast Asia turned public opinion and governments in many countries against the United States and discredited the policy of containment. Certainly, in the years after the American withdrawal all the signs suggested that, weakened by Vietnam and Watergate – the illegal phone-tapping and bugging scandal that led to President Nixon's resignation in 1974 – the United States was in retreat while the Soviet Union was on the march.

163

Soviet policy became more reckless, as ACADEMICIAN OLEG BOGOMOLOV and his colleagues at the Soviet Institute of Economics of the World Socialist System warned at the time of the invasion of Afghanistan. 'We came to the conclusion', says Bogomolov, 'that the policy of extending communism in the Third World was very dangerous for us because we could not win this confrontation. It was not economically bearable for us and it was politically dangerous. Well, we practically contributed much to the formation of an anti-Soviet coalition in the rest of the world. That's why we were against any expansion of our influence in the Third World, and especially in Afghanistan. That's why one week after the invasion we warned our leadership about the possible consequences and suggested the withdrawal of our troops from that country.' Bogomolov's warning, ignored at the time, turned into an accurate prediction. The Soviet invasion of Afghanistan brought together the West and a large number of Islamic countries. It substantially undermined support for the Soviet Union in even the non-Muslim countries of the Third World.

America's failure in Vietnam had been a serious, though temporary, set-back for Washington. It weakened America and undermined its self-confidence. The Nixon administration's attempt to extricate itself from the war through better relations with Moscow and Peking contributed to its espousal of detente. In a sense, though, that war did not end in 1975, because America continued its policy of containment through economic sanctions against Vietnam – a policy that ironically survived the collapse of communism in the Soviet Union.

The Soviet failure in Afghanistan had a far greater impact on the political landscape of the world. It played a major part in undermining Moscow's morale and contributed to the eventual unravelling of the Soviet Union. After nine years of fighting, the Soviet army remained hopelessly bogged down in a guerrilla war fought largely on the terms of the *mujahidin*; nor were there any prospects of a victory. The continuing Soviet military presence in Afghanistan solidified the Islamic countries' opposition to Moscow. Meanwhile, the war was taking its toll also on the home front. 'Afghanistan was the place where you understood vividly and every day that the Soviet system was doing something terribly wrong and that basically it was criminal,' says ARTYOM BOROVIK. 'Here in Moscow you could see the queues, the bad [state of the] economy but you couldn't see the criminal part of the system. The dissidents were in the camps – but the camps were far away and you couldn't see them. There, in Afghanistan, after you saw villages being bombed, you could hardly agree that this country was building the kind of society that the world would want to live under.'

The Soviet withdrawal created an ominous precedent for Moscow. Previously it had been one of the cornerstones of Marxist-Leninist ideology that no country that had embarked on the road to socialism would ever be allowed to turn back. Though formally not a part of the Soviet bloc, Afghanistan was in both its foreign and its domestic policies indistinguishable from Moscow's closest allies. The pull-out from Afghanistan was followed within months by the collapse of communism in Eastern Europe. Soon after that the Soviet troops stationed in the Warsaw Pact countries were also marching home, and the curtains came down on the Kremlin's empire.

Guerrillas of the anti-government UNITA movement in Angola parade in the bush in front of a banner of their leader, Jonas Savimbi, after they defeated a government offensive. (Mavinga, October 1985.)

8

A COLD WAR BATTLEGROUND: ANGOLA

'The United States did not want a communist victory in southern Africa. So, obviously, we had to support the people who were not supported by the communists,' says HENRY KISSINGER, who was Secretary of State during the Nixon and Ford administrations. 'That did not mean that we had an inherent preference of one over another. The strategic interest Angola had for America was to prevent a situation where Soviet military intervention became the dominant element in a continent where civil war was one of the methods of settling domestic conflict. And, indeed, Soviet military intervention then spread to Ethiopia. The only problem for the Soviets was that they began to exhaust themselves in the process. But you can always rely on history to do your work for you, and it was no consolation to Carthage that a few hundred years after it was destroyed the Roman empire collapsed also.'

The conflict between the United States and the Soviet Union in Africa – which became such a prominent feature of the Cold War in the 1970s – was in stark contrast with the respective positions of the two countries at the end of the Second World War. At that time, Washington and Moscow shared the view that the colonial empires of Britain and France should be dissolved. With the exception of Liberia (founded by black Americans in the nineteenth century) and Ethiopia, United States influence in Africa was minimal; Soviet involvement was negligible. There was only one other independent state on the continent, South Africa. But, as the process of decolonization got under way in the 1950s, the scope for superpower involvement widened considerably.

Apart from the ex-colonial powers, the United States seemed a natural trading partner and aid donor for the newly independent states. It had the markets for African produce and the wealth to be able to provide help. Moscow also began to adopt a more positive approach towards the Third World. Stalin had shown suspicion and hostility towards many of the former colonies. They did not fit into his scheme of the world, divided into 'two camps', which allowed for no middle way between the socialist East and the capitalist West. He considered nationalist leaders without radical socialist credentials, such as Nehru of India or Sukarno of Indonesia, as stooges of the imperialist West.

Khrushchev broke with Stalin's policy, and Soviet interest in the developing countries, including those of Africa, acquired a new intensity. The idea of an alliance between the Soviet Union, on the one hand, and the liberation movements and governments of the young states of the Third World became a cornerstone of Soviet foreign policy. In fact, the roots of that idea go back further, to the days of Tsarist Russia, as VASILI SOLODOVNIKOV, a former Director of the Africa Institute in Moscow, explains. 'The main objective was to help people to be freed from colonialism. This idea for Russia was not a new one. In the nineteenth century we helped the Balkan people to be freed from Turkish rule. Our people, if not our government, also gave much help to Ethiopia at the end of the nineteenth century against the invasion from Italy. At the beginning of the twentieth century we were on the side of the Boers during the Boer wars.'

In addition to historical reasons – which had much to do with Russia's attempts to prevent the West European states from taking over the whole of Africa – Solodovnikov also identifies three further reasons for Soviet interest in the African continent: ideology, economic interests and strategic concerns. 'Supporting liberation movements all over the world', says Solodovnikov, 'gave us a chance to recruit liberated countries to our side, to defend our ideology and our policy in the international arena and in our struggle with the West in the Cold War. We had some interest in economic cooperation, of course. We wanted to have our markets because our standards – that is, technological standards – were low and we couldn't export our machinery to European countries; we needed markets in developing countries. We exported most of our machinery to Africa, Asia and even Latin America. Finally, we had some strategic interests because we didn't want the West to surround us, and that's why we needed allies and some good friends in Africa. We also needed some bases for our navy and air force. During the war between Ethiopia and Somalia we sent military supplies to Ethiopia and needed some airports for these.'

These four considerations – great power status, ideology, strategy and trade – sometimes went hand in hand. However, it soon became obvious that, more often than not, the first three were in conflict with Moscow's economic interests. Among American policymakers there was a strong perception that ideology was one of the driving forces behind Soviet expansion in Africa and elsewhere. 'Moscow had a desire to convert as many newly independent African countries as possible to the communist system,' says HERMAN COHEN, who became Assistant Secretary of State for African Affairs in 1989, after a career as a diplomat in several African countries. 'I had a feeling that they sort of had a tally-sheet in the Kremlin, saying how many countries became communist this week.'

Moscow looked on this process from a different angle. The Kremlin's stated policy was to support colonial peoples that were fighting to achieve their independence and, once they had done so, to help these countries stand on their own feet. 'We had no egoistical interests,' says ANDREI ALEXANDROV-AGENTOV, foreign policy adviser to four Soviet leaders in the period 1964–86. 'What the hell did we want to gain in Ethiopia or in Angola or in Ghana? That was the influence of the ideological side of our policy. It was a reflection of socialist internationalism that if a people takes power and proclaims its intention to build a new society, based on socialist principles, it's our moral duty to be on its side.'

However, the ideological simplicity of presenting the Soviet Union as the champion of the developing countries against the imperialist West was complicated by the Sino-Soviet split of the early 1960s. From then on, Moscow had to wage an ideological war on two fronts. 'China insisted on revolutions headed by communists,' says NODARI SIMONIYA, Deputy Director of the Institute of World Economy and International Relations in Moscow. 'They insisted that the struggle must be an armed struggle. We rejected this idea, and from 1960 we published thousands of articles and books, criticizing the Chinese for their adventurism and for their absurd revolutionary ideas. But the majority of left-wing movements found it more pleasant to listen to the Chinese advice because our advice was more cautious. We warned them to be careful because the situation was not yet ready for revolution. They didn't like this idea that you just sit and wait – maybe half a century or maybe a whole century. And the Chinese said no, it's not necessary to wait. Today – right now – you can start the war, you can start seizing political power.'

Soviet caution was dictated by prudence and inertia; in several cases the Soviet Union continued to support non-communist liberation movements with which it had already established relations. Attempting to impose communist regimes on traditional societies could easily backfire. It could also create anxiety in the West about Soviet intentions in the Third World. 'We never imposed socialism on Africa; we proposed the theory of socialist orientation,' says VASILI SOLODOVNIKOV. 'It comes from our institute; in fact, it comes from me personally. I took the definition from Yugoslav scholars; they spoke about it and I liked it very much. And we proposed this idea of socialist orientation in 1966. And when we sent out teams to Somalia or Ethiopia, or when their people came to our institute, I

170

would tell them: "Look, be very careful, cool it, try not to be very quick." Our friends didn't always like this. For instance, the leaders from Mozambique were very much against it and said, "You look on us as a small brother."'

Ultimately, the ideological debates as to whether the Soviet-style regimes in Africa and elsewhere were socialist, or merely followed a socialist orientation, had little relevance. For one thing, the Americans could not distinguish between the two concepts and regarded any country with pro-Soviet policies as communist. Besides, Marxist-Leninist ideology in the hands of the Kremlin was flexible enough to accommodate any changes of policy if that was required by the Soviet Union's great-power interests. The Kremlin enjoyed very good, though mainly economic, relations with Emperor Haile Selassie of Ethiopia, whose feudal monarchy could not be portrayed as a progressive society. In the Arab world Moscow gave its whole-hearted support to radical nationalist regimes, such as Egypt, Syria and Iraq, which for decades suppressed their communist parties. 'We and the Americans were often using ideological cloaks to pursue state interests,' says KAREN BRUTENTS, a former Soviet central committee official. 'And it was quite easy for the Americans to say that they are defending freedom, and for us to say that we are defending national liberation, socialism and so on.'

In practice Soviet policy decisions in African affairs were motivated by pragmatic considerations. These could involve Moscow's assessment of individuals and organizations based on their perceived reliability or loyalty to the Soviet Union. There was often an element of inertia whereby Moscow would stick by the friends it had once chosen. Joshua Nkomo, the leader of the ZAPU liberation movement, which was fighting for an end to white rule in the former Rhodesia (now Zimbabwe), was not a Marxist and nor was his organization the most efficient in fighting the Rhodesian regime, yet he continued to receive Moscow's support. 'When the liberation movement emerged, it was organized by Joshua Nkomo and he was the first who was known in our country,' says VASILI SOLODOVNIKOV,

171

who as Soviet ambassador to Zambia in the late 1970s had frequent contacts with Nkomo. 'Later there were divisions in the liberation movement. Still we continued to support our old friends because we knew them. It's better to support one liberation movement than to choose many; it's not like a supermarket. It was a conservative policy.'

Moscow's main concern was to support countries around the world that were friendly to it, regardless of whether they were communist or not, because, as a superpower, it sought to extend its influence around the world. Of course, a Marxist-Leninist regime was more likely to be a guarantor of continued support for Moscow than a state that was merely friendly, both because of its ideological commitment and because its very survival might depend on close links with the Soviet Union. A less committed ally could be more easily persuaded to change its policy, especially if the United States offered it political or financial inducements.

Strategic considerations also played a part in Soviet policies, even though much of Africa had, on the whole, relatively little geopolitical significance for either superpower. The exceptions were North Africa, particularly the countries involved in the Middle East conflict, the Horn and southern Africa. 'Moscow had strategic interests, particularly in the Red Sea and the Horn of Africa, as a back door to the Middle East, and they felt that they could use military facilities there – which they eventually got in the Dahlak Islands,' says HERMAN COHEN. 'And when the *Trident* submarine became a reality and could reach the Soviet Union from much longer distances, they greatly feared the South Atlantic Ocean and they needed surveillance areas on the West African coast. They had one in Angola which was a bit too far south and they had one in Guinea for a while, but we managed to get that eliminated.'

In terms of economic advantage, Soviet expansion in Africa was a disaster. 'A traditional imperialist power conquers other states, making them colonies or semi-colonies, just to squeeze something from them,' says NODARI SIMONIYA. 'But the Soviet Union was not squeezing anybody; it was the Soviet Union that was the object of squeezing by others. The problem was that even when the Soviet Union conquered some country or controlled it, it failed to benefit from taking its raw materials or resources.' Much of the Soviet Union's failure to draw financial benefits from its relations with African countries had to do with structural weaknesses in its economic and trading system. In any case, the Soviet Union was not very interested in taking advantage of African resources which had traditionally been exported to the ex-colonial powers and the rest of the Western world. For the most part, it did not need the raw materials coming from Africa because it produced them itself.

Moscow could have used its influence – as some Western policy-makers claimed it was planning to do, once it could encircle mineral-rich South Africa – to deprive the West of access to crucial raw materials. Yet, even in Angola, with its rich oil reserves in the Cabinda enclave, the Soviet Union never tried to use this resource as an economic weapon against the West. The Soviet Union did not have the marketing network to sell Angolan oil around the world. And by stopping Angolan oil exports to the West – even if it could have persuaded Luanda to do that – the Kremlin would have ended up paying for a much larger share of the Angolan war out of its own pocket. With Angola enjoying the revenues from its oil exports, Luanda was able to finance part of the war effort, including the payment of the Cuban troops stationed in the country. 'Even in Angola, where the Soviets were very influential,' says HERMAN COHEN, 'it was the United States that was making the money out of the oil, with the Chevron Corporation in control there. The Marxist government of Angola was an excellent business partner. We never had any problems with them.'

However, the American administration did have political problems with Angola. The superpower conflict there began in 1975, when the new revolutionary government in Portugal decided to divest itself of its African empire. At the beginning of the year Lisbon announced that after 320 years of colonial rule, Angola would gain independence in November. Almost immediately a bitter struggle for power began in the country.

Angola, unlike the other Portuguese colonies in Africa, had no unified liberation movement. As the count-down to independence got under way, the three competing liberation movements began to receive increasing foreign aid. The oldest-established of the three, the Popular Movement for the Liberation of Angola (MPLA), for long supported by Moscow, once again began to receive substantial Soviet assistance, and in the course of the year Cuban advisers arrived as well. Meanwhile, China and the United States were stepping up their support for the two other liberation movements: in the first instance, for the National Front for the Liberation of Angola (FLNA), and later for the National Union for the Total Independence of Angola (UNITA). South Africa, whose occupation of South-West Africa on Angola's southern border had for long been condemned by the international community, began to help the UNITA forces. This was because of the MPLA's support for the South-West Africa People's Organization (SWAPO), which was fighting to liberate the country from Pretoria's rule to establish an independent Namibia. 'The government installed by the MPLA had as its first task to guarantee the independence and integrity of national territory and to fulfil its obligations as a member of the Organization of African Unity, whose purpose is the liberation of the whole continent,' says José Eduardo dos Santos, President of Angola since 1979. 'The fact that Namibia had been illegally occupied by South Africa and that South Africa had used that territory as a trampoline to attack liberation movements made the situation in Angola even worse. The apartheid regime wanted to overthrow the MPLA government by force to preserve its dominion over Namibia.'

Who arrived first and in what numbers – whether the Cubans or the South Africans – is a matter of continuing debate. In any case, each side in the Angolan conflict was prepared to invite foreign countries to intervene militarily to prevent its defeat. The MPLA invited Cuban troops and Soviet military advisers; South African troops fought on behalf of UNITA and FLNA, which were also receiving financial support from America.

Cuban President Fidel Castro was prepared to take a bold initiative. 'There is a strong streak of what I would call "Robin Hood" nationalism in Cuban behaviour,' says CHESTER CROCKER, who was American Assistant Secretary of State for African Affairs in 1981–9. 'The little guy is going to take on the big guys and will not get pushed around by Yankees or Russians or anybody else. It would not surprise me if, when all the archives are opened, we find considerable evidence that Castro was leaning quite far forward in his chair – with the help of Portuguese communists – to help insert the Cubans into support for the MPLA as their chosen instrument. The Russians were watching all this and supporting it in a general way, but it would be a mistake to assume that they were giving orders.' SERGO MIKOYAN, the Soviet Latin America expert whose contacts with Castro go back to the beginning of the 1960s, sees the intervention in Angola in a similar light: 'As far as Angola is concerned, it was Castro's idea to intervene there, and he did it without consultations with Moscow because he was afraid that Moscow would be against it. So he first sent his troops in and then he talked to Moscow. It was a case in which we became his pawn.'

What made these developments particularly disconcerting to Washington was the way in which Moscow managed to transfer a large Cuban military force to Angola and exploit it for its own purposes. 'For an imperial power to have its ability to project power without risking its own manpower and running all the domestic and international risks, is a very interesting instrument of policy – as the Brits and others discovered many decades earlier,' says CHESTER CROCKER. 'So Moscow had its Gurkhas; this was unprecedented, and we certainly looked on this as a dangerous escalation in terms of the range of options open for the projection of Moscow's power. We knew about Admiral Gorshkov's blue-water navy plans, we knew about the really major build-up of Soviet naval capability as well as the heavy-lift transport aircraft capability. But what were they going to transport? Ultimately it had to be people on the ground and it turned out to be the Cubans. Of course, there's the long history of US–Cuban bad relations, so this was seen as this guy down in that little island 90 miles off our shores sticking a finger in our eye! And this had become a global instrument. And the bottom line was that Angola was where detente died.'

As it turned out, American involvement in Angola, which would have been the natural response to Soviet moves in the conditions of the Cold War, was suddenly curtailed at the beginning of 1976, following the passing of the Clark amendment, by which Congress banned further assistance to Angola. This was one of the results of the Vietnam and Watergate syndromes in the United States – even though HENRY KISSINGER tried to dispel fears in Washington that Angola might become another Vietnam. Kissinger believes that the Clark amendment exacerbated the conflict in Angola. 'Had it not been for Congress, I believe there would have been a negotiated outcome in which the Organization of African Unity would have asked all outside nations to withdraw. We already had an understanding with the Soviet Union to that effect, and the Clark amendment, by taking us out of the equation, removed the Soviet incentive to do this.'

Although the Americans effectively excluded themselves from active participation in the Angolan conflict for a decade, the Cubans did not have it all to themselves. South Africa became increasingly involved as its leaders argued that the Soviet–Cuban involvement in Angola was part of a domino strategy in southern Africa, which would lead to a 'total onslaught' by Soviet-backed forces on the republic itself. Since the MPLA was giving support to SWAPO, the South African authorities decided to step up assistance to UNITA in Angola itself. South Africa launched a large-scale incursion into Angola in late 1975. 'The action of the South African military forces', says PIK BOTHA, the South African Foreign Minister, 'was aimed at securing the border and stopping the Cubans from coming down too far south and thus producing a real threat to the region.'

As the Cuban-backed MPLA forces defeated the FNLA and UNITA and secured their hold on Angola in early 1976, South African forces were withdrawn from the country. But Pretoria continued to see a danger in the presence of Cuban troops in Angola and in the continued existence of a pro-Soviet government there, and further South African incursions began again from 1978 onwards. They attacked not only SWAPO bases but also MPLA military and economic targets in an attempt to destabilize Angola. To help counter the threat from the UNITA guerrillas and the South African forces, the MPLA government imported more Cuban soldiers, though they were rarely used in combat. 'There were [by the late 1980s] 50,000 Cuban troops armed to the teeth with the most modern weapons,' says PIK BOTHA. 'One cannot say that you could not have introduced Cubans in other areas of southern Africa. And if you look at a map, there was this danger of Angola, Zambia, Zimbabwe and Mozambique becoming Soviet pawns and surrogates. Right across from the Indian to the Atlantic Ocean, you would have had Soviet influence freely doing whatever they wanted and planning whatever they wanted.'

The South African leaders' apocalyptic portrayal of their country's possible future was intended to persuade the West that its interests, too, would be seriously harmed if Soviet-backed expansion was not halted. According to that argument, if a chain of pro-Soviet countries in the region could throttle South Africa and its pro-Western government was replaced by a black nationalist regime, the West would be deprived of the country's substantial mineral wealth, including platinum, manganese, chromium, gold and diamonds. Moreover, Western shipping would be barred from the Cape route around South Africa, which was particularly crucial at times when the Suez canal was closed.

From the West's point of view, these arguments carried little conviction: the example of pro-Soviet states (including Angola in the region) demonstrated that they carried on trading with the West. And why would the Soviet Union risk war with the United States over the Cape route? In any case, giving support to the Whites-only government in South Africa, on the grounds that it was anti-communist would have driven more African states into Moscow's welcoming arms. One did not have to be pro-communist to agree with JOE SLOVO, former General Secretary of the South African Communist Party, that Pretoria was doing its utmost to exploit the Cold War: 'It suited the people who were shoring up apartheid to use the communist bogey, the threat from the Soviet Union, in order to gain support from their Western friends at the height of the Cold War. There was no threat from the Soviet Union to South Africa. There was a threat to the apartheid establishment, the race power bloc, from us – and we were supported by the Soviet Union.'

However, South Africa's arguments found a more receptive ear in Washington when President Reagan's administration took over. America was determined to challenge vigorously Soviet advances around the world and to get the Cubans out of Africa. At the State Department CHESTER CROCKER inaugurated the policy of 'constructive engagement' that involved talks with South Africa as part of an overall settlement in the region. The objective was to gain independence for Namibia, bring about the withdrawal of foreign troops from Angola and find a solution to the Angolan civil war. Many opponents of the apartheid regime accused the Reagan administration of boosting South Africa's prestige by being prepared to deal with it. Chester Crocker disagrees: 'I remember the last time I had an official meeting with the former [South African] President, P.W. Botha, in the mid-1980s. I was carrying a letter from Ronald Reagan and as I walked into his office, he looked at me with cold suspicion and didn't greet me. He simply said: "Why are you here?" What he was saying was that we were pursuing our own interests; we didn't give a licence to the South Africans. We said, if all you want to do is fight, then turn on your soldiers and the Soviets will turn on theirs and we will watch from the sidelines because we are not going to play that game. But if you are interested in reaching out and finding a basis to coexist in your neighbourhood, then we will try to be helpful.'

However, Crocker's diplomacy was slow to produce results. South African incursions into Angola continued and were paralleled by a build-up of Cuban forces in the country. As the Vietnam syndrome wore off in America, Congress repealed the Clark amendment in 1985, after which Washington supplemented its diplomatic effort with renewed assistance to UNITA. It was not until 1988 that the negotiators began to make any real progress, and an agreement was finally reached in New York in December of that year. By the provisions of that accord, South Africa was to grant Namibia independence and Cuba undertook to withdraw its troops from Angola by July 1991. What prompted the opposing sides to agree to end foreign military intervention in Angola? José Eduardo dos Santos says that the setbacks suffered by the South African troops played an important part: 'In 1987–8 the South African forces were not allowed to realize their project of occupying an important part of southern Angola, to provoke the fall of the government and bring a military victory for UNITA. Having failed, South Africa decided to seek political solutions. At the same time, there were profound changes in political thought in the Soviet Union which facilitated the solution of the problem.'

The military situation, however, was more complex and, in the view of Vladimir Kazimirov, who was appointed Soviet ambassador to Angola at the end of 1987, the war against the UNITA guerrillas was unwinnable. 'The principal task of planning was with the Soviet military advisers', says Kazimirov, 'and it was quite obvious even for people like me, with no military experience, that the operations could not produce positive results. Very often these operations were like heavy blows into a vacuum – or directed against cotton-wool. The UNITA troops would disperse, away from the target of these heavy blows, and would start operating elsewhere.'

However, the main inspiration for seeking an end to foreign

179

intervention in Angola came as a result of Mikhail Gorbachev's policies. By the time of the New York accord, the withdrawal of Soviet troops from Afghanistan was well under way. The Soviet President was anxious to settle regional conflicts that had further poisoned relations between the superpowers, and was eager to extricate his country from expensive involvements abroad. (By the end of 1992 the developing countries' debts owed to the former Soviet Union were estimated to amount to $146 billion; little of that was expected ever to be repaid. Angola's debt to Moscow stood at $4 billion.) Gorbachev's policies helped transform old-established adversarial attitudes. 'There is no question that when Gorbachev took off his horns – in South African eyes – it made it much easier for the Afrikaner leadership in South Africa to envisage living in a peaceful, constructive manner with the regions of southern Africa,' says CHESTER CROCKER. 'And that also meant reaching out to negotiate with the ANC [African National Congress], because it put an end to the fatuous illusions of an armed struggle, and there was not going to be a revolutionary solution in South Africa. It was one of the factors.'

Namibia became the first beneficiary in southern Africa of 'new thinking' in international relations when it finally gained its independence from South Africa in March 1990. The Cuban troops completed their withdrawal from Angola ahead of schedule in May 1991. Foreign military intervention in Angola came to an end with the simultaneous demise of the Cold War. Meanwhile, in South Africa, the ANC's imprisoned leader, Nelson Mandela, was released from gaol, and the country embarked on the road towards dismantling apartheid and establishing multi-racial democracy.

After 16 years of civil war in Angola, the prospects of a peaceful settlement appeared on the horizon in April 1991, when the MPLA government and UNITA concluded a peace agreement in Estoril, in Portugal. However, the long-awaited multi-party elections in September 1992 – which were part of the Estoril accord – did not mark the end of the fighting in Angola. Jonas Savimbi's UNITA, defeated at the polls, disputed the results, and this led to the launch of another phase in the civil war. The seeds of the continuation of the conflict lay in political, regional and tribal differences within the country. The superpowers and other outsiders had earlier been given an opportunity to interfere in Angola because of the Cold War division of the world. Foreign interference widened the extent of the fighting and the ensuing devastation, but it was not the original cause of strife. For that reason, the end of the Cold War provided no instant solution to the Angolan civil war. It merely held out a slim hope that outside powers would be more willing to help bring about a settlement, rather than become involved on one side or the other.

An unusual meeting – a former Chairman of the KGB greets a former Director of the CIA. Soviet Communist Party leader Yuri Andropov receives American Vice-President George Bush in Moscow at the time of Brezhnev's funeral, November 1982.

9

THE SECRET WAR

By early 1982 American–Soviet talks in Geneva on intermediate-range missiles in Europe had stalled. PAUL NITZE, one of the most resourceful among American arms control negotiators, began to think of unorthodox ways to find a way out of the impasse. 'It took maybe six months of preparation to really get [the Soviet diplomat, Yuli] Kvitsinsky persuaded that this was something he might want to participate in,' says Nitze. 'And the last problem was that he thought that the KGB might be listening in because I'd proposed that we meet at my apartment. But he said, "No, your apartment is certainly bugged by the KGB, we can't do that." And then I said, "Well, how about Norman Clyne's [Nitze's assistant] apartment?", where we were sitting and talking on the balcony, and he said, "Oh, the KGB might have bugs up in the awning above this balcony." And I said, "Well, how about going for a walk in the woods?" and he said, "Well, how would you know I don't have a listening device in my shoe?" And I thought, "That wouldn't worry me because if something leaked out thereafter, I'd know it was you, not anybody else." And he agreed to this walk.'

Kvitsinsky's apparent concern about the seemingly all-pervasive presence of the KGB (the Soviet Committee for State Security) demonstrates the power of the intelligence services, which underwent a huge expansion during the Cold War. In fact, 10 years before the Nitze–Kvitsinsky 'walk in the woods', America's National Security Agency (NSA) – which monitors electronic communications – had scored a notable success. Helped by a Soviet enciphering error, it managed to report in detail on the Soviet negotiating position at the SALT negotiations.

The beginnings of the CIA (Central Intelligence Agency) go back to the postwar era. At that time the whole idea of setting up a central organization for espionage and analysis in peacetime was a novelty for the United States. At the end of the war the Office of Strategic Services, which combined spying with sabotage and other activities, was disbanded. It was not until 1947 that its successor, the CIA, was established, owing in no small measure to the need to counter what was perceived to be a growing Soviet threat. Thereafter its development – much accelerated by the Korean war – was phenomenal, its resources expanding sixfold between 1948 and 1953.

'The CIA was designed to prevent another Pearl Harbor,' says RICHARD HELMS, who, in his own words, joined the Agency 'on the day the doors opened', rising to become its director in 1966. 'When the CIA was set up, Congress intended that all foreign information coming into the United States government be made available to the CIA – and made available promptly. This material was to be concentrated in one place because it was discovered that Pearl Harbor was caused not by lack of information but by lack of attention to putting it together and forming the mosaic that would have told us that the Japanese were going to attack at Pearl Harbor.'

Besides intelligence-gathering and analysis, the CIA's brief included covert action: a whole range of activities from bribing foreign politicians to planning assassinations, sabotage and assisting coups. Still, its functions were very limited when compared with those of the KGB, which combined intelligence with domestic security.

'The KGB was a vast organization,' says Richard Helms. 'Before it was broken up, it had at least half a million people and when you look at it in terms of its mission and size, it corresponds to what we have in the United States under the following organizations: the

CIA, the Federal Bureau of Investigation, the National Security Agency, the US Customs, the Coast Guard and the Secret Service. Also the core mission of the KGB was to be the sword and shield of the Communist Party.' This KGB 'monster' was something of a state within a state. But its First Chief Directorate, dealing with foreign intelligence – roughly the equivalent of the CIA – employed about 15,000 officers in the 1980s, which was about the same as the number working for the CIA.

As with so many other organizations that have since come to be closely connected with the Cold War, the KGB's origins go back much further in history than those of its American counterpart. While the worldwide ambitions of the United States had been kept in check by the prewar policy of isolationism, Soviet policies even at that time were motivated by a mixture of Marxist internationalism and Russian imperial ambitions. The KGB began life as the Cheka, the Extraordinary Commission for Combating Counter-revolution and Sabotage, formed at the end of 1917 within days of the October revolution. Its foreign department, whose tasks can best be compared with those of the CIA, followed a few months later. Stalin changed the organization's name, structure and leadership on several occasions. After his death it acquired greater continuity, becoming in 1954 the KGB, the Committee for State Security – a name and structure it kept until its dissolution in 1991.

How did the two organizations view their main target?

'The Cold War was a reality', says LEONID SHEBARSHIN, an orientalist who was chief of the KGB's external intelligence in 1989–91, 'and it determined the main directions of our effort as a service. Our main concern was not local happenings, local problems and local politics. Our main concern was what we called our main opponent, that's the United States, with all its ramifications – first of all, the CIA, the State Department, the Defence Department and so on. I don't think we were much mistaken. The Cold War was a real thing.'

OLEG KALUGIN, who became chief of foreign counter-intelligence in 1973, recalls the target in the more ideological terms of the time.

185

'American capitalism – capitalism as such – was enemy No. 1. Of course, as an enemy, it had subdivisions: the CIA was one of the main targets of penetration as the lethal weapon of American imperialism aimed at all freedom-loving people, as we used to say. And then the NATO military-political alliance and then others, like Zionism as a major political force that affected international relations. So we always knew there were no problems with finding enemies.'

For WILLIAM COLBY, who was the CIA's Director in 1973–6, the target was equally obvious. 'I always thought the CIA's main objective was to get inside the Kremlin, not to play games with the KGB. There were elements that you had to contest with them, your counter-intelligence and so forth, of course, but that's just one of the barriers. Your real desire is to know what's going on in the heads of those people making policy in the Kremlin.'

Did you succeed in that?

'Not really. It's a tough target; they were very well disciplined. We had some very good agents: Colonel [Oleg] Penkovsky and some of the others. The rather interesting comparison is, of course, that over the years the CIA had one defector to the Soviet Union; dozens of KGB officers defected to the United States.'

The CIA's record, if judged by open defections, has been very good. Not so that of the British Secret Intelligence Service (MI6) and Security Service (MI5), which suffered many blows to their effectiveness and prestige through betrayals by communists in their ranks, particularly during the early years of the Cold War. One of the defectors was GEORGE BLAKE, who was captured during the Korean war, and began to act as a double agent for the KGB on his return from imprisonment. 'I came to the conclusion', Blake says, 'that the Soviet Union was trying to build a new society where there would be equality, justice and social security, and that that was a noble experiment that should be encouraged and helped. And as my job in the British Secret Intelligence Service (SIS) at that time was obviously to prevent that society from emerging, I felt that I was doing the wrong thing.'

George Blake was among the last generation of Western defectors who decided to work for Soviet intelligence largely for idealistic reasons. Most of those who decided to serve Moscow, including Kim Philby, the most famous among them, were prewar communists, attracted to the cause by the Soviet economy's success in avoiding the Great Depression of the early 1930s and the Kremlin's willingness to stand up to the Nazi threat (until the Hitler–Stalin pact of 1939). After the 1950s, as the communist system gradually lost its appeal, most Western intelligence officers and informers who ended up working for the KGB did so because of money or blackmail.

Defection for ideological reasons became increasingly a one-way traffic, with the movement from the East to the West. OLEG GORDIEVSKY, who joined the KGB in 1962, later decided to become a double agent to help the British. 'Blinded by communist propaganda, we all believed that the West was wrong in everything and the Soviet Union was right in everything. During my first trips to the West I realized that it was the other way round. The West was a sane, just, democratic and liberal society, while the communist countries were societies of insanity, oppression and brutality.'

Working as a double agent was a risky occupation – the more so for a KGB officer because in the Soviet Union the punishment for treason was death. 'At the beginning I was very euphoric about it,' says Gordievsky. 'I felt that now I was an honest man. But then, year after year, I began to feel the ground under my feet becoming hotter and hotter. After three or four years of my cooperating [with the British], the KGB started to feel very distinctly that there was a major source of leakage in the system. And I felt that they were looking for me. I started to feel stress, pressure, fear and nervousness. I started to take sleeping pills and pills for high blood pressure. Eventually I would have become a total wreck. In the end I started to wish there could be an end to it all – some dramatic end – to make a nice exclamation mark at the end of my career. But I never imagined that it would be as dramatic as it was – that the KGB would catch me and then I would escape at the last moment, leaving my wife and children behind.'

CÄCILIE SILBERSTEIN, a Berlin office worker who provided information on East German trade with the developing countries for the West Germans in the late 1950s, believed getting caught was inevitable. 'It's the same thing as dying; but you cannot think about dying all the time. You know it will happen; but you hope it will not happen just now.' For Cäcilie Silberstein the inevitable happened one day in 1959. 'At the enterprise where I worked the entire staff were assembled for a meeting. First there was a discussion about spies in general. Then they said they knew who the spy was in our midst. Then my name was read out and I was arrested there – in public.' Cäcilie Silberstein was sentenced to 12 years' imprisonment. She was set free five years later in exchange for a payment made by Bonn for the release of political prisoners and West German agents imprisoned in East Germany.

Germany was the busiest arena in the contest of spies. The large concentration of NATO and Warsaw Pact forces on German territory provided one of the main attractions; the absence of a language barrier between East and West Germans made the recruitment of agents relatively easy; and before the Wall went up in 1961, Berlin was the only place where movement between the Eastern and Western blocs remained unrestricted. Germany also provided the most spectacular case of espionage, that of Günter Guillaume, the East German agent who worked as Chancellor Willy Brandt's personal assistant in Bonn. His exposure led to Brandt's resignation in 1974.

However, Germany was only one of the many fronts in the worldwide espionage war in which the CIA's primary task was to contribute to the policy of containment. In the early 1950s Washington still viewed Italy, with the largest communist party in Western Europe, as a weak link in the NATO alliance and was concerned about reports of Soviet funding for the Italian communists which greatly exaggerated the amounts actually involved. WILLIAM COLBY arrived in Rome in 1953 with a mission to give secret financial support to organizations that could become a bulwark against communist advance. 'My function was to be the senior officer of our effort to strengthen Italian democracy against the communist effort to subvert it. Our estimate at the time was that there was about $50 million a year coming from the Soviet Union into the Communist Party, the trade unions, the youth groups and the newspapers. Whether our estimate was right or wrong, the Soviets have since confirmed that they were sending money abroad for that kind of political effort. And we were not interested in supporting the Right; we were supporting the Centre because that's where the battle was.'

> But weren't you interfering in the democratic process of another country?

'Yes, we were acting outside the law in giving aid to the political parties and so forth; there's no question about that. But it was a question of necessity because there was no way of doing it legally then. Our whole purpose was to help them to defend their democracy against a very vigorous effort to subvert them.'

Covert action of this kind was also an integral part of the KGB's activities. OLEG KALUGIN was working in the United States in the early 1960s as Radio Moscow's correspondent. 'One of our main tasks', Kalugin says, 'was to discredit American foreign policy in regard to Africa, because in the 1960s several independent African states emerged and Africa was becoming a major political force. Black propaganda methods were used. For instance, we would send hundreds of letters anonymously through the mail to African diplomats and journalists stationed in Washington and New York. We would say things to incite them, like, "You bloody black guys, you'd better get back to Africa." And a day or two later the American newspapers reported that a racist hate campaign was going on in America, and Tass, the official Soviet news agency, would report all over the world the instances of racial intolerance and discrimination in the United States. In fact, [many of] these were provoked by the KGB.'

Dirty tricks were part of the intelligence agencies' armoury. Moreover, both sides engaged in covert action on a much larger scale. One of the bloodiest episodes was the war in Laos, which was fought parallel to the war in Vietnam. In Laos, though, there was no American military presence: the war was prosecuted with the help of the CIA. WILLIAM COLBY, who was there at the time, explains the reasons: 'We had agreed with the Russians, in the Geneva agreements of 1962, that we would keep our forces out of Laos. Now the Russians knew that we were active, of course, but we didn't confront them with it, and as a result they kept their side of the bargain. Their air force left Laos in 1962 and never came back.

'Because we couldn't use the military there, President Kennedy first and then President Johnson turned to the CIA and said, "can you stop the communists from taking over Laos", as they were trying to do. And I think the CIA did a pretty good job there. We had about 350 men there, who helped a force of about 35,000 tribal people, who fought the enemy to a standstill. After 10 years the battle-lines were approximately where they were at first and the North Vietnamese force which was doing the attacking had grown from 7,000 to 70,000. Eventually we reached the same agreement on Laos in 1973 that we had reached in 1962: that we would all remove our forces. We removed ours and the North Vietnamese did not remove theirs; only this time when they resumed the effort there was no opposition from our side.'

One of the KGB's larger operations outside the Soviet Union took place in Hungary in 1956, when Ivan Serov, its Chairman, coordinated the crushing of the uprising and the subsequent campaign of retribution. Serov had arrived in Hungary in the guise of an adviser to the Hungarian interior ministry even before the uprising broke out on 23 October. SÁNDOR KOPÁCSI, the Budapest police chief, met him that day, and discussions were held at the ministry on how to deal with the first demonstrations. Two weeks later Serov personally arrested General Pál Maléter, the Hungarian Defence Minister, and other Hungarian officials as they were holding talks with Soviet officers about the withdrawal of Soviet forces.

The KGB's role went much further. Kopácsi was among the thousands who were arrested after the uprising. 'I was interrogated by a bloodthirsty KGB officer, called Karisov,' says Kopácsi. 'He wanted me to confess that I'd been spying for the Yugoslavs. I told him that the KGB hadn't learnt anything since the 20th Congress of the Soviet CP and that its methods hadn't changed. And what did I get for saying that! I was made to stand in front of a machine gun, as though I was about to be executed. And I had good reasons for thinking that because I could hear constant firing out in the courtyard. I still bear on my wrists the marks of a dog-lead with studs which was used for stretching out my arms. I was interrogated by KGB officers for three months, until January 1957, when Hungarian interrogators took over.'

On the other side of the Iron Curtain the CIA was active in engineering the downfall of governments that were considered harmful to American interests. In 1953 a joint CIA–SIS operation in Iran played a major part in toppling Mohammed Mossadegh – the radical Iranian Prime Minister, who had nationalized foreign oil interests – and in restoring the Shah to the throne. The following year the left-wing regime of Jacobo Arbenz Guzman in Guatemala was overthrown with CIA assistance. In both cases the governments that were subsequently installed pursued right-wing policies through authoritarian and even dictatorial methods.

Attempts to overthrow left-wing governments continued well beyond the 1950s. When Salvador Allende, a Marxist politician, was elected president of Chile in 1970, the CIA intensified its campaign against him. RICHARD HELMS, the CIA's Director at the time, defends the Agency's role: 'It was President Nixon who wanted to upset Mr Allende – it wasn't the Agency. The Agency has no policy-making function. What the Agency was involved in was directed and supported by the United States government.' Allende was eventually toppled by a military coup three years later which brought General Augusto Pinochet's dictatorship to power. Like many other right-wing authoritarian regimes, the Pinochet government enjoyed for a time tacit American support. 'This was part of the containment policy,' Helms explains. 'Were those right-wing dictators going to continue or were the communists going to take over these countries? And the preference for the time being was to back the dictators who were non-communist rather than taking the chance that throwing them out was simply going to make another communist country.'

But how much did the CIA and the KGB contribute to the waging of the Cold War? There were successes and setbacks in equal measure on both sides. One of the early fiascos of the CIA was its joint attempt with the British SIS in 1949–53 to foment an uprising in Albania by sending armed groups of anti-communist émigrés into the country. 'Albania was on the other side of Yugoslavia,' WILLIAM COLBY explains, 'yet it was then an ally of the Soviets. The idea was that if we could break one country out of the Eastern bloc, that might start the process of the others separating from it.' The operation failed because the Albanian authorities had infiltrated the émigré organizations and had located most of the groups almost as soon as they were landed from boats or dropped by parachute.

One of the lessons of the Albanian fiasco was an appreciation of just how difficult it was to go from containment – helping pro-Western regimes survive – to rolling back communism, which was one of the American slogans of the 1950s. Perhaps the most notorious of the CIA's failures – its support for the abortive Bay of Pigs invasion of Cuba by anti-Castro émigrés in April 1961 – was another demonstration of the difficulties involved in putting into practice the doctrine of 'liberation'. Nonetheless, attempts to get rid of Fidel Castro continued unabated and various schemes were invented under a project known as Operation Mongoose. 'This task force was established for the sole purpose of conducting covert action against

192

Cuba,' says WALT ELDER, who was executive assistant to the CIA's director at the time. 'Covert action, as Bill Colby has often described it, "falls somewhere between a diplomatic protest and sending in the marines". There were instances of sabotage. I think we blew up an electric power plant and there was a ship bombed in Havana harbour.

'There was also the unspoken but clearly understood goal of "getting rid of Castro". There were assassination plots – and you cannot fault the CIA for not trying, but they were enormously unsuccessful. One of the plots involved somehow poisoning Castro. Well, it's one thing to have poison pills available; it's another for the right hands to get them to Castro. We had no luck with that whatsoever. And there were harassment schemes. There was one bright idea that if we could induce a drug into his cigar, he would smoke it and his beard would fall off – presumably then the Cuban people would all fall down laughing. This was an indication of the desperation of our efforts.'

Revelations about the CIA's assassination plots created much adverse publicity for the Agency when its activities were investigated by the Senate's Church Committee in the mid-1970s. The generally accepted view was that assassination, while acceptable in wartime, could not be condoned in peacetime. 'We in the Agency didn't see the difference,' says Walt Elder. 'To us the Cold War was war. We thought that these were enemies of our country. And if the [CIA's] Director attends a meeting at the White House and he comes away with the strong impression that the government would be most pleased if somebody were gotten rid of, he thinks that it's his job to think up a way to do this. But there's always a dichotomy in any intelligence agency where you have covert operations on one side and noble-minded analysts on the other.'

Although covert action was the most spectacular among the activities of the intelligence agencies, the daily gathering and analysis of information was more important in the long term. In this area, too, mistakes were made on both sides. In the 1960s, for instance, the

193

CIA underestimated the scale of the Soviet military build-up. In general, its success rate in predicting Soviet moves was no better than that of many think-tanks operating with much smaller resources. However, the KGB had even more failures. Its assessments of Western intentions were often misguided because they were based on a mixture of insufficient knowledge, conspiracy theories and ideological dogma. In 1979 the KGB wildly exaggerated American ambitions towards Afghanistan; some of its officials even claimed that Hafizullah Amin, the Afghan communist leader who had been educated in the United States, was a CIA agent. At the same time the KGB seriously underestimated the likely extent of the American reaction to the Soviet invasion of Afghanistan.

NIKOLAI LEONOV, who became the first head of the newly established department of information and analysis in February 1991, believes the most crucial problem was the lack of coordination between the KGB's many departments. 'All departments of the KGB represented their own realm,' says Leonov. 'Everybody tried to form their own empire. That's why when Kryuchkov was appointed chief of the KGB [in 1988] he decided to create an instrument of analysis for the whole of the KGB. That was the response to the internal problem which reflected the separation of the state into different, practically independent, ministries and organizations.'

Yet the KGB had many achievements to its credit. It enjoyed the advantage of operating in open societies, while its adversary, the CIA, devoted most of its effort to a country that was almost entirely shrouded in secrecy. In the 1940s Klaus Fuchs, 'the atom spy', helped speed up the development of the Soviet atomic bomb by perhaps 12–18 months. One of the KGB's greatest triumphs was its penetration of the British intelligence community in the 1940s and 1950s, which led to the elimination of many British agents in Eastern Europe and undermined Britain's cooperation with the CIA. The KGB was also successful on numerous other occasions. When the Kremlin decided to overthrow Hafizullah Amin, it was the KGB's elite Alpha unit that led the way, storming the Afghan presidential palace in December 1979 and accomplishing its mission with deadly accuracy.

Some of the major achievements of the CIA can be attributed to a combination of advanced technology and analytical skills. RICHARD HELMS explains: 'The CIA designed most of the satellites that were used to photograph the Soviet Union, starting with the *Discoverer* in 1960. This was done by something called the National Reconnaissance Organization (NRO), a combination of the US Air Force and the CIA. But most of the design work on these satellites was done in the Agency as its contribution to the NRO. This was one of the Agency's great achievements because when we came to the SALT I negotiations, the Russians declined to identify what missiles they had. So it was the United States government's figures that were used for the SALT I negotiations and those figures came largely from overhead reconnaissance.'

The Cuban missile crisis was an illustration of both the strengths and the weaknesses of the CIA. The massive naval operation to transport in the utmost secrecy a huge Soviet military contingent to Cuba in the summer of 1962 aroused comparatively little interest among the American intelligence community. Only John McCone, the CIA's Director, began to question seriously what the Soviets' intentions were and in the process to develop a hunch that they must be deploying nuclear missiles – a conviction that was not shared by the rest of the CIA.

'McCone was not only able to combine his practical business sense with this almost unique intuitive leap on the part of an intelligence analyst to put himself in the adversary's mind, but he also had the courage of his convictions,' says WALT ELDER, who was McCone's executive assistant. 'He was finally set in concrete on his views when the [Soviet] surface-to-air missiles began to appear. He said: "They are of no military value, you can take them out with an air strike in five minutes and they are not there to protect the Cuban sugar-cane cutters. What are they there for?" He said, "They must be there to blind us, so that we can't fly our U-2s and they must be putting something in there that they don't want us to see." And he decided that these would be offensive missiles.'

McCone's insistence on the resumption of the CIA's U-2 flights over Cuba led to a major triumph of American intelligence, based on the results of technological advance and espionage. RICHARD HELMS continues the story: 'When it was discovered on October 16 that there were definitely Soviet offensive missiles in the western part of Cuba and we had a photograph of one of the installations, the analysts were able to tell almost immediately that this was an SS-4 MRBM unit because Colonel Penkovsky, who was an agent for British and American intelligence at the time, had provided a manual for the SS-4 which not only explained carefully how the missile worked and how it was to be installed, but also contained a diagram of what an installation of an SS-4 firing range looked like. Therefore, knowing precisely how the installation had to be established, the analysts were able to convey to the President how much time he had to manoeuvre, in other words to make arrangements with Mr Khrushchev over the withdrawal of the missiles.'

During the 1970s the CIA's reputation was badly tarnished by adverse publicity about its covert actions and revelations that it had kept large numbers of American citizens under surveillance. It was brought under Congressional control and its covert operations were severely curbed. However, the CIA managed to weather the storm of the 1970s. It emerged into the Reagan era to become the beneficiary of a huge increase in its budget and, as its critics say, to return to some of its bad old ways in the area of covert action.

The KGB became a victim of the demise of the Cold War. Within weeks of the failed coup against President Gorbachev in August 1991, the KGB empire, which had been at the heart of the Soviet state for 74 years, was dismantled. Its foreign intelligence, security service and border forces were split into separate agencies along Western lines.

However, the KGB's failure to survive the Cold War was no reflection of its record. Its disappearance was related to the fact that the regime whose sword and shield it used to be had collapsed. 'It would be pointless to talk about the successes of the KGB when the country for which the KGB worked is no longer there,' says LEONID SHEBARSHIN, who headed the KGB for 27 hours after the collapse of the August coup. 'The only yardstick for any special service is whether it is – or was – able to implement the policy of the state, for right or wrong. If you look at it from this point of view, Afghanistan was not our failure. We also had friendly regimes in Angola, Mozambique – about Libya I am not so sure – Ethiopia and Yemen. How can you judge a surgeon who performed a successful operation on a patient who died subsequently of other causes?'

High noon of detente. Soviet Communist Party leader Leonid Brezhnev and President Nixon sign a number of agreements, including one on the prevention of nuclear war, during their summit in Washington and San Clemente, California (where the picture was taken), in June 1973. At the end of his visit Brezhnev declared that the Cold War was over.

10

DETENTE AND ITS DEMISE

'Nixon came to the Crimea in July [1974] already on the threshold of impeachment, and it was interesting to observe how Brezhnev treated him. It was a kind of sorrowful tenderness; he thought it was a pity that things had turned out so. By the way, he gave out a command to our mass media not to make a great noise about Watergate, not to offend Nixon. And I remember a comic incident at the end of their meeting when they had a tour on a yacht, along the southern coast of the Crimea. They had a friendly chat, they had dinner and they admired the beauty of the landscape. Then Nixon filled his glass and holding onto the table – partly because of the sea, partly because of the drinks, probably – said: "I want to propose a toast to a new doctrine in foreign policy, the doctrine of mutual trust and lasting peace, the Brezhnev–Nixon doctrine."'

The words of ANDREI ALEXANDROV-AGENTOV, Brezhnev's foreign policy adviser for 21 years, recall one of the high points of detente, the period during which the East–West confrontation of the Cold War gave way to a degree of cooperation. It was a time of annual summits between Soviet and American leaders; there was a huge expansion in East–West trade; there were more contacts between ordinary people on either side of the Iron Curtain which, however, remained firmly in place; and, above all, arms control agreements concluded in those years held out the prospect of a safer world.

The origins of detente

The inspiration for detente – the relaxation of tension – had come from many sources. One of the most crucial was a growing recognition in Washington and Moscow that the nuclear arms race must somehow be regulated. Twelve years before the Brezhnev–Nixon summit in the Crimea, the world had come, perhaps, as close to a nuclear confrontation as it ever would during the Cold War. Yet the sense of relief that greeted the end of the Cuban missile crisis in October 1962 was premature; the rest of the 1960s witnessed a hitherto unprecedented acceleration in the nuclear arms race. COLONEL-GENERAL NIKOLAI CHERVOV, who was one of the Soviet army's leading disarmament experts in the 1980s, describes those developments: 'In 1955 the Soviet Union had 40 [strategic] nuclear delivery vehicles,' Chervov says. 'By 1965 the number had increased 10 times, making it 400. The United States had 400 in 1955 and 1,800 by 1965. Three to five nuclear warheads appeared practically every day. It was a vicious circle: the more weapons you had, the more the other side was increasing its numbers. And the question that arose at that time was whether to continue the stockpiling of weapons or to start negotiations on arms control.'

After a massive expansion, by 1967 the United States had reached its target of 1,056 ICBMs set by the incoming Kennedy administration six years earlier. Meanwhile, smarting from its humiliation over the Cuban missile crisis, the Kremlin had launched an even more prodigious build-up in its force. Between 1966 and 1969, the number of Soviet ICBMs increased fourfold, to reach 1,050, fulfilling Khrushchev's earlier boast about Soviet factories turning out missiles like sausages. VIKTOR KARPOV, the Soviet diplomat who later negotiated the Strategic Arms Limitation Treaty (SALT II) of 1979, says, 'There was a growing understanding that a further build-up of missiles and warheads was useless because the number on both sides was not only enough to stop any intention to use those weapons but, with all those weapons used, the whole of the northern hemisphere would have been destroyed by radiation.'

Within less than a decade of the show-down between Kennedy and Khrushchev over the Soviet missiles in Cuba, the Soviet Union had built up a strategic arsenal that more or less matched the size of the American deterrent. There was no need for further catching up and that – together with technological advances that guaranteed mutual assured destruction – made it easier to start the arms control process. 'Detente was the product of a new situation when parity in nuclear strategic arms had been achieved,' says ALEXANDER BESSMERTNYKH, the former Soviet Foreign Minister. 'That gave the confidence to start a new kind of relationship between the United States and the Soviet Union. Arms control was the backbone of detente.'

Moscow had other reasons, too, for responding favourably to the Nixon administration's gambit in seeking detente. The Kremlin was eager to gain the status of a superpower, to obtain Western recognition for the postwar status quo of a divided Europe and to shore up its faltering economy through importing Western high-technology products.

But what did the American side hope to achieve through initiating detente? When it took office in 1969, the Nixon administration was anxious to extricate America from the Vietnam quagmire. By improving its relations with the two communist giants, Washington was hoping that Moscow and Peking would exercise a moderating influence on the North Vietnamese. In general, America had overextended itself in the cause of containment, and the Nixon doctrine sought to scale down Washington's commitments around the world. America's plan was to establish a linkage between superpower detente and regional conflicts. By drawing Moscow into a closer relationship, it was hoping that the Soviet Union might be prepared to exercise greater restraint in conflicts around the world. Besides, America also wanted to take its share in the expanding East–West trade which was mainly benefiting its European allies.

Yet, after decades of mutual suspicions, could Washington have confidence in Moscow's willingness to fulfil the obligations it would accept under detente? 'Trust wasn't, I think, the issue,' says LAW-RENCE EAGLEBURGER, American Secretary of State under President Bush and a career diplomat with 35 years' experience, 'although it was the issue made by an awful lot of those who argued against the detente policy. My own view of it, and I supported detente, was that you could distrust but you could still manage to try to deal with those aspects of the relationship that were amenable to negotiation and change; and the level of nuclear weapons was clearly one of those.'

Detente did not come out of the blue. There had been previous periods of thaw in East–West relations, starting with the aftermath of Stalin's death, which in 1955 produced a summit in Geneva – the first meeting of the wartime allies since Potsdam 10 years earlier. Earlier that year the Soviet Union, the United States, Britain and France had already agreed to end their postwar occupation of Austria. A second period of mini-detente began after the peaceful resolution of the Cuban missile crisis with the establishment in 1963 of the Moscow–Washington 'hot line' and the conclusion of the partial test-ban treaty. Five years later the non-proliferation treaty was concluded, whereby the United States, the Soviet Union and Britain (but not China at the time or France) pledged to refrain from transferring nuclear weapons or the technologies required to manufacture them to countries that did not belong to the nuclear club.

In the same year American–Soviet arms control negotiations were finally scheduled to get under way. This followed initial Soviet reluctance to consider a ban on anti-ballistic missile systems. But by the summer of 1968 the Kremlin had been persuaded to drop its objections. 'The tragedy is that on the very day in August 1968 that Washington and Moscow were to announce that strategic arms talks would begin that fall, Soviet troops moved into Prague to suppress the Prague Spring,' says PAUL WARNKE, who was Assistant Secretary of Defence in the Johnson administration. 'That of course made it impossible for us to go ahead on schedule. President Johnson tried to revive the idea, but by that point it was clear that he was gone and Richard Nixon was going to be taking over.'

Readiness on both sides to set limits to the nuclear arms race was a key reason for pursuing detente. For Moscow this would mean recognition by the United States as an equal – the final achievement of a long sought-after objective. This would enhance the Soviet Union's reputation around the world and, if detente was pursued the right way from Moscow's point of view, it would also legitimate its rule over Eastern Europe. More than two decades after the end of the Second World War, Soviet wartime conquests had not been recognized. 'Brezhnev personally went through the flames of the war and saw fire and death, towns and villages destroyed, and thousands of people killed,' says ANDREI ALEXANDROV-AGENTOV. 'This could not but leave a deep impression upon his later thinking. That is why one of the decisive components of his foreign policy was preserving and securing – but not broadening – the political and territorial results of the war for the Soviet Union, with an absolutely unconditional fixation over frontiers and over a belt of friendly states along the Western border of the Soviet Union, the existence of which would reduce to a minimum any threat of military attack from the West.'

The European dimension

The two superpowers were not alone in seeking a safer world through arms control and an improvement in relations across the European divide. Two decades after the postwar settlement, the division of the continent could no longer be dismissed as temporary. For Western Europe it was a question of accepting the status quo in the hope that more contacts between the Eastern and Western parts of the continent would reduce the level of military confrontation, bring trade benefits and lighten the heavy hand of the Kremlin's control over its satellites.

France under President Charles de Gaulle had pioneered the detente of the 1960s, partly to show its independence from the United States. In 1966, the year France left the military command of NATO, de Gaulle went to Moscow. 'He was considered at that time a traitor to the Atlantic Alliance,' says JEAN-NOËL DE LIPKOWSKI, French Secretary of State for Foreign Affairs during the late 1960s and early 1970s. 'And in front of all the prominent officials of the Soviet Union he made an amazing speech. He said: "You expect me to break the Atlantic Alliance. You are hoping that I will become neutral. But even if I fight against certain tendencies of the Americans, they are still my friends and I am their loyal ally."' Nevertheless, France's independent policies remained an irritant for the rest of the Western alliance, although relations between de Gaulle and Richard Nixon were very good. Lipkowski recalls that when Nixon's first foreign visit as president took him to France, the American President explained to de Gaulle that he knew he was not anti-American: 'De Gaulle said, "I am not not anti anything, I am just pro-French and what I want for France is the right to disagree. If I can't disagree, I am not an ally, I am a protectorate." And Nixon said: "Of course, General, you are right. An ally should be treated in a decent way. You should have the right to express what you feel." Then we finished the conversation and later de Gaulle turned to me and said: "If I were president of the United States, I am not sure that France would have the right to disagree."'

Within Western Europe there was an even stronger impulse for detente in Germany, the country divided along the fault-line of the Cold War. Bonn's continuing denial of the existence of East Germany had not taken Germany any closer to unification. On the other hand, there was a chance that yielding to the inevitable and accepting, at least for the time being, the reality of the other Germany would lead to better relations between the two German states. That in turn would improve conditions for West Berliners and East Germans. In the second half of the 1960s Bonn began a cautious policy of opening to the East, and this *Ostpolitik* gained momentum in 1969 with the election of a new centre-left coalition government, led by Willy Brandt's Social Democrats.

The new West German government took office a few months after Richard Nixon was sworn in as president in January 1969. Although the two countries shared an interest in pursuing detente, initially it was not clear that they could agree on tactics. EGON BAHR, Bonn's chief negotiator with Moscow and East Berlin, recalls his meeting with Henry Kissinger. 'A fortnight before we formed our government, I went to Washington to explain our intentions to Henry Kissinger', says Bahr. 'And I had the feeling that I wasn't able to convince him. He had real mistrust. First of all, this was the first time the Germans wanted to do something on their own. Number two, nobody knew at that time if we had taken all the necessary points into account. Number three, if there was to be detente, he wanted to make it. Quite clear.'

Washington's misgivings were caused by concern that, through *Ostpolitik*, Bonn might distance itself from the Western alliance. 'Initially we were worried it might lead to the beginning of a German nationalism and a German attempt to play off the West against the East and a resurrection of the traditional German policy that had produced a disaster twice in the century,' says HENRY KISSINGER. 'Within a very short time, however, we accepted the view that this was not the intention of Brandt and, secondly, that the momentum was so much in that direction that we should support it.'

The Washington–Bonn relationship improved as *Ostpolitik* began to produce results and the Americans were edging closer to an agreement with Moscow. After the signing of the Soviet–West German non-aggression pact of August 1970, Bahr recalls: 'I visited him [Kissinger] in Washington again and he started by saying, "Egon, I have to admit this is the first time your government informed us in advance, and it then did what it had really intended to do and it worked. So, my congratulations." And this was the basis', Bahr says, 'for the very close cooperation that was necessary for the Four-Power agreement. This was confidence and friendship.'

Washington's detente gambit

Bonn's opening to the East was based on the notion of *realpolitik*. The American approach to the Soviet Union under Nixon and Kissinger was motivated by a similar spirit of pragmatism. Nixon had established his political reputation on the strength of his anti-communist campaign in the late 1940s; as a politician with impeccable conservative credentials, he could afford to be more accommodating towards Moscow than liberal figures.

Kissinger saw the world primarily in terms of power politics, not ideology. 'His view of Europe was like Metternich's in the nineteenth century,' says MAURICE SCHUMANN, who served as French Foreign Minister during the detente years. 'He always believed that peace depended on a world balance; and he was right. But he believed that this entirely depended on the relationship between the two giants; and there he was wrong. At the same time he was so remarkably clever that he was not a prisoner of his own limits.' JIŘÍ HÁJEK, who was Czechoslovakia's Foreign Minister during the Prague Spring, remembers another example of Kissinger's understanding of *realpolitik* a year before he joined the Washington administration. 'At the beginning of 1968', Hájek says, 'I had the opportunity to meet Mr Kissinger. It was a very interesting conversation. And he just confirmed our position by saying: "Of course, what you are doing is fine, but if you get into conflict with your Soviet friends, I am very sorry to tell you that nobody in the West would help you because it's a problem of the balance of power."'

The Nixon administration's main goal was to stabilize the relationship between the two superpowers, and the most important step towards this was through arms control. Washington was also hoping that a bilateral arms control deal – and according a status of equality to Moscow – would encourage the Kremlin to rein in its North Vietnamese allies. 'We were so strained by Vietnam that we were looking for ways to diminish the confrontation with the Soviets,' says LAWRENCE EAGLEBURGER. In the meantime Washington embarked on its separate detente with China, whose communist government it had refused to recognize from the very beginning. [HENRY] KISSINGER paid a secret visit to Peking in 1971 to prepare Nixon's much-publicized pilgrimage to Mao Tse-tung the following year. 'It was important for the United States', says Kissinger, 'to have a diplomatic dialogue with the most populous nation in the world and with a nation that impinges on all of Asia. By establishing an option towards China, the Soviet Union also became much more tractable in their negotiations. Before that they tried to get a concession for the mere willingness to sit down and negotiate with us. Afterwards they became very eager to have negotiations with us, and the whole fabric of what came to be known as detente only started after the opening with China.'

Detente began just as the confrontation between the two communist giants had reached its most acute phase. Concern over its eastern borders was pushing Moscow towards reaching a deal with Washington on strategic arms. But Brezhnev had a difficult job on his hand trying to line up support for SALT I. ANDREI ALEXANDROV-AGENTOV recalls how the Soviet leader once spent five hours arguing with Marshal Grechko, the Defence Minister: '"Tell me one thing," he [Brezhnev] said, "if we don't sign the treaty, are you sure that it will not be possible for America to stay ahead of us? No, we cannot guarantee that."'

Soviet hardliners found other reasons to attempt to slow down detente. SALT I was to be signed by Brezhnev and Nixon in Moscow in 1972. 'There was much resistance within the ruling circles of the Soviet Union to inviting Nixon to Moscow,' says Alexandrov-Agentov. 'It coincided with a rather harsh phase of the American war in Vietnam, with the bombing of Hanoi and the mining of North Vietnam's main port, Haiphong. There were even people within the Politburo who said, "No, we cannot do it, the people will not understand it. They are killing innocent people and we shall receive them as honoured guests in the Kremlin. No, it's not the right time." Among those saying this was [head of state] Podgorny, who was very active against it. Brezhnev summoned the central committee some days before Nixon's arrival and gave a big and emotional report, trying to convince his audience that it was a politically wise step which would be useful not only for the Soviet Union and for the future of world peace but also for Vietnam.'

There was also vigorous opposition to detente in America among military chiefs, in Congress and among the trade unions. They shared a continuing mistrust of Soviet intentions around the world, argued that SALT benefited Moscow and believed that detente was not merely an expression of America's weakness but also a cause of it. (After the SALT I agreement Senator Henry Jackson, the leading critic of detente, succeeded in getting Congress to pass an amendment that required parity between the number of American and Soviet nuclear weapon launchers in any future treaty.)

One of the leading academic advocates of the case against detente was RICHARD PIPES, a professor at Harvard University. 'Detente was based on very faulty premises from the beginning. And that was the notion of building bridges to the Soviet system. They [the Soviets] always repeated that detente was irreversible. In other words, that we had to acquiesce in the kind of regime they were and in their conquests. The notion that through accommodation we can change them was faulty. To change them you needed a very hardline policy.'

However, in spite of opposition on both sides, the first of the three Nixon–Brezhnev summits duly took place in May 1972. Its centrepiece was SALT I, which consisted of two parts. One was an ABM treaty of unlimited duration, which limited the number of anti-ballistic missile systems each side could deploy to two. (Two years later this was reduced to one each. The Soviet Union installed one around Moscow; the United States never completed its deployment.) The other part of the treaty, valid for five years, limited the number of strategic missiles to 2,400 for the Soviet Union and 1,700 for the United States. The discrepancy between the two figures was due to the American lead in deploying more than one warhead on the same missile – the multiple independently targetable re-entry vehicles (MIRVs) – and because strategic bombers, of which the Americans also had more, were not included in the treaty.

SALT I did not stop the nuclear arms race. On the contrary, taking advantage of the new technological advances provided by MIRVs, between 1972 and the end of the 1980s the United States doubled its number of strategic nuclear warheads and the Soviet Union increased its strength sixfold, with the two sides reaching parity at a level of nearly 12,000 each.

Moreover, MIRVs became a complicating factor that made subsequent reductions in strategic weapons more difficult to achieve. 'Supposing both sides get down to 100 missiles each, and each missile has 10 warheads,' explains PAUL WARNKE, who negotiated the SALT II treaty for the American side. 'That would be an infinitely more dangerous situation than one in which both sides have 15,000 strategic warheads, because if you had 100 missiles each, you would have 1,000 warheads to direct against 100 targets, and each side would have a clear first-strike capability – but at the expense of blowing up 1,000 warheads with incalculable damage.'

Nevertheless, SALT I was one of the crowning achievements of detente. ANDREI ALEXANDROV-AGENTOV considers that 'psychologically it was a turning-point in the consciousness of Soviet and American leaders and the peoples of both countries, from the inevitable animosity to seemingly possible mutual understanding.' The thaw in Soviet–American relations brought a remarkable improvement in the general political mood. YULI KVITSINSKY, one of the senior Soviet disarmament negotiators, recalls the positive atmosphere of the time. 'When Richard Nixon and Gerald Ford were presidents, we achieved a lot of agreements, and the general mood in Moscow and Washington was to make any compromise suitable for both sides. It was a time for courageous, bold and inventive negotiations on both sides because we knew that if you, as a negotiator, did not achieve any results, you would be rather criticized for that and your superiors would step in and do the job for you.'

The improvement in relations was most clearly visible in the frequency of contacts between the American and Soviet leaders. In the 1950s there were two summits; in the 1960s three; and then in the period 1972–4 four. But detente went well beyond the confines of the White House and the Kremlin. It also ushered in an era of East–West cooperation unmatched at any time during the Cold War – until the twilight of the entire era in the second half of the 1980s. 'It was', says Yuli Kvitsinsky, 'a period of very close relationship, the [1975 joint] *Soyuz–Apollo* flight in space, dozens of agreements on all possible things, on medicine, on the construction of buildings in the polar region, visits at the top level and exchanges of scientists.'

Trade was another crucial area where expansion was very substantial. American exports to the Soviet Union increased significantly in the first half of the 1970s after Congress removed many restrictions. American grain became the staple diet of many Soviet citizens. Yet some of Washington's European allies, West Germany and France in particular, were far ahead in the volume of their trade with the Soviet Union. Western governments and banks began to extend credits on a large scale to the Soviet-bloc countries – a process that would leave several East European states debt-ridden by the early 1980s as interest rates shot up on the world's financial markets.

The culmination of detente came in 1975 with the Conference on Security and Cooperation in Europe, held in Helsinki. Brezhnev had been trying for many years to get international recognition for the postwar frontiers in Europe. Such a recognition would, in the Kremlin's view, freeze the division of Germany and would amount to an acknowledgment of the Soviet sphere of influence in Eastern Europe. Bonn's *Ostpolitik* in the early 1970s had already removed the main objections to accepting the realities of the situation. In return the West was hoping to extract some concessions on human rights in the Soviet bloc which, if observed by Moscow and its East

210

European allies, would have undermined the position of the communist regimes. Both sides were keen to expand trade. Moreover, they also showed readiness to discuss conventional troop strength in Europe, although the Mutual and Balanced Force Reduction (MBFR) talks, launched in 1973, dragged on without success well beyond the era of detente.

Brezhnev was prepared to go a long way to achieve his main goal – agreement on the political issues. Curiously, though, the agreement that was supposed to set in concrete the division of Europe achieved by Stalin's troops 30 years earlier coincided with the last time a West European country looked likely to come under communist rule. This followed the Portuguese revolution of 1974, which had put an end to nearly five decades of right-wing dictatorship, and some Western governments feared that a pro-communist regime might be established in Portugal, within the ranks of NATO. In January 1975 JAMES CALLAGHAN, the British Foreign Secretary at the time, visited Moscow with Prime Minister Harold Wilson. Lord Callaghan says: 'I put it quite squarely to Mr Brezhnev with Harold Wilson's consent, "Mr Brezhnev, do you want Portugal or do you want the Helsinki Agreement, because you can have one but you can't have the other, and certainly from our point of view Helsinki is more important. And I would have thought that that should have been your view, too." He undertook to report this back to the Politburo. When we reached Helsinki, not only we but the Germans, Tito from Yugoslavia and others all raised this question. And, I believe, as a result, Brezhnev held back from assisting [Portuguese Communist leader Alvaro] Cunhal as much as he might have done.'

Brezhnev appeared to be on his best behaviour towards Portugal to ensure that Helsinki would not slip from his grasp. But what kind of gain did the Helsinki Final Act and detente in Europe represent for the Kremlin? 'The Helsinki agreement was extremely favourable to the Russians', says JEAN-NOËL DE LIPKOWSKI, 'because we finally legitimized Stalin's conquest of half of Europe. We accepted that and also another paragraph that we would not interfere in events happening in the Russian camp. We were giving the green light to the Russians to do whatever they wanted in that zone.'

The more common view in the West is not so negative about the Helsinki accord. LORD CALLAGHAN takes a pragmatic approach to its significance: 'Everything, when you make an international agreement, is a bargain. History has shown that we got the better of the bargain because communism collapsed. There were some short-term gains in the eyes of Mr Brezhnev, but they didn't last because the question of the frontiers was not a legal recognition but a *de facto* recognition. And nobody in Western Europe had the intention of changing those frontiers by force anyway. Mr Brezhnev merely gained recognition of a fact that already existed.'

What the West gained in return was a commitment by the Soviet-bloc countries to allow the free flow of people and information – an undertaking that none of them began to observe until the late 1980s. The imprisonment of dissidents, censorship of publications and severe restrictions on travel to the West continued, regardless of detente. In any case, during the negotiations that led to the drafting of the Helsinki Final Act the Soviet side showed considerable reluctance to enter into any commitments on human rights. LIPKOWSKI remembers Andrei Gromyko's response to his suggestion that French newspapers should be allowed to be put on sale in Moscow and some other towns. 'Gromyko was a very tough man,' Lipkowski says. 'He was always motionless, as phlegmatic as a British colonel. He said, "That's impossible to accept because then anyone can read the news coming from the West, which is manipulated by the capitalists and is always prejudiced against us. If I push your way of thinking to the extreme, that means that a crazy man could go down the Underground in Moscow and begin selling the Bible." So I said, "Yes, Minister, but we will reciprocate and allow any kind of crazy man to go down the Metro in Paris and sell Karl Marx. Probably you are taking a greater risk because more people would read the Bible." He was furious.'

212

Although the observance of human rights became enshrined in the 'third basket' of the Helsinki accord – the other two dealt with inter-state relations and trade – few politicians in the West at the time either expected the East to abide by it or, indeed, made much fuss over its violation. The issue of human rights was not high on the agenda of the Western architects of detente. Nor did Gerald Ford, who had replaced Nixon as president in 1974, take a more aggressive stance. He had refused to receive Alexander Solzhenitsyn at the White House after the Russian dissident writer's expulsion from his land of birth. The passing of the Jackson–Vanik amendment in the United States Congress in 1974 – which in the case of communist countries linked the granting of most-favoured-nation trading status to their commitment to allow their citizens to emigrate – was very much against the wishes of the Washington administration, which preferred dealing with the Kremlin behind the scenes to help Jewish emigration from the Soviet Union.

It was only with the inauguration of Jimmy Carter as president in 1977 that the cause of human rights gained a strident voice at the highest level of international politics. By then detente was very much on the wane, although Carter himself was eager to continue it. 'The Soviet leadership was very, very uncomfortable about human rights,' says ALEXANDER BESSMERTNYKH, who accompanied Gromyko at many talks as his assistant and later as head of the Soviet foreign ministry's USA department. 'The talks would go smoothly until we came to the subject of human rights. Then there would be an explosion – or dead silence – on the Soviet side because Gromyko had a deep conviction that the human rights issue was a calculated insult to the Soviet system and also a clear-cut interference in Soviet domestic affairs. He wouldn't even take the list of persons the US administration would be talking about – political prisoners or refuseniks. If the Secretary [of State] presented that list, it would drop on the table and then one of Gromyko's assistants would pick it up. He would never touch it.'

Yet President Carter's espousal of human rights as part of

213

American diplomacy was itself made easier by the provisions of the Helsinki accord. The West could take the Soviet-bloc countries to task for failing to observe the stipulations of agreements they had freely entered into. 'The Soviets didn't have the slightest intention of keeping their word', says LIPKOWSKI, 'and thought their system was strong enough to eliminate those tendencies for freedom. Nevertheless, these agreements were used by a bunch of very brave people, the dissidents – like Sakharov and Shcharansky – who took those few lines we had negotiated as a pretext for being the first to assert the freedom of expression. They deserve to be honoured by humanity.'

Detente in retreat

During the Carter years rows over the human rights record of the communist countries complemented other disputes involving regional conflicts and further twists to the arms race. Together they led to the demise of detente in the late 1970s. But detente had made the world appear to be a somewhat safer place – at least on the global, if not the regional, level. However, even at their best, the achievements of detente were limited in scope. HENRY KISSINGER himself is cautious in his assessment: 'The simple-minded version is that detente attempted to achieve the millennium. There was no total peace, therefore detente failed. The fact is that detente, for the purposes that we saw, achieved its objectives. It managed to separate the Vietnam peace movement from the other concerns about peace. It managed to demonstrate to the American public that its government was interested in the relaxation of tension. It achieved a number of major successes in arms control and in other respects. It began to disintegrate because the American domestic situation disintegrated with Watergate.'

Although for sections of the Western public and some politicians detente carried the illusion of a root-and-branch change in East–West relations, it was, in practice, very much a continuation of the Cold War by other means. True, there was greater trust between the

214

two blocs, the superpowers viewed each other as more predictable, and increased trade brought benefits to many. However, there was no let-up in Moscow's ideological struggle against capitalism or in its involvement in regional conflicts, and some Western leaders believed that closer economic and cultural links between the two blocs would undermine the Soviet system.

'Things began to change with the Kissinger detente policy,' says LAWRENCE EAGLEBURGER, 'but they were still within the context of how do we ameliorate the confrontation, not how do we do away with it.' The SALT agreements of 1972 and 1979 did not reduce the size of the two superpowers' strategic arsenals; they simply placed a ceiling on their future growth. There was no change in many of Moscow's basic attitudes. Attempts at arms control – which had earlier foundered owing, in part, to the Kremlin's commitment to a paranoid form of secrecy – could now succeed not because the Soviet leadership was prepared to accept on-site verification but because the development of sophisticated spy satellites had made these less necessary.

Moscow was savouring its great triumph: Washington's acknowledgment of its status as the other superpower. 'The general mood was that we were happy that we had achieved parity with the Americans,' says YULI KVITSINSKY. 'We had sacrificed maybe the lives of two generations for this task. But now the belief was that after we had achieved this parity and nobody was able to threaten us seriously, we should start to give the people a better standard of living and we needed economic and cultural cooperation for that.'

But to the outside world there were no signs of Soviet retrenchment. From the early 1960s to the second half of the 1970s the Soviet Union had sustained a remarkably high increase, estimated at around 5 per cent per annum, in its defence expenditure. Although the Kremlin's secretiveness concealed the exact size of this build-up, the trend itself could not be hidden. 'The limits that were achieved at arms control negotiations', says ALEXEI ARBATOV, a specialist on the Soviet military, 'were compensated for by increased defence spending; the military-industrial complex was provided with a very solid compensation in resources. We started a very expensive build-up on our eastern borders because of the conflict with China; we were also expanding our forces directed against Western Europe; and we were greatly expanding our strategic missile systems. Detente went parallel to the military build-up. And that was probably one of the most important reasons for the collapse of detente.'

The continuing build-up in Soviet military strength coincided with a much smaller increase in American defence spending – much of which was eaten up by the huge cost of the Vietnam war. When GENERAL ALEXANDER HAIG took over as NATO's Supreme Allied Commander in Europe in 1974, he was shocked by the low level of military preparedness among the troops. 'I don't want to over-dramatize the situation,' says Haig, 'but we had just been victimized by 10 years of sterile involvement in Southeast Asia, and to conduct that war the Johnson administration had kept sneaking people out of Europe to fight in Vietnam. The units were under-strength; the equipment was outmoded and in a state of decay; and exercises were not being conducted because they cost money. In Europe this was also the product of detente in the early 1970s.'

The war in Vietnam – the cause of deep divisions in American society – was not the only reason for America's apparent weakness. For much of 1973–4 detente was overshadowed by Richard Nixon's political agony arising out of the White House's attempts to cover up the Watergate scandal. The president was in danger of impeach-ment before he yielded to the inevitable and resigned. During his final year in office his conduct alienated many figures in the Wash-ington establishment. One of them was PAUL NITZE, the author of the policy-setting NSC-68 document from 1950, who resigned from the SALT II delegation. 'I thought Mr Nixon was handling the negotiations largely on grounds of his personal problems in the United States,' says Paul Nitze, 'and that the one defence he had was that he was essential to the conduct of foreign policy and, particu-larly, that his negotiations with the Russians were crucial to US security. I was persuaded that Mr Nixon was doing this for personal purposes and I shouldn't have anything to do with it.'

If anything, American weakness was thrown into greater relief by Soviet assertiveness starting in the mid-1970s. Having achieved parity with the United States, a new globalism appeared in Soviet foreign policy. No place on earth was too far away for Soviet involvement. Even PAUL WARNKE, a liberal member of the Carter administration, was struck by Moscow's new course: 'The Soviets were making hay,' says Warnke, 'and there was a sense that they were trying to take advantage of instability in Africa.' From 1975 Moscow was financing Cuban military involvement in the Angolan civil war; two years later it acted in a similar way to bolster the Ethiopian communist regime in its war with Somalia; and in 1979 Soviet forces moved into Afghanistan.

YULI KVITSINSKY does not accept that Soviet foreign policy was becoming more assertive. 'I never believed in the concept of expansionist Soviet policies because this was more or less a reaction to a certain given situation in Africa, in Asia and so on. It was not a colonialist policy because we never knew how to make our presence in all those areas beneficial for the Soviet Union. We put a lot of money into these areas, but we didn't get either bananas, or raw materials, or anything.' GEORGI ARBATOV, Director of the USA Institute in Moscow since its foundation in the early years of the Brezhnev era, takes a much harsher attitude towards the policies pursued by the Soviet leaders whom he used to advise: 'It was a manifestation of moral and political degeneration that, after entering the path of detente, from 1975 we slipped back into very bad policies.' Arbatov explains the reasons behind the change of course: 'In 1974 Brezhnev became sick and he never recovered completely. It was a weakness of our political system that we lived with a sick leader for eight years; and it was bad for the world. He had a very limited attention span. As to the others, they felt that we had acquired a big military might, it was really parity with the Americans. And the Americans after Vietnam, after Watergate, were not going to interfere – which was

217

true. Politicians with greater vision would never have done it because you cannot play such games with a great power. A great power will recover and then it will take its revenge.'

That revenge was a long time coming. For one thing, the Carter administration was divided over foreign policy. 'On the question of how to deal with the Soviet Union, there was a strategic cleavage within the administration,' says ZBIGNIEW BRZEZINSKI, President Carter's National Security Adviser. The ambivalence of the Carter years was also accentuated by the president's personality and style. Brzezinski believes that even when the administration began to adopt a tougher line towards the Soviet Union in its last two years, it was handicapped by its public image of weakness. 'I think deep down in his heart the President would have preferred – indeed much preferred – accommodation to confrontation', says Brzezinski. 'Even when he was doing what was needed to be done, he didn't quite convey to the American people a sense of commitment and comfort with that posture – whereas Reagan did.'

The ambivalence of the Carter administration was in many ways a reflection of the trauma caused by the Vietnam war to American society. There was a marked reluctance to undertake commitments around the world in support of the policy of containment for fear that such involvement would lead to a repetition of the Vietnam bloodletting. That acted as a spur to Soviet ambitions. 'Our failure in Angola in 1976 was directly a consequence of domestic political concerns here', says LAWRENCE EAGLEBURGER, 'and was very much related to Vietnam and the attitude of Congress to US involvement in those adventures. Angola sent the wrong message to Moscow in the sense that they thought – with some justice – that we lacked willingness to act forcefully to prevent continued takeovers of governments by Marxist movements.'

Yet President Carter had one major foreign policy success to his credit: the Camp David agreement in 1978 brought 30 years of conflict between Egypt and Israel to an end. Significantly, the accord had been reached through the exclusion of the Soviet Union from the peace process. This was an indication that superpower detente was not essential to settling regional conflicts.

Increased Soviet assertiveness round the world – which was to culminate in the invasion of Afghanistan in 1979 – remained a serious concern for the West. Another problem was the continuing Soviet military build-up. In 1977 Moscow began to replace its aged SS-4 and SS-5 missiles of Cuban missile-crisis vintage with the latest SS-20 intermediate-range missiles, each with several warheads, targeted on Western Europe.

NATO had no equivalent weapons, and concern began to grow in West European capitals – the issue was first raised by West German Chancellor Helmut Schmidt – that Moscow might be trying to revive its old game of driving a wedge between NATO's American and European components. Would Washington risk an all-out nuclear confrontation with Moscow, involving the destruction of the United States, simply to respond in the event of an attack by SS-20s on Western Europe by launching its ICBMs against the Soviet Union? To put it bluntly, was Hamburg worth Chicago to the Americans? 'There was no certainty that the Americans would necessarily risk their own destruction for some sort of nuclear blackmail against one of the European countries,' says LORD CARRINGTON, who was British Foreign Secretary at the time. The remedy seemed to lie in the deployment of *Pershing-2* and *Tomahawk* cruise missiles in Western Europe. At the end of 1979 NATO decided to pursue a twin-track policy: to deploy the missiles by the end of 1983 unless the Soviet side was prepared to negotiate them away before then.

Moscow was in no mood for compromise at the time. It argued that the deployment of SS-20s amounted to no more than the modernization of existing weapons. ANDREI ALEXANDROV-AGENTOV now regrets the approach adopted by the Kremlin at the time. 'It was a mistake on the part of Brezhnev and the people around him – and I do not exclude myself – that we simply did not appreciate the scale of anxiety caused in the West. In the eyes of the military it was nothing special. They were glad that they had invented a better model of a rocket that was more effective than the SS-4 and the SS-5. Afterwards there were some discussions in Moscow that perhaps the following year [1979] when Brezhnev was due to go to the GDR for its [30th] jubilee, he should declare some reduction in our forces in East Germany – maybe even partly in nuclear arms – just to make things a little calmer. And here I must be very frank – I don't think I've said it anywhere yet – Brezhnev was for it. Even the ministry of defence was not against. Gromyko was against. Gromyko wanted to hold the trump cards for future negotiations and that was one of the very grave mistakes in our policy in that period.'

The end of superpower detente

The Carter administration's response in the face of increasing Soviet assertiveness was to get tougher. This was a vindication of the views held by ZBIGNIEW BRZEZINSKI, who had been arguing for a more forceful approach even during the first half of Carter's presidency. 'It was under President Carter', Brzezinski says, 'that an actual increase in the budget and in the relationship of defence spending to the GNP was undertaken.' Apart from decisions on new weapons, the Carter years also saw the launch of the Rapid Deployment Force to facilitate quick American military reaction in trouble-spots around the world.

Everywhere detente was lying in ruins. One of the last attempts to salvage something from the rubble was the signing of SALT II at the Carter–Brezhnev summit in Vienna in 1980. The main provisions of the treaty – both sides were now restricted to building up to a ceiling of 2,400 weapon launchers, of which not more than 1,320 could have more than one warhead – reflected the guidelines laid down nearly five years earlier at the Vladivostok summit between Brezhnev and Ford.

However, even SALT II became – at least formally – a victim of the reaction against detente. It was due to go for ratification before the Senate in Washington, but in the summer of 1979 it was held up by reports about the presence of a Soviet brigade of soldiers in Cuba. There was a strong public reaction in the United States, even though, as PAUL WARNKE – who negotiated much of SALT II – puts it, 'there were those who felt you could invite them over to Disneyworld and they'd all defect; eventually, McGeorge Bundy pointed out that the brigade had been there since the Cuban missile crisis and had been accepted by the United States.'

In the end Carter did not submit SALT II to the Senate; as Warnke says, its ratification 'was basically killed by Afghanistan', a view that his Soviet counterpart, VIKTOR KARPOV, largely shares. 'I can understand that the mood in the Senate was very negative to the treaty because its ratification would show to the whole world that everything is O.K., everything is under control and at the same time the Soviet forces in Afghanistan would stay there.'

Although SALT II was not ratified, successive American administrations decided to abide by it, which proves, according to PAUL WARNKE, that 'it was a very good deal from the standpoint of the United States'. But after its lingering illness in the second half of the 1970s, superpower detente was now clinically dead. (However, detente in Europe, especially in the area of trade, survived.) A whole range of contacts – American–Soviet and international – were cut off or severely curbed. In the wake of the Soviet invasion of Afghanistan, Washington responded by cutting back grain exports to the Soviet Union. It also placed a ban on exports of high-technology products. International sport – a traditional Cold War battleground for sportsmen and women – acquired an even greater political dimension with the United States and many other Western countries boycotting the Moscow Olympics in 1980. Four years later the Soviet Union and its allies retaliated by staying away from the Los Angeles Olympic games.

The spirit of mutual trust was now replaced by mutual suspicions. America under President Reagan was determined to build up its military capability as a sign of its readiness to challenge Soviet moves around the world with much greater vigour. Washington wanted to negotiate from a position of strength. The newly revived suspicions poisoned the atmosphere at arms control talks, which proved abortive throughout the early 1980s. At the Geneva talks on Intermediate-range Nuclear Forces (INF) – which were held to deal with the thorny issue of the SS-20s and the *Pershing-2* and cruise missiles – even the problem-solving skills of Paul Nitze and YULI KVITSINSKY failed to produce a successful outcome. 'When I started the negotiations with Paul Nitze in Geneva,' says Kvitsinsky, 'the general belief in Moscow was that the Americans did not want any compromise. And when I tried without any instructions to use all methods to find a compromise, I was very often accused of naivety. They told me, "Do you believe Nitze is instructed to achieve an agreement? No, he is instructed to play for time and then sever the negotiations."'

As the talks got bogged down, Kvitsinsky accepted Nitze's suggestion that they should have an informal discussion and there followed their famous 'walk in the woods' in the Jura mountains outside Geneva. Its product was an informal document that would limit both sides to 75 intermediate-range missiles. Moscow would have to dismantle many of its SS-20s already in place; but Washington, which had yet to deploy its missiles, would refrain from deploying the *Pershing-2*, whose speed (less than 10 minutes from launch to target) made it particularly dangerous in Soviet eyes.

However, with the spirit of detente dead, the informal Nitze–Kvitsinsky proposal came to nothing. Moscow did not seize this opportunity, thereby sparing Washington the embarrassment of having to decide about a deal that fell short of President Reagan's preferred 'zero option', which involved having no land-based intermediate-range missiles in Europe at all. 'The main reason' why Moscow opposed the deal, Kvitsinsky believes, was its 'deep mistrust towards Reagan and his goals. He said at that time a lot of strange things about local wars in Europe, pre-emptive strikes and so on, which was by no means inspiring for those who advocated an agreement with him.' President Reagan's rhetoric and policies did not change until after Mikhail Gorbachev had become leader of the Soviet Union. An INF agreement had to wait until 1987, when a version of the 'zero option' was adopted. A new era of East–West trust produced a deal that was considerably better than the one coming out of the Geneva woods.

Soviet Communist Party leader Mikhail Gorbachev and President Reagan listening to their interpreters during their first summit in Geneva, November 1985. They soon realized that they could do business with each other.

11

THE GORBACHEV
FACTOR

'We had all been used to the Cold War for some time – for 40 years', says LORD CARRINGTON, NATO's Secretary-General in the mid-1980s, 'and I think we all found it rather difficult to think, Did he [Gorbachev] really mean it? Was he genuine? Was it a ploy? And, of course, it all happened in the end so quickly that most of us were taken by surprise. I wouldn't have believed it, when I left NATO in 1988, if you had told me that what has happened since was going to happen. In fact, I would have asked you to go and see a doctor. And yet it all happened. And I suppose the beginning of it was the Berlin Wall and the fact that the Soviet Union didn't intervene in East Germany.'

More than anything else, perhaps, the breaching of the Berlin Wall in November 1989 symbolized the collapse of the Soviet empire in Eastern Europe. Mikhail Gorbachev, whose predecessors had invested so much effort in acquiring and retaining control over this region, now acquiesced in its loss. By the end of the 1980s, new thinking had already changed the nature of East–West relations out of all recognition. Trust had replaced suspicion in dealings between the superpowers. Major arms reduction treaties had already been concluded or were close to being signed. For all practical purposes, the Cold War was drawing to a close. Finally, any lingering fears that a restoration of the old-style communist regime would endanger these achievements were quashed with the failure of the abortive coup against Gorbachev in August 1991.

The second Cold War

The contrast between the early and late 1980s could not have been greater. Soviet–American relations in the first half of the 1980s were at their lowest ebb in a generation. The demise of detente – which had much to do with Moscow's continuing arms build-up and its greater assertiveness around the world – had created a strong backlash in America. Already in its final year the Carter administration had started to spend more on the military, a move that was accelerated under President Reagan. 'We were in 1980 finishing a decade in which we had gone down in military investment over 20 per cent in real terms and this happened to be the second decade of Soviet expansion,' says CASPAR WEINBERGER, who was President Reagan's Defence Secretary from 1981 to 1987. 'When we took office in January of 1981, I believe the President – I certainly – was absolutely astounded at this gap that actually existed when we got our classified briefings. And it was growing in every way. And that was something that gave them encouragement, so we had to do something about it.'

Were you going to build up your force to match the Soviet expansion or to achieve superiority?

'We never said either one. In fact, I was very explicit in saying we were not going to try to get a tank for a tank and an artillery piece for an artillery piece. They had an enormous lead. Now some of this was over-equipment; they had introduced new systems and kept a lot of the older things in their inventory. What we were trying to do was to make as clear as possible to them that we were resolved to regain military strength: a military strength that was necessary if we wanted to deter what we believed then – and what I believe now – was their old idea of world domination. They always talked about how they had to protect the homeland but as they put increasingly wide arches of defence around the homeland they got further and further out into the world.'

The huge American military build-up – the largest since the Korean war – coincided with the deployment in late 1983 of American *Pershing-2* and cruise missiles in Western Europe in response to the Soviet SS-20s. Earlier that year President Reagan had announced his Strategic Defence Initiative (SDI) to develop a protective shield, based on laser and particle beam weapons, against ballistic missiles. If successful, such a project would have had to be countered by the Soviet side either with more ICBMs, to make sure that the defences could be overcome, or by the development of a similar system. Many Soviet and American scientists shared the view of ROALD SAGDEYEV, President Gorbachev's scientific adviser, that SDI – in its original concept – was a piece of 'science fiction' that was not really feasible: he 'recommended not to reciprocate'. Gorbachev was not so sure and SDI remained, in his eyes, one of the main obstacles to arms control for several years.

Reagan's advocacy of these measures to boost America's military strength was part of his broader approach of taking a firm stand against the Soviet Union. In language reminiscent of the vintage Cold War rhetoric of the early 1950s, the President branded the Soviet Union an evil empire and predicted that communism would end up on the ash-heap of history. 'Ronald Reagan reinitiated the ideological war which, in my view, turned out to be fundamental to the end of the Soviet empire,' says RICHARD PERLE, American Assistant Secretary of Defence during 1981–7. 'I think he had a strategic purpose. He understood intuitively that the root of the Soviet problem, from the point of view of the Soviet leadership, was a lack of legitimacy in that society. They governed by force, by repressive measures; they would never have survived in an open election. And he understood that if you chipped away at that legitimacy, it would weaken the empire and, perhaps, even bring about its demise.'

Ronald Reagan's tendency to lecture the Soviet leaders extended even into the Gorbachev era, when Soviet–American relations began to improve as a result, in part, of the personal rapport established between the two leaders. Yet the early Reagan–Gorbachev summits were not entirely without difficulties. 'Sometimes our meetings began with Mr Reagan suddenly starting to express his opinions like giving a lesson without a preamble,' MIKHAIL GORBACHEV recalls, 'or pretending to do this. Once or twice I asked the President not to do this and to realize who was sitting opposite him – to realize that we were in a position of equality, and that he was not my teacher or prosecutor, and that if he wanted to continue in this manner we would have no dialogue, but if we could reach agreement I would be ready to go further. We had to go through this. Nevertheless, I had the impression that here was a statesman who was able to move towards us and to take decisive steps, even the most difficult steps.'

'Reagan was a complete change in the whole system of the relationship between the United States and the Soviet Union,' says YULI KVITSINSKY, the Soviet arms control negotiator whose talks in Geneva in the early 1980s appeared to be leading nowhere. 'Everything got sharply articulated. We all of a sudden felt that we were adversaries and we had to expel each other from certain positions in Europe, Asia and so on. All those problems, Angola and so on, would have under other circumstances been more or less marginal. One way or another, after a period of time we could have agreed on their resolution. But the mood in the last years of the Brezhnev era and the first years of Reagan was a confrontational one. The tone was changed and the tone, as the Germans say, makes the music.'

Gorbachev's early policies

When Mikhail Gorbachev became the leader of the Soviet Union in March 1985, few would have expected him to change not only the tone but also the tune. His geriatric comrades in the Politburo, who had seen three of their number die in the previous 30 months, would certainly not have elected Gorbachev general secretary if they had realized the scale of the changes his policies would bring. 'One can see many Gorbachevs,' says NIKOLAI SHISHLIN, who served as a central committee foreign policy specialist in the 1980s. 'The Gorbachev of 1985 was quite different from the Gorbachev of 1990 or 1992. His colleagues thought, O.K., let Gorbachev be our leader; he is more active, he is younger, he has more physical force and he will play our old games but more actively, and it will bring good results. And at the beginning Gorbachev tried to improve the situation, not to change it. But then, step by step, he had come to understand that it was impossible to improve a broken and false system. It was necessary to say farewell to this system.'

Even the slogans associated with Gorbachev's policies indicated only a gradual change in his objectives. First it was acceleration, *uskorenie*, then it became restructuring, *perestroika* – a term less far-reaching in its implications than full-scale reform. The initial goals were limited. 'At the beginning the aim of *perestroika* was a radical perfecting of the existing system,' says ALEXANDER YAKOVLEV, one of the architects of this policy. 'We were talking about changing the rules of politics so that there would be alternative candidates in elections; changing priorities in industry; and giving freedom to artists in their creative activity. But all that reform was to be within the existing system, which was to remain socialist. But once we started, we stumbled into the opposition of the whole system. And unfortunately it wasn't immediately that we realized that if you want to change this system, you should change it altogether and not just try to reform it.'

Better relations with the West were a precondition for the success of the domestic reforms Gorbachev was planning to intro-duce. It was essential to restore a degree of trust between the superpowers if arms control treaties were to be concluded, which, in turn, would make it possible to reduce defence expenditure. A return to the policy of closer cooperation would also reopen some of the trade channels with the West that had dried up, particularly in the areas of high technology. Gorbachev recognized that the time had come to revive detente and, unlike his predecessors, he was willing eventually to make very substantial concessions.

Nevertheless, in the foreign policy field, too, Gorbachev showed no signs at first of the momentous transformation he was going to inaugurate. 'Initially Gorbachev's point of view was rather traditional; he had inherited it from previous generations of Soviet leaders,' says ANATOLI CHERNYAYEV, who became Gorbachev's foreign policy adviser in 1986. 'That view was based on the confrontation between the two systems. But he realized that we should somehow pursue new policies so that it would be much safer for us to live together, if not actually to be friends. At first, his idea was that we should cooperate with the United States on the level of disarmament – and everything else would follow. But later on he realized that all matters were closely linked together. If, for example, we say that human rights are our internal matter and you should not interfere in that, let's just carry on with disarmament, that's an absolutely mistaken course. Everything should be tackled together in a package. As soon as he realized that, he managed to achieve the major breakthrough in our foreign policy.'

However, that breakthrough was still two years away when Gorbachev made one of his most inspired moves by appointing EDUARD SHEVARDNADZE in place of the veteran cold warrior Andrei Gromyko, who had been foreign minister for 28 years. Shevardnadze, who had been Georgia's Communist Party leader for 13 years and had little experience in international affairs, shared Gorbachev's determination to change things and his ability to inspire trust among Western leaders. 'As regards foreign policy,' says Shevardnadze, 'the way people's thinking had been formed over decades was that there was a traditional enemy with whom you had to be ready to fight. If you were not ready, he would destroy you. Overcoming these stereotypes, coming to the conclusion that this wasn't your enemy but your partner, was extremely difficult.'

Gorbachev's earliest foreign policy initiatives in the spring and summer of 1985 included a freeze on the deployment of further intermediate-range missiles in Europe and a moratorium on underground nuclear tests. Although both moves were designed to inspire a greater degree of trust, neither was particularly radical. Similar measures had been taken by previous Soviet leaders, and the Reagan administration – the most stridently anti-communist in 30 years – needed a great deal more persuasion that Mikhail Gorbachev was a man they could do business with.

The persuasion on a personal level began in Geneva in November 1985 – the first Soviet–American summit since the Brezhnev–Carter meeting in Vienna six years earlier. Gorbachev was well suited to begin the charm offensive. Two years earlier he had already made a good impression on Margaret Thatcher, the British Prime Minister whose tough anti-communist stance had earned her the title of the 'Iron Lady' in Moscow.

'Mr Gorbachev showed greater flexibility and less suspicion than his predecessors,' says ANDREI ALEXANDROV-AGENTOV, who in 1986 ended 22 years as foreign policy adviser to four successive Soviet leaders. 'He was more apt to understand the point of view and interests of his partner – something that was partly characteristic of Brezhnev, too, but much less so of Khrushchev with his explosive nature. And then, of course, he had a greater inclination not only for compromise but also for making concessions.'

New thinking in action

The Geneva summit produced no substantive results. However, it did begin, in less tangible terms, the process of establishing trust between the leaders of the superpowers. Initially, a great deal of prejudice still had to be overcome. 'In Geneva, Gorbachev and his surroundings paid more attention than necessary to Mr Reagan's age,' says NIKOLAI SHISHLIN, who attended the summit. 'Besides that, they were victims of our own propaganda, saying, "Mr Reagan, yes, he is the President but he is an actor and he is a puppet. Big business is the real owner of the United States and the constructor of American foreign policy." But, step by step, changes came. And after Geneva, [the 1986 summit in] Reykjavik was really a big leap; though many observers considered the results there quite poor, it constructed a framework for a new era. And after that relations between Gorbachev and Reagan became more and more warm. They sent letters and congratulations to each other on different occasions; they appeared on TV – here in Moscow at the time, seeing Reagan on Soviet TV, that was a shock! After [the 1988 summit in] Moscow I think they became almost friends. And I do remember how they shook hands, how they addressed each other in Moscow, it was really a warm atmosphere, very friendly, very cordial.'

The feeling of trust was all the more important given the two leaders' contrasting personalities. Gorbachev, then in his mid-50s, well-acquainted with the nitty-gritty of foreign policy issues, was a dynamic figure who was often the initiator of new ideas. Reagan, who was more than 20 years his senior, had a more intuitive grasp of policies and had little interest in complex arguments or matters of detail. 'I remember once when somehow there was a gap in protocol and they were left together for several minutes in the Oval Office [of the White House],' says GENNADI GERASIMOV, a former Soviet foreign ministry spokesman. 'I was there by chance. Reagan started to talk about a story which he'd read in the *Reader's Digest* about a man who was so fat he couldn't move around at all and how this man was reducing his weight and he'd started to move around his room and what an achievement that was – something like that. Gorbachev couldn't understand why Reagan was telling him this story. They were on different wavelengths in my view. But they were great leaders in the sense that they stopped the Cold War.'

The second Reagan–Gorbachev summit, in Reykjavik in October 1986, was among the most dramatic meetings of its kind, because following the American President's proposal that Washington and Moscow should phase out all their ballistic missiles over a 10-year period, Gorbachev unexpectedly suggested that all nuclear weapons should be eliminated. But to the disappointment of both leaders, no deal was made because of Gorbachev's continued insistence that work on SDI should be limited to laboratory research – a concession Reagan was not prepared to make.

However, 1986 had already produced one substantial agreement to reduce tension in Europe. A month before the Reykjavik summit took place, the 35-nation CSCE gathering in Stockholm had agreed on confidence-boosting measures in the military sphere. These required advance notification to be given of any major troop movements. The Warsaw Pact agreed, for the first time, to mandatory on-site inspections of its forces by representatives of NATO and neutral countries. The new approach was a reflection of Gorbachev's policy of *glasnost*, openness, that was rapidly gaining ground at home.

The real change in East–West relations began in the wake of the Reykjavik fiasco. 'You can attribute the shift in foreign policy to the beginning of 1987,' says ANATOLI CHERNYAYEV. 'It fully and finally emerged during Gorbachev's first visit to the United States in December 1987, when he had an opportunity to meet the military and industrial elite, ordinary people and top members of the administration. He realized that these were quite decent people whom one could deal with.' MIKHAIL GORBACHEV himself recalls the significance of the occasion: 'I had my first direct contact with Americans and I was really glad about that. I met very interesting, very lively, uninhibited people who had the same way of thinking as we had and they were looking forward to a change in the relations between our two countries. This was a driving force for further thoughts on my part and it strengthened my feeling that we were on the right path and that public opinion was ready for it.'

The 'new thinking' espoused by Mikhail Gorbachev sought to bring to an end the adversarial relationship between East and West that had characterized the Cold War. In its fullest version it was to replace the contest between the two blocs – which continued even under detente – with a genuine form of partnership. 'Before 1985–6 Soviet foreign policy was based on ideological principles,' says VADIM ZAGLADIN, a long-time Soviet foreign policy official who became Gorbachev's adviser in 1988. 'Accordingly, the world was divided into two different systems, and the socialist system was supposed to grow while the capitalist system was correspondingly going to shrink. And everything proceeded from that. After Gorbachev came to power we had to abandon that principle because it did not reflect the reality. But Gorbachev himself couldn't say that in public for a very long time, because in the Soviet leadership at that time only one or two persons shared this opinion. Only at the end of November 1987 could Gorbachev acknowledge the fact that while contradictions between the two systems existed, nobody had the right to a monopoly of the right decisions.'

Besides the fact that the old, ideological thinking no longer reflected reality, MIKHAIL GORBACHEV also came to the realization that it was downright dangerous, because of its emphasis on confrontation. 'We had to create new relations together,' Gorbachev says, 'but for that we needed to understand that the stake placed on confrontation had yielded nothing. It had only led to a situation where the world was divided into opposing camps. It was a policy of blocs, confrontation and the arms race. This policy had only led us to the edge of a precipice. And we found new paths by realizing that we were all part of one civilization and that we lived in one interconnected world. The new thinking was born, and out of the new thinking came the new policy.'

One of the milestones in 'new thinking' was the Washington summit. It produced the INF treaty, which required the United States and the Soviet Union to destroy all of their land-based intermediate-range missiles. By eliminating an entire class of weapons, the INF treaty went far beyond the scope of SALT I and II, which had merely placed ceilings on the deployment of strategic weapons. PAUL WARNKE, a consultant to the State Department in 1979 when NATO decided to respond to the Soviet deployment of SS-20s, believes the INF treaty vindicated NATO's firm stance. 'The Soviets had got exactly what they deserved – a greater number of missiles in Western Europe – and it worked. They began to recognize that this was an unstable situation and, as a consequence, much to our surprise and, I think, to the disappointment of some in the Reagan administration, they accepted the zero option. Some of the Reagan administration officials found it very difficult to take a "yes" for an answer.'

The INF deal on President Reagan's terms – its provisions reflected his 'zero option', first proposed in 1981 – had been made possible by three concessions Mikhail Gorbachev was now prepared to make. He dropped his insistence on limiting work on SDI to the research laboratories; he no longer required the British and French nuclear deterrents to be included in a deal; and he undertook not to redeploy the dismantled SS-20s in Siberia, a move that America's allies in Asia and China would have regarded as a threat to their security. Moscow's improved relations with Peking had made it easier to accept this stipulation.

It had taken ten years since the beginning of the SS-20 deployment to reach an agreement about their dismantling along with the American cruise and *Pershing-2* missiles. The initial Soviet move had greatly exacerbated East–West relations; had created discord within NATO; had given rise to the most widespread public protests in Western Europe against any weapons deployment in the case of the cruise and *Pershing-2* missiles; and had created extra worries for the Kremlin. 'We spent an awful lot of effort on putting nuclear weapons there and probably just as much effort on getting them out again,' says LORD CARRINGTON. 'It all happened during my period, pretty well. Half the time I was trying to put them there, the other half trying to get them out. Much better out than in.'

The INF treaty was only one among a number of significant arms control agreements. In the field of conventional weapons, 15 years of discussion (1973–88) during both the detente and the second Cold War periods had failed to bear fruit at the MBFR talks in Vienna. Revamped under the title of Conventional Forces in Europe (CFE), and given the specific task of taking away the capacity for surprise attack, these long-deadlocked arms reduction talks suddenly regained momentum. All the more so after Mikhail Gorbachev announced large-scale unilateral reductions in Soviet army strength in December 1988. Two years later the CFE treaty was signed at a grand ceremony in Paris, attended by leaders of 34 countries, as part of the CSCE process, which now became the framework for far more genuine security and cooperation in Europe than at the Helsinki conference 15 years earlier. The asymmetrical reductions meant in practice up to 50 per cent cuts on the part of the Warsaw Pact countries, as against around 10 per cent for NATO, to bring about parity in terms of tanks and heavy artillery. These cuts, and a separate agreement for reducing each superpower's military strength to 195,000 troops in Central Europe, would have been momentous a few years earlier. But by November 1990, when the CFE treaty was signed, these accords were rapidly losing their significance. Moscow had already agreed to withdraw all its forces from eastern Germany by the end of 1994, and the fast-disintegrating Warsaw Pact had only six months of life ahead of it.

The momentum of arms reduction continued right up to the end of Mikhail Gorbachev's rule – and beyond. START I, signed at the end of July 1991, envisaged a 30 per cent reduction in the nuclear warhead arsenals of the United States and the Soviet Union by the year 2000. Within 18 months it was superseded by START II, which specified that each side was to cut its nuclear warheads by a further two-thirds to between 3,000 and 3,500 by 2003. In the process all ICBMs with multiple warheads – the mainstay of the Soviet deterrent – were to be eliminated.

In the space of three or four years the Cold War thinking and practice of over four decades faded away. Much of the attention focused on the arms reduction process as the most crucial aspect of the move away from a world of confrontation. Yet, the very fact that America and the Soviet Union were, by the late 1980s, acting like partners and not like adversaries meant that relations between them were expanding over a much broader area. 'During the Cold War, relations between the US and the Soviet Union were 85 per cent military and strategic,' says ALEXANDER BESSMERTNYKH. 'But at the end of the 1980s we were turning to real normality in relations between the two countries.' Normality meant agreements on trade, science, the environment and a whole range of other issues.

Reagan and Gorbachev

The transformation of the Soviet–American relationship under Mikhail Gorbachev was crucial in bringing the Cold War to an end. In barely five years the Soviet leader had succeeded in untying the many Gordian knots in superpower relations. The Soviet leader's political skills, his ability to inspire trust and prove himself flexible on important issues, clearly had a great deal to do with this. Credit was given where it appeared to be due. In the late 1980s Western capitals visited by the Soviet leader were swept by a wave of 'Gorbymania'. Gorbachev's popularity around the world far exceeded and outlasted the support he had enjoyed at home, where his economic reforms were failing to produce any improvements.

But what had prompted Gorbachev to set out on this new path? He was a generation younger than his predecessors, the first Soviet leader not to have lived through the trauma of the Second World War as an adult or to have worked in a high party office under Stalin. His realization that the Soviet Union could not go on the way it had been for many years was palpable from the very beginning of his years in office. However, the major changes in foreign policy had to wait until a year or two after Gorbachev began his term as General Secretary of the Communist Party. 'This new thinking came about in our country after Chernobyl,' says YULI KVITSINSKY. 'It's one thing theoretically to sit at a computer and to tell how many warheads you need, and it's quite another when you experience what it's like. And Chernobyl was in this respect a grave lesson, which very convincingly proved that all this ideology of the Cold

War and the use of nuclear weapons was, to put it mildly, a theoretical exercise or, if you choose to be explicit enough, it was just madness.'

Advocates of Reagan's hardline policies of the early 1980s advance another reason for Gorbachev's change of course. They argue that Moscow was forced to realize that it could not compete with the United States when it came to a massive build-up in military forces, including the new challenge posed by SDI. GENERAL ALEXANDER HAIG was President Reagan's first Secretary of State. 'Our defence build-up was important, especially after a wave of Soviet imperialism,' says Haig, 'but I don't want to overdramatize that. It was not the causal contributor to winning the Cold War; that was the result of the internal contradictions in Marxism-Leninism, which was doomed to failure from the beginning. But I think standing up, building up our defences in the early 1980s made a major contribution.'

But was it the aim of the American administration to exhaust the Soviet economy through another round in the arms race?

'Not really, no,' says CASPAR WEINBERGER. 'Certainly I didn't have it. I was not in the least interested in bankrupting anybody and with the Soviet form of government at the time with no public opinion, no debates, no polls, no discussions and no votes you could not in effect change their policy by anything short of convincing their leadership they could not win a military action against the United States or NATO, and that is what we were acquiring our military strength for. In the course of doing that they did become convinced they couldn't win. And the only real thing I gave Gorbachev credit for – and I'm not a fan of Gorbachev – was for being smart enough to see that they had to change to convince us that they were going to be a kinder and gentler country; a different country with a different agenda.'

Politicians associated with the detente period take a markedly different approach. 'President Reagan is very much to be commended for his role – but his role began in Geneva in 1985,' says PAUL

WARNKE, who was a senior arms control negotiator under President Carter. 'The tremendous defence build-up had no effect except that it impoverished the United States and further impoverished the Soviet Union. It did not play any sort of constructive role as far as the ending of the Cold War is concerned. All it did was to postpone that ending.'

EGON BAHR, one of the leading European advocates of detente, adopts an even harsher approach to the Reagan administration's early policies. 'The greatest stabilization of the Eastern system was created by the arms race. Without Reagan's policy I'm convinced we would have had the breakdown two years earlier. Because if the West started a big arms race – and it was ahead in technology – the East had to follow with not as good technology but bigger numbers. This was strengthening the military people, this had the power of discipline – and the discipline of the East–West conflict was also a discipline for the West. We were convinced after the first stage of detente that our task was to neutralize the only point in which the Eastern camp was strong – the purely military point. When I met Gorbachev for the first time – it was six weeks after he became General Secretary – I found that he had reached the conclusion that for economic reasons the gap between East and West would increase and therefore he had to bring down military spending. And he was confronted with Mr Reagan, who had started the latest arms race. From this point of view, it's very probable that we lost two or three years.'

EDUARD SHEVARDNADZE, whose contribution to the implementation of the new Soviet foreign policy was second only to Gorbachev's, is also adamant in denying that Reagan's tough policies played a part. 'The decisive moment was what we began,' says Shevardnadze. 'It was impossible to break up the Soviet Union from the outside – neither Reagan nor Hitler could do it. This began from the inside with *perestroika* and democratization, this is how the process began. When arms reduction began, that did play a role. SDI and all those things could, on the contrary, have been used as an excuse to strengthen the Soviet Union. We could have said that Reagan started SDI and we had to tighten our belts to give an appropriate response.'

The ending of the Cold War is undoubtedly the most important achievement of the second half of the twentieth century. Politicians of different hues want to take credit for it or, at least, for having prompted Gorbachev to adopt the policies which played a crucial part in unravelling more than four decades of global confrontation. Yet the conflicting claims of Western 'hawks' and 'doves' are perhaps more complementary than they may seem at first glance. In the longer term, detente provided the seeds that would germinate in the policy of East–West partnership in the late 1980s by establishing a network of links – political, economic and cultural – between the two sides. Brezhnev's policy of trying to provide both guns and butter for the people relied for its success on massive infusions of Western technology for the ailing Soviet economy. Several East European countries – above all, Poland, Hungary and East Germany – became dependent on the West as a lifeline for their economies and were particularly hard hit by the down-turn in East–West relations in the early 1980s.

Reagan's tough policies, which combined the arms build-up with a determined effort to deny Moscow access to advanced technology and a wide range of strategic products, presented the Soviet leadership with a difficult choice. They could try to match the USA's arms spending and revert to the pre-detente policies of Eastern-bloc economic self-sufficiency. That would have resulted in a sudden and possibly calamitous reversal in the gradual improvement in living conditions and would have had to be policed by a return to more intense repression. The alternative was to mend fences with the West by a genuine commitment to cooperation.

Reagan presented the Kremlin with a challenge by seeking to withdraw – often in the face of West European opposition – the benefits of detente that were most prized by Moscow. He could not have done that if detente had not been in place already. Although the

Western cold warriors and advocates of detente were not aware of it, the effect of this may well have been the same as the combination of the 'tough guy' and the 'nice guy' working together to persuade the Soviet leaders to mend their ways.

While a succession of orthodox communist leaders remained in charge in the Kremlin in the early 1980s, there was no guarantee that Reagan's policy would succeed. Admittedly, Romania's return to acute hardship and severe repression under President Ceauşescu presented a cautionary example of what would happen in case of a return to Stalinist practices; yet the milder option of tightening discipline was actively implemented in the Soviet Union under Andropov, whose KGB experience had left a strong imprint on his thinking. Even Gorbachev began his period in office by continuing a high level of military spending and introducing tough disciplinarian measures – including the economically disastrous anti-alcohol campaign. Ultimately, he proved to be of a different mettle from his elderly predecessors. His flexibility and imaginative approach led him to adopt 'new thinking', which helped contribute to the transformation of Soviet–American relations. That, in turn, was one of the crucial changes which brought the Cold War to an end. 'I think that I did manage to do something towards this, something major,' says MIKHAIL GORBACHEV. 'But I don't think that if there had been no Gorbachev, it wouldn't have happened. It would have happened anyway. There would have been an Ivanov here, or a Major there, or I don't know who else. The need was there, and the logic of the historical process showed that something must happen. We had reached the limit. This had to be understood and expressed in adequate policies.'

Gorbachev and Eastern Europe

The forging of an East–West partnership was one of the two earthquakes that shattered the contours of the Cold War landscape during the Gorbachev years. The other one was the collapse of the

241

Soviet empire in Eastern Europe, which also made possible the unification of the two Germanies. As in other areas of Soviet action, there was little to indicate in 1985 that dramatic changes would soon be on the way. 'Gorbachev wanted to build new relations with the socialist countries of Eastern Europe to make them more flexible, equal and mutually beneficial,' says VALERI MUSATOV, a former Eastern Europe specialist with the central committee in Moscow. 'He suggested that meetings of communist party general secretaries should be held more often. His agenda was to deepen economic, scientific and technological cooperation within Comecon. But in a year or two he lost interest in such meetings. Maybe it was because his partners – the old guard in the socialist countries – showed opposition and the meetings became a formality.'

A change of style in Moscow's relations with its allies was apparent almost from the moment MIKHAIL GORBACHEV was elected to succeed Chernenko. 'Before 1985 there was only one type of relationship,' says Gorbachev. 'The model of the Soviet Union was imposed; it was to be followed by the socialist countries. But even at the first meetings at Chernenko's funeral in the narrow circles of the first secretaries, I said, "Let's think about new relations. We recognize for you – and we hope you recognize for us – the right to make decisions and to take responsibility for those decisions." This is how the Brezhnev doctrine, as it is called, was buried.'

Although Gorbachev adopted a new tone in his dealings with East European countries, he did not immediately stop the long-standing Soviet practice of interfering in their affairs. Back in 1984 Erich Honecker, the East German leader, had planned to visit West Germany in the wake of the deployment of cruise and *Pershing-2* missiles in Western Europe. He was anxious to protect his country's trade links with Bonn, but Moscow had placed a virtual freeze on East–West relations as a sign of its disapproval of the missile deployment, and Honecker was told not to make the trip. 'This was an example of Soviet domination,' says GÜNTER SCHABOWSKI, who was one of Honecker's colleagues in the East German Politburo.

'In 1986, when Honecker made a second attempt to wrest an agreement from the Soviets to visit Bonn, Gorbachev reproached him on the grounds that it was impossible to make deals with the "rocket Germans". Gorbachev said, "Our people wouldn't understand that, Erich."' It was only a year later – when Soviet foreign policy had been shifted into a different gear – that Honecker was finally allowed to go on his pilgrimage to Bonn.

However, Gorbachev's main problem with his Warsaw Pact allies was not so much to keep them from fostering close links with the West, but to persuade them to adopt their own versions of his *perestroika*. Eastern Europe's elderly leaders gathered all their strength to oppose him. Todor Zhivkov of Bulgaria had been in power since 1954; János Kádár of Hungary since 1956; Nicolae Ceauşescu of Romania since 1965; Gustáv Husák of Czechoslovakia since 1969; Erich Honecker since 1971; and Wojciech Jaruzelski of Poland (who along with the less enthusiastic Kádár was the only reform-oriented leader) since 1981. Gorbachev gradually dispensed with the Soviet leaders' practice of dictating policy to their East European comrades or replacing those who failed to obey. Instead, he was relying on more diplomatic means, hoping that the force of decades of in-grained habit – aping whatever the latest policy shift happened to be in Moscow – would persuade the East European leaders to follow his example. 'There was no pressure,' says BOHUSLAV CHŇOUPEK, Czecho-slovak Foreign Minister from 1971 to 1988. 'It was just mentioned as an example to you that "we will in the Soviet Union take such and such steps". I never heard from Gorbachev or Shevardnadze, even in talks held in private that "you must do it". Never. But, of course, the influence of these reforms in our countries was tremendous.'

The collapse of the Soviet empire

However, Gorbachev had a way of putting his message across to the old age pensioners' club that formed the East European leadership. 'Twice he spoke with Kádár about the necessity for new people in the

Hungarian leadership,' says VALERI MUSATOV. 'It was a discussion, a friendly talk, containing a few broad hints. It was the same story with Husák. It was very direct talking, but Gorbachev was not brutal; he only dropped a few hints about responsibility for the future. The decision was made by the relevant Politburos.' Husák was the first to go, although his replacement, Miloš Jakeš, was no more of a reformer than his predecessor. More significant was the departure of János Kádár from the leadership of the Hungarian party in May 1988. From then on Hungary, along with Poland, became the testing-ground for reforms that went well beyond Gorbachev's *perestroika* and were soon to herald the transition to democracy.

In Poland the Solidarity trade union had survived seven years of persecution by the communist authorities. Then at the end of 1988 General Jaruzelski, under pressure from growing public discontent, decided to try the policy of accommodation in place of repression. Solidarity was recognized and partially free elections were held in June 1989. To the astonishment of the authorities, Solidarity won all the seats, except one, it was allowed to contest. The communists were then abandoned by their satellite parties, and this led in September to the formation of a government under non-communist leadership, the first time this had happened in Eastern Europe in over 40 years. Moscow did not intervene, raising hopes elsewhere in the region that the end of Soviet domination was on the way.

Equally momentous changes were taking place in Hungary. There reformers within the communist leadership had actively embarked on a course of dismantling the party itself. This took place in October 1989, when the Communist Party was transformed into a Western-style social democratic organization. Earlier the Hungarian leadership had already promised fully-free multi-party elections for 1990. The gradual transition to democracy in Poland and Hungary heightened expectations among people living in the more hardline communist states that there was a chink of light at the end

244

of the long dark tunnel of one-party rule even for them. Hungary provided more than just a precedent for change. Back in May 1989 Hungarian and Austrian officials had taken wire cutters to the barbed wire along their common border, making the first hole in the Iron Curtain. Then in September, as tens of thousands of East Germans anxious to settle in West Germany assembled in Hungary, Budapest broke ranks with the Eastern bloc and allowed the East Germans free passage via Austria.

While so many of his countrymen were abandoning East Germany, Erich Honecker remained adamant that there would be no reforms. As late as October 1989, Gorbachev failed to convince Honecker that reforms were essential. 'Gorbachev did not want to go to Berlin, but it was impossible not to because it was the [40th] anniversary of one of our closest allies,' VALERI MUSATOV explains. 'His discussion with Honecker was very bad because Gorbachev began to speak about the concepts of *perestroika*, political and economic reforms, but Honecker stopped him and asked, "Has your population got enough food, bread, and butter?" He had visited the Soviet Union in the summer. And he asked Gorbachev, "Do you know how the population of the GDR live?" Because among the socialist countries the GDR had the highest standard of living. And the discussion stopped. Two days later demonstrations started in East Germany. Gorbachev said, "This is the beginning of the end" – and he left for Moscow.'

The East German regime tried to stem the exodus by banning travel to Hungary. Foreign travel for East Germans was now virtually limited to the hardline communist state of Czechoslovakia. The East German refugees immediately began heading for the West German embassy in Prague. 'In those days, through those narrow streets, hundreds and hundreds of people kept on coming,' says JAN URBAN, who was then a human rights activist in Prague. 'There were cars abandoned in the streets with their keys still in the ignition. When the police blocked the main entrance to the embassy compound, people just started to climb over the railings. The embassy itself and its gardens turned into the biggest refugee camp in Eastern Europe.'

The refugees were eventually allowed to go to West Germany. Meanwhile hundreds of thousands of East Germans were demonstrating each week, demanding democracy and the right to travel. East Germany was heading for a revolution. The question on everyone's mind was whether Soviet troops would intervene again, as they had done in 1953. 'The order from Moscow, from the ministry of defence, to all commanders in East Germany was to stay in their barracks and not interfere in East Germany's affairs,' says VALERI MUSATOV.

Without Moscow's active involvement, the collapse of the Honecker regime was only a matter of time. Honecker resigned 10 days after Gorbachev's visit, but his successor, Egon Krenz, came from the same stable and failed to inspire any more trust. The unrest continued, leading to the collapse of the East German government in early November. Then on 9 November Günter Schabowski announced that from the following day people would be allowed to travel abroad freely. Many East Germans understood this to mean that the Wall was coming down. 'I first heard it on the radio as I was going to sleep,' says CÄCILIE SILBERSTEIN, an East Berlin office worker. 'Then I heard many cars down in the street and as I opened the window I saw one headlight after another. And there I understood that the Wall must have been opened and I went down with a jacket thrown over my pyjamas. But I'd left my glasses at home and I couldn't fill in the visa form at the Wall. So I went home to get my glasses and also to get dressed properly. By the time I got back to the Wall a huge crowd had already gathered there. And nobody asked me for a visa any more.'

With the city practically reunited for the first time since 1961, Berlin was gripped by the spirit of euphoria. Within days an estimated three million East Germans had crossed into West Berlin. Thousands began to chip away at the Wall using pickaxes, chisels and hammers. 'The GDR was doomed to collapse the moment its border was opened,' says YULI KVITSINSKY, who was Soviet Ambassador to West Germany at the time. 'There was no way to preserve this republic as a viable state.' Indeed, within weeks of the Wall coming down, preparations got under way not only for holding multi-party elections in East Germany but also for bringing about the unification of the two German states. This took both East and West by surprise. Soviet policy-makers, for long wedded to the idea of keeping Germany divided, had to revise their thinking. There were, though, a few exceptions. One of them was VYACHESLAV DASHICHEV, who had been appointed chairman of an advisers' council in the foreign ministry two years earlier. 'In November 1987 I put on the agenda for the first time since the 1950s the question of German reunification, but I met a great deal of resistance. I was told the German question was closed and not debatable. But among Shevardnadze's personal staff there were some clever people who understood that because the division of Germany was one of the main causes of the Cold War, it was necessary to consider whether the new doctrine of the "common European home", proclaimed by Gorbachev, was possible under the circumstances of a divided Germany and a divided Europe.'

Initially Moscow was hoping that a more democratic East Germany might survive. It soon became obvious, though, that the momentum of German unification could not be stopped. This prompted Gorbachev to agree that the Soviet Union should place no obstacles in the way of Germany's unification. Hardliners in the Soviet leadership remained opposed to the moves towards bringing the two Germanies together. 'There were different discussions at the time about the fact that Germany, once it was united, should not be a member of any political alliance or military bloc,' says YEGOR LIGACHEV, who was still in the Politburo in 1990. 'There was a suggestion for the Soviet troops to remain in Germany in the longer term. The process of unification should have been more planned, more stable and more legal, and we could have used our military presence there – without actually using tanks – to ensure this. It should have been just a matter of using our political weight. We could have used political and economic levers and our military presence in East Germany.'

However, with Gorbachev at the height of his powers and enjoying the greatest degree of international prestige during his years in office, the hardline opposition in the Soviet Union was in disarray. Unification went ahead as planned, with the negotiations between the four wartime allies and the two Germanies, known as the 'two-plus-four' talks, bringing about the necessary international guarantees for a united Germany. But what did the Soviet Union gain by going along with the process of German unification? 'We couldn't afford to be in a position of opposition to a future united Germany, because the relationship with this leading European state was a key question for any Russian policy,' says YULI KVITSINSKY,

Alexander Dubček, the man who tried to give communism 'a human face', and the dissident playwright Václav Havel toast the victory of the 'Velvet Revolution' in Czechoslovakia. (Prague, November 1989.)

who supervised the 'two-plus-four' negotiations on behalf of the Soviet government. 'It was a defeat for the former Soviet policy in Europe, but it was the optimal solution for the Soviet Union under the new circumstances. It was an investment – a rather courageous one – in the future. It's my conviction that we had no other choice and no other possible pattern of action which would have suited our strategic interests better than the one we chose at the time.'

While Germany was racing towards the unification date of 3 October 1990, the rest of the Soviet bloc was coming apart at the seams. The collapse of the Berlin Wall had already been followed by the velvet revolution in Czechoslovakia, and the anti-Zhivkov coup in Bulgaria by the bloody revolution in Romania, which had led to the overthrow and execution of President Ceauşescu.

In the first half of 1990, as multi-party elections were held throughout the region, East Europeans began to grapple with the intricacies of democracy. Initially, the newly elected non-communist governments were reluctant to upset Moscow by suggesting that the military and economic organizations of the Soviet bloc should be dismantled. But as President Gorbachev and the Soviet leadership became increasingly involved in the problems of the internal Soviet empire, the East Europeans began to realize that independence was now within reach. They could see no point in perpetuating Comecon. They wanted to reorient their trade towards the West; and, in any case, economic conditions in the Soviet Union were even more catastrophic than in Eastern Europe. The Warsaw Pact, for its part, was seen as one of the cornerstones of the Soviet imperial grip on Eastern Europe and, as such, it was a humiliating symbol they wanted to do away with. Both organizations disappeared not with a bang but a whimper. 'The final session of Comecon was held in Budapest in the summer of 1991,' says VYACHESLAV SYCHEV, its last secretary. 'It took less than one hour to sign all the documents to put an end to the activities of the organization.'

After more than four decades of tight control over the region, Moscow finally allowed the countries of Eastern Europe to go their own way. It had not encouraged them to do so. Gorbachev would have preferred to preserve a community or alliance of equal partners in the region. However, matters had escaped Moscow's control after the Soviet leadership decided to allow the East Europeans to pursue their own policies. 'Non-interference was my major principle,' says ALEXANDER YAKOVLEV, Soviet central committee secretary for international affairs at the time. 'I was absolutely convinced that interference in the affairs of the socialist countries was damaging both them and my country. But still I was hoping for a more evolutionary way of development and not for the explosive way that actually happened.'

East and West were equally surprised at the lack of any Soviet response to the collapse of Moscow's influence and power in Eastern Europe. The new Soviet policy of allowing self-determination for its allies had reached its logical conclusion. Moreover, Moscow could not afford to undermine the trust it had successfully built up in Washington by behaving as an old-fashioned empire and trying to put down the East Europeans' efforts to gain independence. In any case, the poor state of the Soviet economy and the increasing movement towards independence within the Soviet Union itself made Eastern Europe less and less relevant in Moscow's eyes.

The cost of maintaining that empire had also mounted over the years and was no longer making much sense. 'When the time came, the Soviet leaders were ready,' says NIKOLAI SHISHLIN. 'They understood that it was impossible for the Soviet Union to remain in a position where it was the constructor of all the failures, mischiefs and faults in the countries with which we were so tightly connected. And besides that there was a strong conviction that we had to think about ourselves. Maybe even some egotistic ideas were in the air. "To hell with them! Let's think about ways of improving our own life." And there was another idea. "Are they our supporters or are they our burden?" And so Moscow was calm as it watched how communism in Central and Eastern Europe collapsed. But it was the same bell which tolled for changes in the Soviet Union and for the collapse of communism in the Soviet Union itself.'

That funeral was to take place in Moscow two years later, following the attempted hardline communist coup against Gorbachev in August 1991. The coup failed and Boris Yeltsin, the Russian President whose courage in confronting the tanks did more than anything else to ensure its defeat, used it as an excuse to disestablish the Communist Party. Without the party bureaucracy, the increasingly ramshackle Soviet Union fell apart at the end of 1991. President Gorbachev, whose policies had done so much first to debilitate and then to kill off the Cold War, was left with no country to lead.

Berlin – the day after. Jubilant Berliners on top of the Wall in front of the Brandenburg Gate, 10 November 1989. It was just hours after the Wall was breached, and hundreds of thousands of East Berliners began to stream across to West Berlin.

12

FROM YALTA TO MALTA – AND BEYOND

The Cold War climate

'I was eight years old when Nikita Khrushchev came to the United States in 1959,' says SUSAN EISENHOWER, President Eisenhower's granddaughter. 'And I remember being told by my mother that we had to quickly get dressed because Grandad was bringing the Soviet Premier to the farm from Camp David during the summit. Khrushchev handed out little Red Star pins to all of us and we thought it was wonderful; in fact he pinned them on, himself, and that upset my parents a great deal. I remember them collecting them up and saying, "You are not wearing these to school, this man is not our friend." My mother said that he'd just given a speech, saying that he would bury us. And when my brother was showing great enthusiasm for Khrushchev, my father told him, "Well, if the Russians take over the United States, we'll be the first family that's shot."'

The Cold War mentality that emerged in the second half of the 1940s held sway for more than four decades – the era that was signposted by the Yalta conference of February 1945 and the Bush–Gorbachev summit in Malta of December 1989. For most people in the East and West this mentality consisted of a profound mistrust of those on the other side of the 'Iron Curtain' and of an underlying concern about conflict between the two opposing camps, possibly involving the use of nuclear weapons. The 'Iron Curtain' was very much a construction in people's minds; for most East Europeans, the 'enemy' was their communist leadership or the Kremlin, which had incorporated their countries into the Soviet empire. Communists in the West regarded their governments or the capitalist class as the main adversary.

Concern about an East–West confrontation turned into fear at times of crisis, such as those over Berlin, Cuba and the Middle East, when it seemed that the Cold War might turn into a hot war of devastating proportions. The NATO and Warsaw Pact countries – supposedly safe behind their nuclear deterrents – were the most prone to this paranoia because they were aware that they would be the primary target for a possible nuclear strike by the other side.

In the early 1980s, as President Reagan combined a huge arms build-up with a stridently anti-communist tone, sections of the Kremlin leadership were swept by a spirit of war psychosis, which reached fever pitch in November 1983. That occurred just before the deployment of cruise and *Pershing-2* missiles in Western Europe and it coincided with the NATO exercise 'Able Archer', one of the periodic tests of communications and command procedures for the use of nuclear weapons in the event of war. The American admin-istration learnt about Moscow's fears through the reports of Oleg Gordievsky, the KGB officer based in London who was working as an agent for the British. His duties included watching out for any signs of unusual activity around government buildings and nuclear missile bases. 'We knew from Gordievsky that there was extreme paranoia in Moscow that, on reflection, was probably quite danger-ous,' says RICHARD PERLE, the American Assistant Secretary of Defence at the time. 'I think there was a more sober and sensible attitude in this country. We didn't think that we were close to a war.'

For some, including members of the Soviet top brass, the pros-pect of a possible military confrontation involving the superpowers remained on the cards even during the mid-1980s. 'I remember sitting in the office of Army General [Valentin] Varennikov, who was one of the Soviet commanders in Afghanistan,' says ARTYOM

254

BOROVIK, a journalist who paid his first visit to Afghanistan in 1986. 'In Varennikov's office in Kabul I saw not only maps of Afghanistan but also a map of Central America and I asked him why it was there. He said "Artyom, if America makes a wrong move here and they invade this country from Pakistan, there will be an immediate answer in Central America, from Nicaragua and from Cuba. We know what we'll be doing there."'

Nearly three decades earlier, Khrushchev's first visit to the United States in 1959 had provided reassurance for American policy-makers anxious to see into their enemy's mind. 'My father told me that as far as the administration was concerned, they were rather happy to have Khrushchev there,' says SUSAN EISENHOWER. 'And that was the reason, which is wonderful; they determined that he loved life and that he was not a kamikaze, so this brought a great deal of reassurance. He was a practical man and he was probably using ideology for his own purposes, but he genuinely loved life.'

The Cold War mentality was sustained through propaganda and repression. The threat of attack or subversion was perceived as coming not just from an outside power but also from within – from the fifth column, whose plain-clothes troops were regarded as furthering the interests of the adversary. In the United States communists, radicals and a broad range of people with real or imagined left-wing sympathies became the target of persecution in the late 1940s and early 1950s, the era associated with Senator Joseph McCarthy's campaign against alleged communist subversion. GILBERT GREEN, who was on the national committee of the Communist Party of the United States, was sentenced to five years' imprisonment in 1949 for conspiracy to overthrow the government. 'I was not conspiring to overthrow anything,' says Green. 'First of all it would have been ridiculous to think of a small organization with probably 20,000–25,000 members trying to overthrow the government. The whole purpose of the arrests and the prosecution of persons was to perpetuate the view that America had to be armed to the teeth because of the external danger and also an internal one

255

from those who supported the external enemy, namely the Soviet Union.'

The large-scale and systematic persecution of political dissenters in the United States – which was sustained with the help of substantial sections of the media – coincided with the most tense period of the Cold War. 'The American media were divided into two groups', says JOHN CHANCELLOR, a veteran NBC (National Broadcasting Corporation) commentator. 'One group that worried about spies under the bed and the group that worried about missiles on the horizon. The spies-under-the-bed crowd went away in about the mid-1950s. The witch-hunt people, the red-scare people, the don't-trust-your-neighbour people, they just didn't sell – thank God for capitalist journalism. Nobody was really interested in that after a while. The missiles-on-the-horizon people are in many ways still with us today. Their arguments were more credible.'

One of the targets of McCarthy's witch-hunt was the State Department, which, like other institutions, he denounced as a hotbed of communist subversion. He also blamed it for losing China to the communists. State Department officials branded as communists were forced out of their jobs and were harassed publicly. This campaign coincided with the final phase of Stalin's murderous rule in the Soviet Union. A memorial plaque in the entrance hall of what used to be the Soviet foreign ministry in Moscow – it now houses the ministry's Russian successor – commemorates the hundreds of Soviet diplomats who were sent to prison or labour camps, many of them to be shot, during the Stalin era.

In the Soviet Union and the rest of the Eastern bloc the persecution of political dissenters was always an integral part of the political system. After Stalin's death the intensity of repression abated. Opponents of the regime were no longer executed; instead, they were imprisoned or dismissed from work. 'Being a dissident was a way of life,' says JAN URBAN, an activist in the Czechoslovak Charter 77 human rights movement in the 1980s. 'You couldn't do it half-way. It had its very strict rules and you were not allowed to make a mistake. It created an absolute distrust, an alert that lasted 24 hours a day. My family had to learn not to ask what I was doing, where I was going. And at a certain stage I had to make it very clear to the security authorities that I couldn't be blackmailed with my family, which was very tough. I learnt to live with fear. I learnt to distrust people when necessary and risk trusting other people when it was necessary or unavoidable.'

In the Soviet Union dissidents were denounced as agents of Western imperialism. Any serious criticism of the Communist Party's policies amounted to treason in the eyes of the regime. So strong was the hold of this enemy image that was projected onto those who disagreed with official policies that, even in private discussions, Soviet leaders did not deviate from the accepted phraseology. 'These are the minutes from a meeting of the Politburo that took place on 9 August 1985,' says YELENA BONNER, the widow of Andrei Sakharov, the most famous of Soviet human rights campaigners. 'I want to quote Gorbachev directly. "Now a few words on another subject. At the end of July, Sakharov – a man not unknown to all of us – asked me to grant permission for his wife, Bonner, to travel abroad to see relatives and receive medical treatment." Then we have Chebrikov, who was chairman of the KGB, saying, "Sakharov's behaviour is determined by the influence of Bonner." And Zimyanin – another member of the Politburo – says a very amusing thing about me: "You can't expect any decent behaviour from Bonner. She's a great beast in a skirt, a henchman of imperialism." That was the level of understanding of the highest in the state.'

Pervasive ignorance of the other side was one of the hallmarks of the Cold War mentality. In Moscow the leadership remained a victim of its own black propaganda about the United States well into the Gorbachev era. GENNADI GERASIMOV, the Soviet Foreign Ministry spokesman in the late 1980s, has an anecdote to illustrate this: 'I was told a story – and I think it's true – that when one of the old guard members of the Politburo, by the name of [Viktor] Nikonov, who was in charge of agriculture, visited the United States for the first time in 1986 or '87 he was shown a supermarket. And he was convinced that this was a Potemkin village, specially made for his visit, and it was very difficult to prove to him that this was not the case. People brought up in the system could really not believe that this kind of abundance of goods in an American supermarket could really exist.'

ALEXANDER BESSMERTNYKH, the former Soviet Foreign Minister, has an equally incredible tale to tell about ignorance on the other side. 'After Reagan was elected President, a lot of people came to Washington from different parts of the country who were so unbelievably conservative that they couldn't see any other shades than black or white. So in order to get to know Reagan's people, we arranged a dinner for them in a club next door to the Soviet embassy in Washington. It was a beautiful dinner, we had nice talks. Then we had a team of youngsters from our school in Washington, dancing and singing and providing entertainment for the crowd. And there was a lady sitting next to me and she said, "Where did you get those children?" And I said "They are our children." And she said "No, they can't be Russian children because they are nice-looking." Some of those people who came with Reagan thought all the Russians must be ugly. It took them maybe a year to get used to the fact that Russians were normal. That was something we had to deal with – people who knew nothing about the Soviet Union, suspecting it even biologically, not only ideologically.'

The high level of mutual ignorance between the Soviet Union and the United States was far less characteristic of the superpowers' European allies who lived in close proximity to one another. The citizens of the two Germanies, in particular, had every opportunity to become acquainted with each other: in the case of the East Germans, mainly through the West German media, in the case of the West Germans also through travel. But, starting during the detente period and then accelerating in the 1980s, the combined effects of the information explosion and of increased opportunities for travel began to break down the walls of ignorance all across the ideological divide.

While the predominant tone of the Western media was anti-Soviet, there was nothing to prevent the expression of a wide range of views about the communist countries – some of it sycophantic in the extreme. From the other side of the Iron Curtain, the West was subjected to relentless criticism, though its tone became somewhat milder during detente. It was only under Mikhail Gorbachev that the decades of mistrust created by hostile propaganda were beginning to draw to an end. The policy of *glasnost* in the Soviet Union played an important role in this by allowing the publication of a much broader spectrum of opinions. Conscious efforts were also made to foster a greater sense of credibility and truthfulness about reporting on each other. GENNADI GERASIMOV was involved in some of these new-style activities. 'We organized meetings between the Soviet propagandists and the American propagandists from the United States Information Agency,' says Gerasimov. 'We had four or five annual meetings discussing propaganda exercises against each other and we stopped inventing stories, such as, for instance, that AIDS was something that had escaped from American laboratories.'

Ideology versus great-power interests

By the time Soviet and American officials were discussing how to put an end to hostile propaganda campaigns, the Soviet ideological drive had largely exhausted itself. Soviet policies and their articulation began increasingly to resemble the Western liberal model – which Gorbachev described as 'universal human values'. That was a far cry from the ideological struggle which had been such an integral part of the Cold War.

Ideology as a means of mobilizing political support was a particularly powerful motivating force on both sides in the postwar years at the time when the Soviet empire spread in Eastern Europe and communism was also conquering parts of the Far East. Thereafter, Marxism-Leninism was largely in decline in the countries under communist rule – but elsewhere, in parts of Asia, Latin

America and Africa, it remained strong until well into the 1970s.

Where communists were in power, the collapse of Marxism-Leninism as an ideology came well before the Soviet empire and the Soviet Union itself disappeared. In Eastern Europe, in particular, where access to the West made comparisons with the Western way of life and ideas easier to make than in the Soviet Union, the flirtation with Marxism had largely come to an end by the late 1960s. That process was accelerated by the disillusionment that followed the crushing of the Prague Spring and, with it, the hope for establishing 'socialism with a human face'. In the West the pragmatic brand of Euro-communism managed for a time to arrest the decline of communism in some countries.

Meanwhile, in the Soviet bloc countries Marxism-Leninism had become an empty dogma, expounded on festive occasions as part of a quasi-religious ritual. 'Although the communist ideology was completely exhausted, the leaders of Eastern Europe and the Soviet Union couldn't get rid of it because it was the only principle of legitimacy of their governments,' says LESZEK KOLAKOWSKI, the Polish-born philosopher and former Marxist who has written the most detailed history and critique of Marxism. 'So no matter whether people believed in it or not, it was necessary. There was one point on which they insisted to the very end and that was the idea of communism as the radiant future of mankind. Nobody took that seriously. And their second point was the idea that communism was historically inevitable – a natural stage following capitalism. And this they wanted people to believe in because it was the ideology of apathy and hopelessness. People were told, don't try to change anything, don't try to revolt, to reform, because it's historically inevitable.

'The ultimate destruction of communist ideology came when people noticed that this system was losing – it was losing the war in Afghanistan. This is why the collapse of communism in Europe took the form of the domino effect. Once it started, it was bound to be imitated because it encouraged people that there was no historical law that determined that you could not get out of this dreadful system.'

But how important was ideology in the formulation of foreign policy during the four decades of superpower confrontation? 'Ideology certainly played a part in the Cold War. After all, any big power with messianic tendencies has need of ideological trappings,' says OLEG TROYANOVSKY, who joined the Soviet diplomatic service in 1944. 'For Britain it was the "white man's burden", for the United States it was "make the world safe for democracy" or "manifest destiny". For the Soviet Union it was the time of socialism throughout the world, and in the first years after the revolution this was taken seriously. One of our lawyers told me that, in some regions of Russia right after the revolution, when sentences were passed for some crime or other, you could be sentenced to five or ten years – but a lighter sentence was that you would go to prison until the world revolution. The idea was that the world revolution was just outside the door. But, little by little, it became a more or less theoretical thing, just like the second coming of Christ. You preach it, you are supposed to believe in it, but no one really takes it seriously. Ideology then took second place to national interests, sometimes it was just to cover up for national interests.'

ANDREI ALEXANDROV-AGENTOV, the veteran Soviet foreign policy adviser, agrees with Troyanovsky in seeing a gradual weakening in ideological motivation: 'Ideological motives, rather characteristic for a leader like Khrushchev, were not for Brezhnev.' Many former Soviet officials are even more dismissive about ideological motivation. 'We lived in an era of confrontation with the West. The entire globe was the arena of this confrontation,' says LEONID SHEBARSHIN, former head of the KGB's foreign intelligence directorate. 'We stepped back – our opponents immediately occupied the vacated space. Wherever we could, we would try to occupy the space ourselves. And what had ideology to do with that? [Emperor of Ethiopia] Haile Selassie was one of the best friends of the Soviet Union and his ideas were hardly progressive. So if you look at the core of things, you will see that it was geopolitical considerations, real politics not ideology, that determined our policy in the Cold War on both sides. I don't think that the nature of a regime ever bothered the Americans or the British. That was all for public consumption. You remember what Eisenhower said about Somoza? "Yes, he's a son of a bitch, but he's our son of a bitch."'

On the American side ideological thinking – which faded into the background somewhat, especially during detente – regained momentum during the Reagan era, when many senior administration officials shared their president's strongly anti-communist thinking. One of the leading theoreticians among them was JEANE KIRKPATRICK, the US representative at the United Nations in the first half of the 1980s. 'I never really viewed the UN basically as a US–Soviet contest,' says Kirkpatrick. 'I viewed the UN very much in Cold War terms, if you will, as a democracy-versus-communism kind of contest. A contest of "-isms" more than that of countries or of governments.' For his part, PAUL NITZE, the pragmatic arms control negotiator, attributes the collapse of communism not to its economic inefficiency but to its being 'a disease of the soul'.

For much of the Cold War Washington and Moscow were equally keen to justify their foreign policy actions on ideological grounds. Of course, there were great differences between individual leaders: Reagan's anti-communism proved much more enduring than Nixon's; Brezhnev was more pragmatic than Khrushchev. But to a great extent they all felt at home in the world of *realpolitik*. America maintained cordial relations with Yugoslavia, Romania and, eventually, China – three communist countries that were singled out for favourable treatment because they were independent (or in the case of Romania, semi-detached) from Moscow. The Soviet Union had extensive contacts with a whole range of right-wing, often semi-feudal, authoritarian rulers such as the Shah of Iran, King Hassan of Morocco and King Mohammad Zahir Shah of Afghanistan, whose country was for long one of the largest beneficiaries of Soviet aid.

Washington could, of course, argue that by maintaining good

relations with the independent communist countries, it was weakening Moscow's international authority and thereby undermining the mainstay of communism; and the Soviet Union could claim that by making its presence felt in countries with very different social systems, it was extending its influence around the world to the benefit of socialism. Ideology and national interest were, therefore, closely intertwined; but, in general, in the taking of practical political steps great-power ambitions seemed on most occasions to play the more important role.

The MAD world

These superpower ambitions clashed around the world in a number of regional disputes; every continent, except Europe (and Australia), had its own Cold War battlegrounds. In Europe the guns facing each other across the two parts of Germany stayed silent. The Warsaw Pact had a clear superiority in terms of conventional weapons over NATO, and it is tempting to assume that the nuclear deterrent played a major part in preventing conflict between the two blocs. If that is the case, then nuclear weapons ensured one of the most peaceful periods in European history. Military action during the Cold War took place either within the same alliance (the Soviet attack on Hungary in 1956 and the Warsaw Pact invasion of Czechoslovakia in 1968), or involved a NATO country (Turkey) and a neutral state (Cyprus, whose northern part was occupied by Turkish troops in 1974).

But was it the notion of mutual assured destruction (MAD) that maintained the peace in Europe and kept the superpowers at arm's length? 'That's like asking the husband and wife who have a lot of disputes but have successfully stayed together for 45 years what was it that kept them together,' says THOMAS SCHELLING, one of the leading theoreticians of nuclear deterrence. 'We do know that nuclear war didn't happen and, in my opinion, we were never close to a nuclear war. We do know that the Soviets behaved in an exceedingly cautious way. They made a terrible mistake at the time of the Cuban crisis and I think in some ways the US government overreacted. But something kept us from ever coming close to nuclear war and, whether you call it MAD or something else, it was the notion that there are so many nuclear warheads on both sides that you can never possibly believe you can launch an attack and get away with it.'

Deterrence was the great orthodoxy of the Cold War. However, it did not go entirely unchallenged. From time to time the anti-nuclear movement, particularly in Western Europe, emerged demanding either unilateral nuclear disarmament or at least substantial reductions. The Campaign for Nuclear Disarmament (CND), which began life in the 1950s, reached the height of its popularity in the early 1980s, when huge demonstrations were held in Britain (and Western Europe) against the deployment of American intermediate-range missiles. 'CND was a fundamentalist movement, that is to say, it just said "no" to nuclear weapons,' says E.P. (EDWARD) THOMPSON, the historian and anti-nuclear campaigner. 'It rejected the ugliest vocabulary ever known to history – that bad language of diplomacy saying, All right, if you go beyond that line we are going to eliminate millions of you.' Thompson also believes that while the notion of deterrence may be rational when discussed by policy planners in a calm environment, in times of heightened international tension it is no guarantee of avoiding a nuclear war. 'Politicians are not rational creatures. Deterrence was a very strong disincentive to using nuclear weapons by either side but that isn't sufficient because there can be surges of irrational emotion among the populace and amongst their politicians which go beyond rationality.'

Another danger presented by the sheer number of nuclear weapons was that of accidental use. 'We've had hydrogen bombs dropped in the ice in Alaska, we've had crashes in the Mediterranean with hydrogen bombs, we've had missile launches in America and in one bizarre incident the commander of the base actually had to drive a jeep over the missile lid because he feared that the systems were out of control,' says BRUCE KENT, who was Secretary General

264

of CND in the early 1980s. 'So when you think of some 30,000 nuclear weapons on each side and an enormous string of human beings with their human fallibility down the line, I think that nuclear war was indeed a major threat and possibility. Just looking at it as an insurance broker, you would say, Yes, there had to be a major risk of a nuclear war with all these things in those numbers in so many hands.'

As Chernobyl demonstrated, nuclear accidents can be devastating. However, THOMAS SCHELLING does not think that accidents or false alarms would have triggered off an all-out nuclear war. 'While there may have been false alarms, they were not of the kind that had much likelihood of leading to war, for two reasons. First, since the mid-1960s the US has had such an immense capability to withstand nuclear attack and retaliate that there would never have been a need to launch on the basis of warning rather than adequate demonstration. Second, a lot of military people are sceptical of alarm systems. I think it was General Thomas Power back in the early 1960s who was chief of staff of the air force who was asked, "What would you do if the ballistic missile early warning system gave you notice of an attack? Would you launch strategic air command?" And he said, "No, you launch it and you guarantee war." It's the characteristic of most military leaders that they are very reluctant to take precipitate action on the basis of some fancy electronic warning system.'

Although the world was a dangerous place with thousands of nuclear weapons on both sides, few leaders of any country with a nuclear deterrent ever seriously contemplated giving it up. Reagan, who discussed that possibility with Gorbachev at the Reykjavik summit, was one of the exceptions. He believed that with the development of SDI it would be possible to abandon nuclear weapons. 'Ronald Reagan hated nuclear weapons and believed in the benefits of a nuclear-free world,' says RICHARD PERLE, Assistant Secretary for Defence under Reagan. 'I had a long conversation with him shortly after I left the Defence Department in the early summer of 1987; it was a sort of farewell meeting. And I went to that meeting with one purpose in mind: to try to talk him out of the argument that the world would be better off without nuclear weapons. So I tried to talk him out of it – and I failed utterly. He was quite committed, quite determined. He believed that nuclear weapons were a scourge and should be eliminated.'

Perle's main argument against a nuclear-free world was that the United States simply could not trust Moscow to comply with any agreement on the elimination of nuclear weapons. 'Imagine the temptation of signing up for an agreement for a nuclear-free world knowing that the United States and the democracies would comply fully with it and understanding that if you hid a couple of hundred weapons away somewhere you would wind up with a nuclear monopoly and in a position to dictate to the whole world. No, I was convinced that the temptation would not be resisted. And indeed, without mentioning names, I sat in on one meeting with President Reagan and the head of government of a European state friendly to the United States and listened to that person say, "I would cheat." So you could imagine what you could expect from the Russians.'

Perle was not the only politician to be horrified by the idea of a possible American–Soviet agreement on abandoning nuclear weapons. The West Europeans were concerned about the implications of the Reykjavik discussions. Would Britain and France be obliged to join a deal between the superpowers on eliminating nuclear weapons? And in the absence of such weapons, what would prevent the Soviet Union from launching an attack against Western Europe, given its superiority in conventional forces? Once nuclear weapons had been invented, attempts to get rid of them were fraught with danger.

After the Cold War

With the passing of the Cold War, fears of an all-out nuclear confrontation between the superpowers receded. But almost immediately new dangers appeared on the horizon. The dissolution of the Soviet Union led to instant nuclear proliferation because, in addition

266

to Russia, three other former Soviet republics, Ukraine, Belarus and Kazakhstan, acquired part of the former Soviet nuclear arsenal. Although these last three agreed to dismantle their nuclear weapons or surrender them to Russia, a whole range of problems involving the cost and logistics of such an operation emerged, and progress on carrying out this undertaking was painfully slow. Wrangling over these details gave a fresh meaning to 'nuclear blackmail', since the new nuclear powers sought to obtain the best possible deal from the West to help pay for the dismantling of their weapons of mass destruction.

The dispersal of former Soviet nuclear weapons and know-how also gave rise to fears that other countries might try to acquire some of these weapons. 'In the West we have this notion that nuclear weapons are not to be used and I don't think it ever occurred to the Soviets to use nuclear weapons,' says THOMAS SCHELLING. 'This is an immensely valuable taboo and it goes all the way back to Hiroshima. Whether it appeals to Saddam Hussein or Gaddafi or Kim Il-sung, I don't know. Until all the weapons of the former Soviet Union are safely gathered together in safe storage or dismantled, there are an awful lot of nuclear weapons out there and we have to be scared.' Given these dangers, PAUL NITZE, the doyen of American arms control negotiators, remains a prudent man. When asked if he believes the time has come to get rid of his family's nuclear fall-out shelter on his Maryland farm, his answer is a firm 'no'; he believes at present 'the prime dangers are confusion and disorder'.

Reagan's much-criticized SDI may now be adapted to counter a possible threat from one of the would-be nuclear powers or deal with the accidental launch of nuclear missiles. In fact, American and Soviet scientists have held discussions in preparation for working together on providing a protective shield against such an eventuality.

In the conventional field the Soviet threat has also gone. So, has the time come to get rid of NATO? Army General VLADIMIR LOBOV, the last Chief of Staff of the Warsaw Pact, certainly believes so. 'Since the Warsaw Pact doesn't exist any more and since the threat to

Western Europe and to the world at least from our side is over, I don't see much reason in NATO still being there. Russia has made several very important pledges that it doesn't have any territorial or other claims on any other state.'

GENERAL ALEXANDER HAIG, NATO's Supreme Commander in Europe in the late 1970s, remains a pessimist who takes exactly the opposite point of view. 'If I had felt a need in 1950 for an alliance, in the year 1992 I feel a greater need because of the growing uncertainties. Today if you turn to the CIS, it's a far cry from a successful democratic outcome, and while we must do all we can to help Mr Yeltsin succeed, we must never lose sight of the fact that an authoritarian reaction could set in, and with such a reaction comes the return of imperialism; because it's always the product of a dictatorial regime to create foreign devils.'

LORD CARRINGTON agrees in seeing a continued future for NATO. This would serve two purposes: it would help keep the West together to counter the increasing uncertainties in Eastern Europe and elsewhere in the world and prevent a splintering of the Western alliance which could lead to an exacerbation of existing tensions over trade and other issues. 'Like it or not, fear does drive people into each other's arms. Once that's removed, the imperative to collaborate very closely does disappear. If we really want the United States involved in the defence of Europe and in seeking to maintain a world level of good behaviour, decency and peace, we've got to make sure that the Americans feel it's worthwhile being around. One of the ways you could do this is to give NATO a more political role; after all, it's the only organization in which the Americans have an opportunity to talk to their European friends.'

To judge by the number of countries that are eager to join it, NATO is more popular than ever. Most of the former Warsaw Pact countries would like to come under the protection of its security umbrella because they are concerned about uncertainties to the East, and at least some of them are worried that they might be dragged into the war in the former Yugoslavia. NATO has been reluctant to

268

provide any security guarantees to its new friends, fearing that a region with existing and potential trouble spots would involve it in too many high-risk commitments.

However, relations between NATO and its Cold War adversaries have changed out of all recognition. 'The Hungarian ambassador in Brussels asked to see me once to present a Warsaw Pact communiqué,' says Lord Carrington. 'That was really, on the whole, a fairly harmless exercise. But the NATO governments said in no circumstances was I to meet the Hungarian ambassador. And the wretched man had to drive up to the gates of NATO, hand the communiqué over to a guard and then he was shut out and had to go back to Brussels. Now my successor spends a lot of time not just in Budapest but in Moscow and Kiev and everywhere else.'

The importance attached to NATO's continuing role has highlighted the failure of the CSCE to fulfil the hopes attached to it at the time when the end of the Cold War seemed to signal a new and more active role for cooperation within the 'common European home'. Notwithstanding the creation of new conflict-prevention and human rights centres, the CSCE has remained firmly in the background in the international attempts to deal with the Yugoslav imbroglio. It has lacked the relative compactness of the European Community to coordinate peace efforts and trade sanctions; and it could not match the universality and practical experience in peace-keeping of the United Nations.

For more than four decades the United Nations was an arena of confrontation and propaganda battles between the two superpowers. It was not until the end of the 1980s that it acquired the role its founders had intended for it – a forum for cooperation among the countries of the world. The first great test of that new era was the aftermath of the Iraqi invasion of Kuwait in 1990. In a move which a few years earlier would have been unimaginable – Moscow used to regard Baghdad as a close friend – the Security Council unanimously condemned Iraq and sanctioned the use of force by UN member states against Iraq to drive it out of occupied Kuwait.

With the passing of the Cold War, the nature of conflict in the world has changed. Although there are still a handful of communist states left, the only significant one, China, is determined to forge the closest possible economic links with the rest of the world. 'Problems that will arise now are not conflicts between communism and capitalism but are mainly focused on economic friction between the up-and-coming countries and the capitalist countries, and among the capitalist countries,' says YASUHIRO NAKASONE, the former Japanese Prime Minister. 'What has happened between Japan and the US will happen all over the world.'

The relationship between the United States and its West European allies is also changing. The European Community is becoming more assertive in defending its interests. That could not have come about in the era of East–West confrontation when the Western allies felt they had to stick together. (France's independent policy was the exception that proved the rule.) 'Our common market could never have been stabilized without German unification,' says CLAUDE CHEYSSON, a former EC Commissioner. 'As long as there was no unification, the Germans were completely dependent on the Americans and you can only have a European union between countries that are really independent and masters of their own destinies. The Americans are our allies, but they have not known the kind of suffering that we have known. So Germany had to be free of the American influence, otherwise the European union could never have worked.'

With the emergence of a more assertive and self-confident Western Europe, and with the continued growth of Japan's economic strength, the world is being divided into three large trading powers. However, America's military supremacy is not in doubt. But does the fact that the United States is now the only superpower left represent any danger? 'It doesn't bother me in the slightest that, to a large extent, the United States is the dominant power in the world,' says EDUARD SHEVARDNADZE, the former Soviet Foreign Minister. 'As the new world order is being established, an advantage

270

built solely on military power doesn't give one the chance to dictate one's will to others. And new giants have appeared, Germany and Japan, and these countries should become permanent members of the UN Security Council. Then there would be a different correlation in the balance of political forces.'

The new strains in relations between the economic giants have arisen mainly in the area of trade. The long-drawn-out GATT negotiations are an illustration of the conflicts among the Western trading powers. The prospects for protectionism have increased with the end of the bipolar world; the discipline imposed on the Western world by the challenge of the Soviet superpower has largely disappeared. However, the danger of a return to the trade wars of the 1930s has been lessened by the high degree of interdependence in commerce and communications in the present-day world. The global economy has become so internationalized that protectionist measures are likely to rebound more often than not on those attempting to introduce them.

The economic problems of the former Soviet Union and its one-time allies are incomparably greater than those of the Western world and they may pose an increasing threat to stability, particularly in Europe. 'It's one of the tragedies of our time that the end of communism – and the return in Eastern Europe to the market system – is being seen as an exercise in hardship,' says JOHN KENNETH GALBRAITH, the eminent American economist. 'Democracy and capitalism are being seen by many people as entailing a degree of economic suffering which is not tolerable. And I would very much like to see help from the Western countries that would minimize that suffering. It's help that we can well afford to give.'

Part of the economic aid former communist countries so much need should have come from the peace dividend, the money that in the past was spent on the military build-up to protect the West against a potential Soviet threat. Yet with the involvement of many Western countries in peacekeeping efforts, ranging from the former Yugoslavia to Cambodia and Somalia, much of the expected peace dividend has yet to materialize. 'The world is spending $850 billion a year on weapons,' says BRUCE KENT. 'Nearly half the world's scientists are engaged in military production or research. And yet every year 15 million children under the age of six die of starvation. And there are 36 military conflicts going on in the world today.'

Most of these conflicts have been less affected by the end of the Cold War than was expected at the time the superpowers ended their involvement. The pull-out of Soviet troops and the defeat of the communist regime in Kabul have not stopped the civil war in Afghanistan; nor has the withdrawal of Cuban and South African troops from Angola prevented their one-time Angolan allies from carrying on the fighting. The main difference is that the rival factions are no longer being armed to the teeth by the superpowers and their proxies, although weapons are still being supplied by outsiders eager to make a profit.

However, the end of the Cold War has ushered in new conflicts which might not have arisen otherwise. This applies, in particular, to regions that were models of stability during the era of East–West confrontation. Eastern Europe is the part of the world that has been most affected by the demise of the Cold War. The countries of the region have been freed of Soviet control; their economies have been adapting themselves to capitalist practices once again; and simmering ethnic tensions have given rise to serious conflicts, including

Croatia, July 1991: the ethnic cleansing begins. Croats flee the town of Kostajnica from advancing Serbian forces. As the war in the former Yugoslavia spread, far more harrowing scenes of refugees were to follow.　　•

wars. There is little to remind East Europeans of the increasingly distant era that was inaugurated by the Yalta conference in 1945 and was symbolically brought to an end at the time of the Malta summit between Presidents Gorbachev and Bush in December 1989 – which coincided with the death throes of communism in Eastern Europe.

'We are going back into a situation in which global stability of the kind that we were used to throughout the Cold War is simply a thing of the past,' says Lawrence Eagleburger. 'Now that may have been the stability of the graveyard and was clearly dominated by the fear of both superpowers and their client states that if something got out of hand, the consequences could clearly lead you to a nuclear war and that, therefore, caused a kind of conservatism on both sides that maintained a certain balance and stability. That's gone and Yugoslavia is just one example of the consequences of the disappearance of the bipolar world. The Yugoslavs would not have come apart at the seams if they had felt that the Soviet Union was still a military threat that would take advantage of instability in Yugoslavia if it occurred. We see it now in the Central Asian Republics of the former Soviet Union, in Armenia and Azerbaijan, and we could go through a long list of these.'

The wars in the former Yugoslavia and the economic crisis that has accompanied the demise of communism in Eastern Europe have created a refugee problem that would have been unimaginable during the Cold War, when almost all communist states kept their citizens firmly behind the Iron Curtain. The fighting in Croatia and Bosnia in 1991–3 transformed two million people into refugees. Stefan Heym, the German writer who used to live in the shadow of the Berlin Wall, warns that 'the economic and political situation will force millions of people away from their homes; there will be an irresistible march and you won't be able to hold them back at the border; even if you build another Wall, they'll scale it.'

Behind what used to be the Iron Curtain, the transition to democracy is encountering major problems. George Soros, the Hungarian-born American billionaire who by early 1993 had set up

17 foundations in Eastern Europe and the former Soviet Union to help bring about the shift to democracy, is pessimistic about the current prospects. 'Communism was a universal closed system and my idea was to help the transition to an open society,' says Soros. 'But the natural tendency is for the universal closed system to break up into particular closed systems based on some other idea, namely the idea of national or ethnic identity. So the major thrust is in that direction and it's those who are pushing in that direction who find me their enemy. They are a little bit more virulent than the old communists, who actually didn't believe in their own dogma.'

The return to earlier patterns of conflict based on ethnic and national divisions, which were swept under the carpet during the Pax Sovietica of the Cold War, is one of the most ominous developments in Eastern Europe. During the era of Soviet domination conflict in the region arose from opposition to Moscow's rule – whether direct or through the imposition of regimes under its control. The conflicts that have emerged since represent a return to the past and make Eastern Europe more like many other trouble-stricken parts of the world. They also remind LAWRENCE EAGLEBURGER of the ethnic tensions – particularly in the Balkans – which contributed to the outbreak of the First World War. 'There's one fundamental difference between now and 1914,' says Eagleburger. 'There isn't now a potential civil war in Western Europe in which the Germans will try to exploit those ethnic tensions against the French or the British or *vice versa*. I mean you don't go to World War III because somebody shoots the functional equivalent of Franz Ferdinand today. But it doesn't mean it's going to be an easy world to live with.'

The period of the Cold War was a unique combination of global confrontation between two superpowers, sustained by ideological enmity, that was made all the more potentially dangerous – but was also kept in check – by the looming presence of nuclear weapons. The euphoria that greeted the passing away of that era has not survived for long. The West – or the Western set of values – has triumphed, but it has to live with many of the new dangers that have emerged as a result of the East's defeat. The United States is now the only superpower left, but in economic terms Japan and Germany – with their low military spending over the years and few outside commitments – have won the Cold War. The new world order is beginning to resemble more and more the old world disorder with its seemingly intractable local conflicts in which the Cold War certainties of right or wrong and friend or foe have little relevance.

Yet, along with the tragedy of Yugoslavia and the emergence of other conflicts, the end of the Cold War has also demonstrated a remarkable degree of success in transforming the political map of Europe. German unification took place peacefully in 1990. Czechoslovakia split up in 1993 without any of the traumas of the former Yugoslavia. Above all, the break-up of the outer Soviet empire in Eastern Europe in 1989 and of the inner Soviet-Russian empire in 1991 were both accomplished peacefully to the extent that the colonial power concerned did not resist these processes. Compared with the bloodshed that marked the end of the British, French, Dutch and Portuguese empires, this was a remarkable achievement. (However, Russia itself might disintegrate, and that could be accompanied by considerable bloodshed.) Moreover, with the end of the Cold War the victims of wars and civil strife are receiving greater protection and more humanitarian aid than they would have done in the past in countries as far apart as Cambodia, Bosnia and Somalia.

'Immediately after the Berlin Wall, Eastern Europe and Mr Gorbachev, there was a kind of euphoria in the world in which everybody thought the millennium had arrived,' says LORD CARRINGTON, who for a time headed the international effort to bring peace to Yugoslavia. 'Very shortly afterwards now it's clear that the millennium hasn't arrived. Although we may have got rid of one problem, we have a whole lot of other ones. And in a way all these problems are going to be as difficult as the Cold War – but they are not as threatening in the sense that they will not bring World War Three.'

COLD WAR
CHRONOLOGY,
1945–93

1945
4–11 Feb   Stalin, Roosevelt and Churchill meet at Yalta.
8 May   End of Second World War in Europe.
26 June   UN Charter signed in San Francisco.
17 July–2 Aug   Stalin, Truman and Churchill/Attlee meet at Potsdam.
6–9 Aug   Atomic bombs dropped on Hiroshima and Nagasaki, Japan.
14 Aug   Japan surrenders.

1946
15 March   Churchill's 'Iron Curtain' speech.

1947
10 Feb   Paris peace treaties signed.
12 March   Truman announces 'Truman Doctrine'.
5 June   Inauguration of Marshall Plan aid package.
5 Oct   Cominform set up.

1948
16 April   OEEC set up to coordinate Marshall Plan.
June   Soviet ban on traffic between East and West Berlin; start of Berlin airlift.
2 Nov   Truman wins US Presidential election.

1949
18 Jan   Comecon set up.
4 April   North Atlantic Treaty signed by 11 countries, including US, Britain and France.
May   End of Soviet blockade of Berlin, and of airlift.

1949, cont'd

23 May   FRG established.
29 Aug   USSR explodes its first atomic bomb.
7 Oct   GDR established.

1950

25 June   North Korean forces invade South Korea.

1952

1 June   East–West German border fortified.
3 Oct   Britain's first atomic bomb test.
1 Nov   US explodes first H-bomb.
4 Nov   Eisenhower wins US Presidential election.

1953

5 March   Stalin dies.
17 June   East German workers' uprising in Berlin.
27 July   Korean war ends.
12 Sept   Khrushchev becomes CPSU leader.

1955

9 May   West Germany joins NATO.
14 May   Warsaw Pact set up.

1956

14 Feb   Opening of CPSU 20th Congress, at which Khrushchev denounces Stalin on 25 February.
17 April   Cominform dissolved.
23 Oct   Start of Hungarian uprising.
31 Oct–7 Nov   Anglo-French offensive in Suez.
4 Nov   Soviet forces attack Budapest.
6 Nov   Eisenhower re-elected US President.

1957

15 Feb   Gromyko becomes USSR Foreign Minister.
4 Oct   USSR announces launch of its earth satellite, *Sputnik-1*.

1959

16 Feb   Castro becomes Prime Minister of Cuba.
15 Sept   Khrushchev starts US visit.

1960

13 Feb   France explodes first atomic bomb.

1960, cont'd
1 May US U-2 spyplane shot down over USSR.
16 May Four-Power summit in Paris.
Aug Soviet technicians recalled from China.
8 Nov Kennedy wins US Presidential election.

1961

12 April Soviet astronaut Yuri Gagarin becomes first man in space.
13 Aug East Germany seals its border with West Berlin.
17 Aug Start of construction of Berlin Wall.

1962

22–27 Oct Cuban missile crisis.

1963

20 June US and USSR agree to set up hotline.
26 June Kennedy visits Berlin.
25 July US and USSR sign nuclear test-ban treaty.
22 Nov Kennedy assassinated; succeeded by Johnson.

1964

15 Oct Brezhnev replaces Khrushchev as leader of CPSU.
16 Oct China explodes first atomic bomb.
3 Nov Johnson wins US Presidential election.

1965

Feb/March US–Viet Cong conflict escalates into Vietnam war.

1966

1 July French forces withdraw from NATO military command.

1967

27 Jan US, USSR and Britain sign treaty banning nuclear weapons from outer space.
5–10 June Six-Day War in Middle East.

1968

30 Jan Start of Viet Cong's *Tet* offensive.
1 July US, USSR and Britain sign nuclear non-proliferation treaty.
20–21 Aug Warsaw Pact troops occupy Czechoslovakia.
5 Nov Nixon wins US Presidential election.

1969

March	Major Soviet–Chinese border clashes.
21 Oct	Brandt becomes West German chancellor.
17 Nov	US–USSR SALT first round opens in Helsinki.

1971

10 April	US ping-pong team arrives in China.
25 Oct	China admitted to UN; Taiwan expelled.

1972

21 Feb	Nixon begins visit to China.
10 April	US and USSR sign convention outlawing biological weapons.
22 May	Nixon begins visit to Moscow.
26 May	US and USSR sign SALT I treaty.
7 Nov	Nixon re-elected US President.
21 Dec	East and West Germany sign Basic Treaty.

1973

27 Jan	Vietnam peace treaty, signed in Paris, takes effect.
March	US troops withdraw from Vietnam.
Oct	Arab–Israeli October (Yom Kippur) War.
23 Dec	Gulf oil producers double prices.

1974

9 Aug	Nixon resigns; succeeded by Ford.
24 Nov	Ford and Brezhnev agree on outline for new strategic arms control pact.

1975

30 April	Vietnam war ends.
17 July	Joint US–USSR *Apollo–Soyuz* space flight.
1 Aug	Helsinki Declaration signed.
Nov	Angolan civil war starts.

1976

2 Nov	Carter wins US Presidential election.

1977

Oct	USSR begins deployment of SS-20 missiles.

1979

1 Jan	US and China establish diplomatic relations.
18 June	Carter and Brezhnev sign SALT II treaty.
25 Dec	Soviet forces invade Afghanistan.

1980

4 Jan	US stops grain sales to USSR.
July	International boycott of Moscow Olympics.
22 Sept	Iran–Iraq war starts.
4 Nov	Reagan wins US Presidential election.

1981

13 Dec	Martial law imposed in Poland.
29 Dec	US imposes economic sanctions against USSR.

1982

16 March	Brezhnev announces freeze on deployment of SS-20 missiles west of Urals.
10 Nov	Brezhnev dies; succeeded by Andropov as leader of CPSU.

1983

March	Reagan announces start of SDI programme.
21 July	Martial law ends in Poland.

1984

17 Jan	Start of NATO and Warsaw Pact conference on disarmament.
9 Feb	Andropov dies; Chernenko becomes CPSU leader.
Aug	Most Warsaw Pact countries boycott Los Angeles Olympics.

1985

4 Feb	Reagan calls for tripled spending on SDI programme.
10 March	Chernenko dies.
11 March	Gorbachev becomes leader of CPSU.
7 April	Gorbachev announces moratorium on missile deployment in Europe.
2 July	Gromyko succeeded as USSR foreign minister by Shevardnadze.
21 Nov	First Gorbachev–Reagan summit in Geneva.

1986

Oct 11–12	Gorbachev and Reagan hold Reykjavik summit.

1987

25 June	Gorbachev outlines reform of Soviet economy.
8-10 Dec	Gorbachev and Reagan summit in Washington; INF treaty signed.

1988

16 July	Warsaw Pact calls for 3-stage reduction of conventional forces in Europe.
20 Aug	Iran–Iraq war ends.
8 Nov	Bush wins US Presidential election.

1989

10 Jan	Cuban troops begin withdrawal from Angola.
15 Feb	Soviet troops complete withdrawal from Afghanistan.
4 June	Solidarity wins Polish parliamentary elections.
10 Sept	Hungary allows East Germans across the border into Austria.
2 Oct	Start of pro-democracy demonstrations in East Germany.
7 Oct	Hungary's Socialist Workers' Party votes for its own dissolution.
9 Nov	East Germany opens its border with West Germany.
10 Dec	Non-communist government takes power in Czechoslovakia.
22 Dec	Ceauşescu's government overthrown in Romania.

1990

11 Feb	Mandela released from prison.
18 March	Free elections in East Germany.
21 March	Namibia gains independence.
9 Aug	Iraq annexes Kuwait.
3 Oct	Germany reunites.
19–21 Nov	CFE arms reduction treaty by NATO and Warsaw Pact countries at Paris CSCE summit.

1991

16 Jan–8 Feb	Gulf war.
June	Start of wars in Slovenia and Croatia.
29 June	Comecon dissolved.
1 July	Warsaw Pact disbands.
31 July	Bush and Gorbachev sign START I.
19–21 Aug	Hardliners' coup attempt in USSR.
29 Aug	Supreme Soviet suspends CPSU.
8 Dec	CIS established, ending USSR.
25 Dec	Gorbachev resigns as President of the USSR; the USSR formally disbands.

Post-Cold War

1992

April   War breaks out in Bosnia.
25 April   Communist government falls in Afghanistan

1993

3 Jan   Bush and Yeltsin sign START II.

BIOGRAPHIES

ALEXANDROV-AGENTOV, ANDREI – Soviet foreign policy *éminence grise*; *b* 1918. Influential foreign policy adviser to Brezhnev, Andropov, Chernenko and Gorbachev before retiring in 1986.

ALEXEYEV, ALEXANDER – Soviet diplomat; *b* 1913. Arrived in Cuba under guise of TASS correspondent 1959. Counsellor, USSR embassy to Cuba, 1960–62; ambassador to Cuba 1962–8.

ARBATOV, GEORGI – Soviet official and politician; *b* 1923. Adviser on US to successive USSR governments. Director, USSR (Russian) Institute of US and Canadian Studies, 1967– . CPSU Central Committee 1981–90.

BAHR, EGON – West German Social Democratic politician; *b* 1922. With Brandt, one of the architects of *Ostpolitik*. Chief negotiator of treaties with USSR and East Germany 1970–72.

BALL, GEORGE – US government official and lawyer; *b* 1909. Under (deputy) secretary of state 1961–6; resigned over Vietnam war. Member of Kennedy's ExComm crisis committee: advised caution during Cuban missile crisis.

BEREZHKOV, VALENTIN – Soviet diplomat and journalist; *b* 1916. Adviser and interpreter to Molotov 1940–44. Editor, Soviet journals 1945–79.

BESSMERTNYKH, ALEXANDER – Soviet diplomat and politician; *b* 1933. Spent almost entire career in US or dealing with US affairs. USSR ambassador to US 1990–91. USSR minister of foreign affairs January–August 1991.

BLAKE, GEORGE – British intelligence officer; *b* 1922. Jailed for 42 years (a year for each British agent said to have died because of Blake's betrayal) in 1961 for giving information to the USSR. Escaped from jail in 1966 and smuggled to USSR.

BOTHA, PIK – South African politician and diplomat; *b* 1932. MP 1970– . South Africa's UN ambassador 1974–7. Minister of foreign affairs 1977– .

283

BOTVINNIK, MIKHAIL – Soviet chess champion; *b* 1911. Seven times USSR chess champion 1931–52. World champion 1948–57, 1958–60, 1961–3.

BRZEZINSKI, ZBIGNIEW – Polish-born US government official and political scientist; *b* 1928. President Carter's national security affairs assistant 1977–81.

BUNDY, MCGEORGE – US government official and political scientist; *b* 1919. National security affairs assistant to presidents Kennedy and Johnson 1961–6; played major role in Cuban missile crisis.

BURLATSKY, FYODOR – Soviet academic, politician and journalist; *b* 1927. Influential under Khrushchev; 'establishment liberal'.

CALLAGHAN, LORD (JAMES) – British Labour politician; *b* 1912. Chancellor 1964–7; home secretary 1967–70; foreign secretary 1974–6; prime minister 1976–9. The only 20th-century British politician to hold all four senior offices of state.

CARRINGTON, LORD (PETER) – British Conservative politician and official; *b* 1919. Foreign secretary 1979–82; resigned following Argentine invasion of Falkland Islands. Secretary-general of NATO 1984–8. EC's mediator for Yugoslavia 1991–2.

CHERNYAYEV, ANATOLI – Soviet official; *b* 1921. Deputy head, international department, CPSU central committee, 1970–86. Foreign policy adviser to Gorbachev 1986–91.

CHERVOV, COLONEL-GENERAL NIKOLAI – Soviet soldier; *b* 1923. Armaments expert; chief of the legal and treaty department, USSR armed forces general staff, throughout the 1980s.

CHEYSSON, CLAUDE – French politician; *b* 1920. EC commissioner for development aid 1973–81. Mitterrand's first foreign minister 1981–4.

CHŇOUPEK, BOHUSLAV – Czechoslovak official and diplomat; *b* 1925. Ambassador to USSR 1970–71. Foreign affairs minister 1971–88.

CHOMSKY, NOAM – US political radical and doyen of theoretical linguistics; *b* 1928. Professor of Linguistics, MIT, 1966– . Strong critic of US foreign policy.

COHEN, HERMAN – US government official and diplomat; *b* 1932. Ambassador to Dakar, Senegal and Gambia 1977–80. Assistant secretary of state for African affairs 1989– .

COLBY, WILLIAM – US intelligence official; *b* 1920. Chief, Far East division, CIA, 1963–8. Director, CIA, 1973–6.

COUVE DE MURVILLE, MAURICE – French politician and diplomat; *b* 1907. Ambassador to Egypt, US and FRG. Foreign minister 1958–68. President of North Atlantic Council 1967–8. Prime minister 1968–9.

CROCKER, CHESTER – US government official; *b* 1941. Assistant secretary of state for African affairs 1981–9. Responsible for negotiating Namibian independence.

DIENSTBIER, JIŘÍ – Czechoslovak journalist, dissident and politician; *b* 1937.

Imprisoned for political activities 1979–82. Spokesman for Charter 77 1985–6. Foreign affairs minister 1989–92.

DOS SANTOS, JOSÉ EDUARDO – Angolan politician; *b* 1942. Fought for MPLA against Portuguese 1970–74. MPLA central committee secretary for economic development 1977–9. President of Angola 1979– .

EAGLEBURGER, LAWRENCE – US government official and diplomat; *b* 1930. Ambassador to Yugoslavia 1977–81. Deputy secretary of state 1989–92; secretary of state 1992–3.

FLORIN, PETER – East German politician and diplomat; *b* 1921. Ambassador to Czechoslovakia 1967–9. State secretary, foreign ministry, 1969–73. Appointed deputy foreign minister and permanent representative at UN 1973.

FULBRIGHT, WILLIAM – US Democratic politician; *b* 1905. Senator 1945–74; chairman, Senate foreign relations committee, 1959–74. Opponent of Vietnam war.

GALBRAITH, JOHN KENNETH – World-renowned US economist; *b* 1908. Director, US strategic bombing survey, 1945. Director, office of economic security policy, state department, 1946. Professor of economics, Harvard University 1949–75.

GARTHOFF, RAYMOND – US government official and diplomat; *b* 1929. Soviet affairs assistant, state department, 1961–8; deputy director, state department, 1970–73. Ambassador to Bulgaria 1977–9.

GERASIMOV, GENNADI – Soviet official and Russian diplomat; *b* 1930. Spokesman, USSR foreign ministry, 1986–90: 'the man who put the soundbite into Soviet politics'. Russia's ambassador to Portugal 1991– .

GORBACHEV, MIKHAIL – Soviet statesman; *b* 1931. Official in Stavropol region 1955–78. Member of CPSU Politburo 1979–91. General Secretary of the CPSU 1985–91. USSR head of state 1988–91. Winner of the Nobel peace prize 1990. Architect and master builder of Soviet domestic reforms and 'new thinking' in foreign policy.

GORDIEVSKY, OLEG – Soviet intelligence officer; *b* 1938. Head of KGB office in London 1982–5. Worked as a double agent for Britain until his defection in 1985.

GRÓSZ, KÁROLY – Hungarian politician; *b* 1930. Prime minister 1987–8; general secretary of HSWP 1988–9, after ending Kádár's 32-year rule.

GYSI, GREGOR – East German politician; *b* 1948. Communist reformer. Chairman SED 1989; chairman PDS 1990–93. Charismatic lawyer who defended dissidents.

HAIG, GENERAL ALEXANDER – US politician and soldier; *b* 1924. Fought in Korea and Vietnam; White House chief of staff 1973–4. Supreme Allied commander Europe, NATO, 1974–9. Secretary of state 1981–2.

HÁJEK, JIŘÍ – Czechoslovak politician and diplomat; *b* 1913. Dubček's foreign minister April–September 1968.

HAYTER, SIR WILLIAM – British diplomat; *b* 1906. Ambassador to USSR 1953–7.

HEALEY, LORD (DENIS) – British Labour politician; *b* 1917. As Labour Party's international secretary 1945–52, tried to bolster social democrats in eastern Europe. Defence secretary 1964–70.

HEGEDÜS, ANDRÁS – Hungarian politician and academic; *b* 1922. Prime minister 1955–6. Fled to Moscow during uprising; later became critic of communist government policy.

HELMS, RICHARD – US intelligence official and diplomat; *b* 1913. Director CIA 1966–73. Ambassador to Iran 1973–6.

HEYM, STEFAN – German writer; *b* 1913. Fled from Nazi persecution in Germany 1933. Lived in US until 1952 when he went to GDR, where he became a critic of the communist government.

JARUZELSKI, GENERAL WOJCIECH – Polish politician and soldier; *b* 1923. Minister of defence 1968–83. Chairman, Military Council for National Salvation, 1981–3, after introducing martial law. President of Poland 1985–90.

KARPOV, VIKTOR – Soviet diplomat; *b* 1928. Acting chief Soviet arms negotiator at SALT II 1978–80. Head, arms limitation and disarmament department, USSR foreign ministry, 1986–91.

KHRUSHCHEV, SERGEI – Russian scientist and historian; *b* 1933. Son of Nikita Khrushchev; began career working on missile design. Applied for US citizenship 1992. Has written two books on his father.

KILLICK, SIR JOHN – British diplomat; *b* 1919. Served in Germany, Ethiopia and US; ambassador to USSR 1971–3; permanent representative to NATO 1975–9.

KINDLEBERGER, CHARLES – US economist and government official; *b* 1910. Chief of division, German and Austrian economic affairs, state department, 1945–8; Professor of economics 1948–81.

KIRÁLY, MAJOR-GENERAL BÉLA – Hungarian historian and soldier; *b* 1912. Imprisoned as alleged conspirator 1951; Commander, Hungarian National Guard 1956; escaped to Austria and then US. Professor, City University, New York, 1968–82. Hungarian MP 1990– .

KIRKPATRICK, JEANE – US diplomat and political scientist; *b* 1926. Permanent representative to UN 1981–5. Professor of government, Georgetown University 1978– .

KISSINGER, HENRY – German-born US government official and political scientist; *b* 1923. One of the architects of detente; famous for his 'shuttle diplomacy'. National security affairs assistant to presidents Nixon and Ford 1969–75; secretary of state 1973–7. Nobel Peace Prize 1973.

KOLAKOWSKI, LESZEK – Polish-born professor of philosophy; *b* 1927. Expelled from Warsaw University 1968; then worked at universities in Britain, Canada and US.

KOMÁREK, VALTR – Czechoslovak official; *b* 1930. First deputy prime minister 1989–90. Head, forecasting institute, Czechoslovak academy of sciences.

KOPÁCSI, SÁNDOR – Hungarian police official; *b* 1922. MP 1953. Police chief, Budapest, 1953–6. Sentenced to life imprisonment 1958; amnestied 1963. Emigrated and settled in Canada 1975.

KÜHN, DETLEF – West German political scientist; *b* 1936. Became director, Federal Institute for Inter-German Issues, 1972.

KVITSINSKY, YULI – Soviet diplomat and politician; *b* 1936. Specialist on arms control and German affairs. Chief, Soviet arms control delegation, 1985–6; 'walked in the woods' with Paul Nitze 1982. USSR ambassador to FRG 1986–90.

LIGACHEV, YEGOR – Soviet official; *b* 1920. Gorbachev's deputy 1985–8, and hardline opponent. CPSU central committee: head, personnel and ideology, 1983–8; head, agriculture, 1988–90. Politburo member 1985–90.

LIPKOWSKI, COMTE JEAN-NOËL DE – French diplomat and politician; *b* 1920. Secretary of state for foreign affairs 1968–72, 1973–4.

MALAN, GENERAL MAGNUS – South African politician and soldier; *b* 1930. Chief of defence staff 1976–80. Minister of defence 1980–91; prominent role in South Africa's involvement in Angolan conflict.

MCNAMARA, ROBERT – US government official; *b* 1916. Played pivotal role in Cuban missile crisis and in Vietnam war; advocate of nuclear deterrence through MAD. Defence secretary 1961–8; resigned over Vietnam. President, World Bank, 1968–81.

MIKOYAN, SERGO – Soviet journalist and academic; *b* 1929. Son of former USSR president. Research fellow of Russian academy of sciences.

MLYNÁŘ, ZDENĚK – Czechoslovak politician; *b* 1930. CP central committee secretary June–November 1968. Signed Charter 77; went into exile 1977.

NAKASONE, YASUHIRO – Japanese politician; *b* 1917. LDP member, House of Representatives. Prime minister 1982–7. Resigned from LDP over Recruit share scandal, rejoined 1991.

NITZE, PAUL – US government official; *b* 1907. Most experienced US arms control negotiator; known to Soviets as the 'silver fox'. Advocated fourfold increase in US military spending 1950. US SALT delegation 1969–74; head, US INF delegation, 1981–3; went for 'walk in the woods' with Kvitsinsky 1982.

NOWAK, JAN – Polish-born broadcaster; *b* 1913. Courier, Polish wartime resistance. Director, Polish service RFE, 1951–76. Moved to US 1977; consultant to US government.

NYERS, REZSŐ – Hungarian economist and politician; *b* 1923. Father of Hungary's 1960s economic reforms. Finance minister 1960–62; HSWP central committee secretary 1962–74; minister of state 1988–9.

PERLE, RICHARD – US government official; *b* 1941. Assistant secretary of defence 1981–7. Represented hardline US approach to arms control.

ROBERTS, SIR FRANK – British diplomat; *b* 1907. Head, foreign office central department, 1941–5. Attended Yalta conference 1945. Minister at Moscow embassy 1945–7. Ambassador to USSR 1960–62, to FRG 1963–8.

SAGDEYEV, ROALD – Soviet physicist; *b* 1932. Head of laboratory, Siberian Institute of Nuclear Physics, 1961–70; director, Institute of Space Research, 1973–88. USSR People's Deputy 1989–91. Married Susan Eisenhower (president Eisenhower's granddaughter) in 1990.

SCHABOWSKI, GÜNTER – East German politician; *b* 1929. East German politburo, full member, 1984–9; CP chief, Berlin, 1985–9. His announcement on 9 November 1989 that people would be allowed to travel freely led to Berlin Wall coming down.

SCHELLING, THOMAS – US economist; *b* 1921. Staff member, Rand corporation, 1958–9. Professor of political economy, Harvard University, 1958–90.

SCHUMANN, MAURICE – French politician and writer; *b* 1912. Secretary of state for foreign affairs 1951–4; foreign minister 1969–73.

SCHÜTZ, KLAUS – West German Social Democratic politician; *b* 1926. Mayor, West Berlin, 1967–77. Close friend of Brandt.

SHEBARSHIN, LEONID – Soviet intelligence official; *b* 1935. Worked for KGB in Pakistan, India and Iran 1960s–early 1980s. Head, KGB foreign intelligence, 1989–91. Was head of KGB for 27 hours in August 1991 after coup.

SHEVARDNADZE, EDUARD – Soviet politician; *b* 1928. USSR minister of foreign affairs 1985–90 and November–December 1991. USSR Politburo 1985–90. President, Georgia, 1992– . Instrumental in creating new era in Soviet foreign policy.

SILBERSTEIN, CÄCILIE – East German translator; *b* 1932. Spied in East Berlin for the West 1957–8. Imprisoned 1959–64.

SITARYAN, STEPAN – Soviet politician and economist; *b* 1930. First deputy chairman, Gosplan, 1986–9. Deputy chairman, USSR council of ministers, 1989–91.

SLOVO, JOE – Lithuanian-born South African communist politician; *b* 1926. General secretary SACP 1987–91. Commander, ANC military wing in 1970s. First white member, ANC national executive committee 1985– . Wife assassinated 1982.

SOROS, GEORGE – Hungarian-born billionaire, businessman and philanthropist; *b* 1930. Settled in US 1956. Since 1984, has established numerous foundations in eastern Europe to bring about transition to democracy.

SYCHEV, VYACHESLAV – Soviet official and scientist; *b* 1933. Secretary, Comecon, 1983–91.

TELLER, EDWARD – Hungarian-born US physicist; *b* 1908. 'Father of the hydrogen bomb'. Assistant director, Los Alamos Scientific Laboratory, 1949–52. Strong advocate of SDI to president Reagan.

TROYANOVSKY, OLEG – Soviet diplomat and official; *b* 1919. Molotov's interpreter after 1945. Aide to Khrushchev early 1960s. Permanent representative to UN 1977–86; ambassador to China 1986–90.

URBAN, GEORGE – Hungarian-born British broadcaster; *b* 1921. General director, RFE, 1983–6. Adviser to Lady Thatcher on east European affairs.

URBAN, JAN – Czechoslovak dissident, journalist and politician; *b* 1951. Chairman, Civic Forum, 1989–90, when he retired from politics.

VÁSÁRHELYI, MIKLÓS – Hungarian politician and writer; *b* 1917. National government press chief 1956. Imprisoned for involvement in uprising 1957–60.

WARNKE, PAUL – US government official lawyer; *b* 1920. Assistant defence secretary, international security affairs, 1967–9. Chief US negotiator, SALT, 1977–8.

WEINBERGER, CASPAR – American official; *b* 1917. Defence secretary 1981–7; advocate of US military build-up. Given honorary British knighthood 1988.

YAKOVLEV, ALEXANDER – Soviet official and historian; *b* 1923. One of the architects of *perestroika*. Ambassador to Canada 1973–83. Promoted *glasnost* while in charge of CPSU propaganda department 1985–8; politburo member 1987–90.

ZAGLADIN, VADIM – Soviet official; *b* 1927. Secretary, USSR Supreme Soviet foreign affairs committee 1981–9. Adviser to Gorbachev 1988–91.

ZUMWALT, ADMIRAL ELMO – US naval officer; *b* 1920. Commander, US naval forces, Vietnam, 1968–70. Chief, naval operations, 1970–74.

ABBREVIATIONS

ABM	anti-ballistic missile
ACC	Allied Control Council (Germany)
ANC	African National Congress
CFE	Conventional Forces in Europe
CIA	Central Intelligence Agency (US)
CIS	Commonwealth of Independent States
CMEA	*see* COMECON
COMECON	Council for Mutual Economic Assistance
CND	Campaign for Nuclear Disarmament (Britain)
CPSU	Communist Party of the Soviet Union
CSCE	Conference on Security and Cooperation in Europe
FDP	Free Democratic Party (West Germany)
FRG	Federal Republic of Germany/West Germany
GDP	gross domestic product
GDR	German Democratic Republic/East Germany
GNP	gross national product
H-bomb	hydrogen bomb
HSWP	Hungarian Socialist Workers' Party
ICBM	intercontinental ballistic missile
INF	intermediate-range nuclear forces
KGB	Committee for State Security (USSR)
LDP	Liberal Democratic Party (Japan)

MAD	mutual assured destruction
MBFR	Mutual and Balanced Force Reduction talks
MEP	Member of the European Parliament
MIRV	multiple independently targetable re-entry vehicle
MIT	Massachusetts Institute of Technology
MPLA	People's Liberation Movement of Angola
NATO	North Atlantic Treaty Organization
NBC	National Broadcasting Corporation (US)
NLF	National Front for Liberation of South Vietnam
NSC	National Security Council (US)
OEEC	Organization for European Economic Cooperation
PDS	Party of Democratic Socialism (Germany)
RFE	Radio Free Europe
RL	Radio Liberty
SAC	Strategic Air Command (US)
SACP	South African Communist Party
SALT	Strategic Arms Limitation Talks
SAM	surface-to-air missile
SDI	Strategic Defence Initiative
SED	Socialist Unity Party (East Germany)
SLBM	submarine-launched ballistic missile
START	Strategic Arms Reduction Talks
Stasi	(*Staatssicherheit*) Office of National Security (East Germany)
SWAPO	South West Africa People's Organization
TASS	Soviet News Agency
UNITA	National Union for the Total Independence of Angola
VOA	Voice of America

FURTHER READING

Arney, George, *Afghanistan* (Mandarin, London, 1990)

Ash, Timothy Garton, *We the People: the Revolution of '89 witnessed in Warsaw, Budapest, Berlin and Prague* (Granta in association with Penguin Books, Cambridge, 1990)

Bowker, Mike, and Williams, Phil, *Superpower Detente: a reappraisal* (RIIA/Sage Publications, London, 1988)

Gaddis, John Lewis, *The United States and the Origins of the Cold War, 1941–47* (Columbia University Press, New York, 1972)

Havel, Václav, *Summer Meditations: on politics, morality and civility in a time of transition* (Faber, London, 1982)

Hersh, Seymour M., *Kissinger: the price of power – Kissinger in the Nixon White House* (Faber, London, 1983)

Hogan, Michael J., *The End of the Cold War: its meaning and implications* (Cambridge University Press, Cambridge, 1992)

Knightley, Phillip, *The Second Oldest Profession: the spy as bureaucrat, patriot, fantasist and whore* (Pan Books, London, 1986)

Lendvai, Paul, *The Bureaucracy of Truth: how communist governments manage the news* (Burnett Books, London, 1981)

Lundestad, Geir, *East, West, North, South. Major Developments in International Politics, 1945–90* (Norwegian University Press, Oslo, 1991)

Maclear, Michael, *Vietnam: The Ten Thousand Day War* (Thames Methuen, London, 1981)

Newhouse, John, *War and Peace in the Nuclear Age* (Vintage Books, New York, 1990)

Nove, Alex, *An Economic History of the USSR* (Penguin Books, Harmondsworth, rev. edn 1982)

Oberdorfer, Don, *The Turn: how the Cold War came to an end – the United States and the Soviet Union, 1983–90* (Cape, London, 1992)

Rothschild, Joseph, *Return to Diversity: a political history of East Central Europe since World War Two* (Oxford University Press, Oxford, 1989)

Roxburgh, Angus, *The Second Russian Revolution* (BBC Books, London, 1991)

Somerville, Keith, *Foreign Military Intervention in Africa* (Pinter, London, 1990)

Turner, Henry Ashby, Jr, *The Two Germanies since 1945* (Yale University Press, London, 1987)

Ulam, Adam B., *Dangerous Relations: the Soviet Union in world politics, 1970–82* (Oxford University Press, Oxford, 1983)

INDEX

PICTURE CREDITS

―――――――

We are grateful to the following for permission to reproduce the photographs in this book:

Page no.

xii	Popperfoto
26	H. Cartier-Bresson, Magnum Photos
32	Popperfoto
52	Popperfoto
57	Cornell Capa, Magnum Photos
75	Semyon Raskin, Magnum Photos
78	David King Collection
92	Erich Lessing, Magnum Photos
95	Popperfoto
114	Popperfoto
118	Hans J. Burkard, Network Photographers
140	Peter Marlow, Magnum Photos
160	Stuart Franklin, Magnum Photos
166	Popperfoto
182	Popperfoto
198	Popperfoto
224	Peter Marlow, Magnum Photos
248	Ian Berry, Magnum Photos
252	Popperfoto
272	Luigi Baldelli, Katz Pictures
cover	Michel Euler, The Associated Press Ltd